The Big Picture

The Big Picture

Building Blocks of a Christian World View

Brian Harris

Paternoster:
thinking faith

First published 2015 by Paternoster
Paternoster is an imprint of Authentic Media Limited
PO Box 6326, Bletchley, Milton Keynes, MK1 9GG.
authenticmedia.co.uk

British Library Cataloguing in Publication Data

A catalogue record for this book is available from the British Library

ISBN 978-1-84227-856-7
978-1-84227-342-0 (e-book)

Cover Design by David McNeill (www.revocreative.co.uk)

Dedicated to Rosemary
Wife, mother of our three children, follower of
Jesus, and my best friend . . .

Contents

Foreword

Francis S. Collins, one of the world's leading geneticists, shares in his introduction to *Belief: Readings on the Reason for Faith* how he travelled from the position of an atheist studying quantum mechanics in a PhD programme at Yale University to studying medicine, encountering life and death issues that were 'wrenchingly real'. He later read C.S. Lewis's *Mere Christianity* and 'the door to the possibility of God began to open' and he started to 'see that the signposts had been around [him] all along'.[1]

Brian Harris, however, takes us on another journey. He asks the provocative question whether the church in general and Christians in particular strut around like Hans Andersen's emperor in new clothes, arrogant and proud, and yet the secular world views us as naked and irrelevant. He contends that Christians have too often failed to grasp and comprehend the brief of the Christian faith and offered instead a pale reflection of a Christ follower as defined in Scripture. The fact that the Christian message is often muted and influences less and less of our world speaks of the glaring nakedness and vacuity of the presentation of our faith. Harris offers a fresh study on possible contours and building blocks that might 're-clothe the emperor'.

Harris comes to the problem of a defective Christian world view and impotent spirituality, not as a spectator standing at a distance; instead, he rolls up his sleeves and enters into the *sheol* of the world's doubt, pain and hopelessness and asks penetrating and probing questions. Where does one find an authentic and robust Christian spirituality today incarnated with orthopraxis and orthopathy? Where are the emperor's clothes? His breadth of international experience drawn from living through the struggles of apartheid in South Africa and residing for two decades in the Pacific Rim, New Zealand and now Perth, Australia, provide rich testimony and illustration in addressing the issue. His vocational pilgrimage in South Africa,

New Zealand, and Australia has followed two parallel trajectories: lecturing in academic institutions and simultaneously nurturing churches as a pastor. He writes as an able theologian whose PhD studies the work of the late Stan Grenz, and as a pastor who understands the pulse of his flock.

In 2011, Carson-Newman University invited Harris to lecture and spend a mini-sabbatical in our Greer House for International Scholars. While leading a graduate seminar on 'Spirituality and Worship', Harris began writing his first work, in what will now become a trilogy with Paternoster: *The Tortoise Usually Wins: Biblical Reflections on Quiet Leadership for Reluctant Leaders*. This work has been well received.

His second work, *The Big Picture: Building Blocks of a Christian World View*, does not follow the traditional roads of defining a Christian world view dogmatically, according to the different 'isms', but journeys across fresh paths and landscapes. For Harris, the contours of a Christian world view are not some restrictive straitjacket, but rather broad lines of faith where the Christian ought to live with nurture, love, faith and hope amidst the messiness of life. Harris's world view is earthed in Scripture and the life of Christ. Using a rugby metaphor, he sets out fifteen 'line in the sand biblical passages' that act as a lens through which we understand our faith and life. Harris recognizes that the relationship between Christianity and culture is complex, and yet all humans are created in the *imago Dei* and pose life's ultimate questions irrespective of their cultural soil. He posits that culture may act as friend and a foe: one may hear the voice of God in today's younger post-Christian generation that embraces values more congruent with the contours of a Christian world view, and at the same time, the idols of our culture, such as money, sex and power, may seduce and entrap. The author reminds his reader that a Christian world view finds biblical evidence for an intentional creation in which you and I have a role to play. Despite the Fall and the shame, we have an honour and nobility. We are wonderfully and fearfully made, and yet we are also fallen creatures that must share the view that grace is a 'cross-shaped reality'. Drawing from a Trinitarian model, Harris urges and spells out what it means for the church to be a community of surprise, embrace and witness. A Christian world view recognizes that the faith community is to 'build a world with a better name . . . better for all creatures great and small'. Harris declares that 'You can't believe in Easter and live timidly'. He challenges the church to throw off the charge of being 'morally suspect' and to change our welcome posture from 'behave, believe, belong' to 'belong, believe, behave'. Incarnation precedes any invitation by the church to belong and we are reminded that 'both Bethlehem's cradle and Calvary's Cross speak of the divine "yes" to humanity in spite of its indifference , cruelty, and fallenness'. Jesus does not cloister away in a safe place but comes out into the public place and dies a death of disgrace with reckless love. We are to live and work in the secular marketplace and celebrate the gift of work and vocation, for William Buechner reminds us that 'the place God calls you is the place where your deep gladness and the world's deep hunger meet'.[2]

The Big Picture is written with a clarity and simplicity of style similar to that of the late John Stott and with the flair, humour, and freshness of a work of N.T. Wright. This book offers the university student an excellent primer, the pastor a light along the way of ministry, and the thoughtful church member and teacher, rich fare. At the conclusion of each chapter the reader finds a series of trenchant questions fielded by a group of Christ followers who have in their own lives yearned for the 're-clothing of the emperor'.

Dr David Crutchley
Chair of Religion
Carson-Newman University
Jefferson City
Tennessee

Preface

Do we really need another book on Christian world view? After all, there are a fair few of them, most of them wisely alerting us to the folly of different 'isms', and guiding us back to a biblical vision of reality. And such texts do indeed have a valuable place. But I have tried to approach things a little differently in *The Big Picture*.

I am genuinely concerned that the Christian faith is poorly understood by its adherents. I often have a sinking feeling that if Jesus were to revisit this planet, he would feel a need to birth something fairly different from the church as it currently exists. As I read the Gospels, I do not get the feeling that the Jesus portrayed in its pages would sit calmly through the average church service and give a beaming affirmation at the end, 'This is exactly what I had in mind.'

Not that everything is wrong with the church – indeed there is much that is right, and I am grateful to the various church congregations who have helped to nurture my own faith and practice. But for all their strengths, the average congregation would quickly acknowledge their conviction that there is far more to the faith than they grasp or experience. Sermons seem to take so long to say so little. The big picture is often lost by a fixation on local concerns and programmes, many of which seem to accomplish little more than keeping us busy.

In *The Big Picture* I try to paint the larger contours of the Christian faith. To be sure, there are many smaller lines that could be added – but it is a mistake to sweat the small stuff when the larger picture is in danger of disappearing.

This, then, is a book that tries to unpack the major themes that flow together as we try to understand a Christian world view

(some prefer to spell it worldview – whatever). I very intentionally speak of *a* Christian world view rather than the silly arro-
gance that suggests that this is *the* Christian world view. The faith
is far too rich and profound to neatly tuck it away into a few tidy
boxes that purport to capture all that Christianity is about. Not
that anything goes – which is why I find the image of contours
helpful. Contours demarcate the broad territory within which our
thinking roams, without tying us to a precise spot. You quickly
sense when you wander too far from their embrace, but they do
not trap you within stultifying confines that mark the death of
all creativity and imagination. Contours say, 'This is your terrain.
Explore it.' And explore it we do in *The Big Picture*.

Many books on Christian world view spend a great deal of time
talking about alternates to a Christian world view. I have chosen
not to go this route, as I think that a robust understanding of
the Christian faith is more important that outlining threatening
alternatives – alternatives which often turn out to be little more
than straw men. I would rather readers have a clear grasp of the
big blocks of a Christian world view, than a caricature of some
alternate perspectives. A firm understanding of our own faith is
our greatest asset when we enter a world of differing beliefs and
perspectives.

So what are our contours? Section A of the book sets the scene,
the opening chapter asking if like the emperor in the Hans Christian Andersen story, we strut around proudly, confident of our
stance and beliefs, but actually appearing to be naked and shallow
to unimpressed onlookers. The chapter suggests some areas
where our thinking is often muddled, and promises to unpack
each at chapter length as the book progresses. The second chapter
explores the role of the Bible in constructing a Christian world
view, and proposes fifteen orienting passages to help guide us in
our quest. Chapter 3 examines the ever-perplexing relationship
between Christianity and culture, arguing that at any one time
culture conveys both the voice of the divine and the demonic.
Differentiating between the two is not always as easy as we might
assume, but our fifteen orienting passages can help us in the task.

With the scene set in section A, section B dives into an exploration of the building blocks of the Christian faith. Chapter 4 tackles
the ever-tricky question of creation and how to understand the

opening chapters of the Bible. It repeatedly affirms the differ-ence between believing in an accidental or an intentional crea-tion. Chapter 5 explores the mystery of our humanity – that we are simultaneously beings made in the image of our Creator, and yet beings who have been impacted by the Fall, and who have forgotten our true name and true home. Chapter 6 examines what is perhaps the greatest wonder of all – the grace of God, which comes to us as a cross-shaped reality. We naturally need to know about the God discovered in Scripture, and chapter 7 invites us to reflect on what it means to worship a God who is triune, a God revealed to us as Father, Son and Spirit. Chapter 8 moves into daring territory, suggesting that our mandate to build a world with a better name, remains. Chapter 9 asks where the Christian story heads, and argues that eschatology, rather than providing an excuse for escapism, should orientate our actions in the present.

If the emperor is to be clothed, we need more than a grasp of the building blocks of faith. We need a sense of how what we believe will work out in practice. Section C helps to provide this. Chapter 10 wonders what genuinely hospitable churches, shaped by the incar-nation of Jesus, might look like, and how openness to the other might impact our ministry. Chapter 11 closes the book by asking what it might mean to clothe the emperor at work. It examines what a clear sense of vocation and calling could mean, and applies this in two areas, education and economics. It does not suggest tidy answers, but invites the reader to the humility of the life lived listening for the still, small voice of God – a voice which continues to speak, even in the messiest and most broken of life circumstances.

Naturally I hope you will find *The Big Picture* helpful. When writing, I had in mind the many thoughtful Christians I encounter as I speak and teach in Australia and beyond. They have asked for a book addressing the questions explored in this text. More than a few have said they will examine its contents in their home groups, and I hope that the questions at the end of each chapter will help to facilitate many rich discussions.

I also had in mind those who are committed to living out their faith in the workplace. Do make sure to read the final chapter – I think it will prove helpful.

I am not the font of all wisdom on the Christian faith, and am so grateful to a range of theologians from around the world who agreed to answer my interview questions found at the end of each chapter. I deliberately chose a diverse (but always gifted) group. Usually they agree with me – at times they do not. So be it! The Christian faith is not a suffocating straightjacket, and on topics of such magnitude it is healthy that we don't simply parrot each other mindlessly. I am delighted that each adds to the topic discussed, and hope that their contribution will encourage you to examine some of their publications.

I have the privilege (and privilege it is) of serving both as the principal of Vose Seminary (where we train current and future church leaders) and as Pastor at Large for the Carey Movement – the latter a church and school planting missional movement. They are settings that allow for rich discussion and reflection, quickly earthed in the reality of a Christian faith lived out in an increasingly secular society. To all at Vose and Carey – thank you. Your friendship, support, questions and comments have shaped so much of this book.

This book is the second of three that Paternoster has contracted me to write. Each is on a topic close to my heart. The first, *The Tortoise Usually Wins*, explores the nature of Christian leadership, and was written with a special empathy for quiet and reluctant leaders. I continue to believe that if we unleash the potential of these sometimes overlooked leaders, it will be for the good of us all, and am delighted that the book has been so well received. The second, *The Big Picture* explores the big building blocks of a Christian world view, hopefully helping to correct the shallow understanding of faith that is so widespread. The final book planned for the trilogy is *When Faith Turns Ugly*. Toxic expressions of faith are a major issue not adequately addressed, and my hope is that this work will contribute to an embrace of the kind of faith Jesus envisioned when he promised us life in all its fullness. I am grateful to Paternoster for their support and encouragement in this writing project, and especially to Dr Michael Parsons for his practical guidance and his enthusiastic affirmation.

Dr David Crutchley has written the foreword to this work. He has been a good friend over many years. It was while I was on a mini sabbatical at Carson Newman University, where David is the Chair of Religion, that this trilogy began. I will not forget the kindness and warmth I was shown whilst there.

I have dedicated *The Big Picture* to Rosemary, who I married on 29 November 1980. The years have slipped by joyfully and adventurously. I cannot imagine life without her. We have raised three wonderful children, ministered in three countries, and continue to delight and astonish each other. I am truly blessed.

Brian Harris
Vose Seminary, Perth, Australia
April, 2014

Section A:

Setting the Scene, the Bible and Culture

1.

The Emperor's New Clothes: On Acknowledging our Nakedness

You probably know the story. An arrogant emperor is anxious to impress his subjects with a wonderful new wardrobe. Unknown to him, the tailors he has selected are somewhat suspect, and suggest to him an offer too good to be true. They will dress him in the finest suit of clothes, the beauty of which will be apparent to all – all, that is, except the ignorant, the foolish, and those unfit for their position. To them the outfit will be invisible. Never doubting his own wisdom, the emperor readily signs up for the deal and is soon fitted in his new attire. If you remember the Hans Christian Andersen tale, you will recollect that that consisted of absolutely nothing. A stark naked emperor is soon parading amongst his subjects who, anxious lest they be considered stupid, promptly 'ooooh' and 'aaaah' at the supposedly stunning (but actually non-existent) garments. The awkward façade is only ended when a child calls out, 'But he isn't wearing anything at all!' The obvious honesty of the assessment wins the day, and a horrified emperor is forced to face his rather embarrassing nakedness.

First published in 1837, this Danish tale has been translated into over one hundred languages, evidence that there is something about the story that speaks to us at a deeper level. Interestingly enough it is sometimes alleged that Andersen wrote it after reading the seventh letter to the churches in Revelation, the church in Laodicea. Apparently he was struck by the image of Revelation 3:17 where John writes, 'You say, "I am rich . . . and do not need a thing." But you do not realise that you are wretched, pitiful, poor, blind and naked.' As Andersen reflected on someone not realizing they were naked, the story pieced its way into life.

Our opening question is a disturbing one. Could it be that the church, and more particularly Christians, strut around like that deluded emperor proclaiming to have the best that life offers, whilst onlookers lower their eyes and wonder why they are parading around naked?

Alister McGrath has written, 'Too often, traditional apologetics has sought to commend Christianity without asking why it is that so many are not Christians. It seems relatively pointless to extol the attractiveness of the Christian faith if this is not accompanied by a deadly serious effort to discover why it is obviously so unattractive to so many people.'[1]

Sadly McGrath's assessment that many find the Christian faith unattractive might be valid. At an anecdotal level, I remember as a social work student meeting with a mother and her 18-year-old son. The son had attacked her with a broken bottle after she had objected to his selling $50,000 of her jewellery to help fund a growing addiction. It was my role to listen to the story and help find a creative way forward. In the midst of much discussion the mother suddenly suggested, 'Why not start going to church? That is probably what you need.' Her son instantly replied, 'Oh please, I have more than enough problems as it is.'

That conversation took place over thirty years ago, but I still remember the spontaneity of the association. For that young man the thought of participating in a church was an additional difficulty. Not for one second did he contemplate that it might provide a path to solve his very real problems, problems he was desperately anxious to overcome. I remember the sadness I felt when I heard his comment. It has not left me. Something is wrong. The emperor has no clothes.

Lest you think that a comment made over a generation ago is of little current significance, I suspect that the only thing that has changed is that today no one would bother to suggest that church attendance might help solve a crisis. We who know Jesus to be the source of our life, hope and delight, must ask, 'Why?'

The thesis of this book is that current representations of Christian faith are often far removed from the life of faithful Christ following envisioned in the Scriptures. It came into sharp focus for me a few years ago. A church I was assisting was trying to devise a new mission statement, and contemplated 'Making people wholehearted followers of Jesus'. As I wandered around the different groups evaluating this proposal, I heard one cynic say, 'We should be more honest. Our statement should be "Making people boring for Jesus!"' The rest of the group giggled in agreement. When such comments become our default drive, and improbable descriptors like 'boring' become a norm for the followers of Jesus the Christ, something has gone badly wrong. We need to evaluate the reality of 'what is' in the light of 'what is supposed to be'. Painful though it might be, it is only in facing our possible nakedness that we are likely to find a path back to the 'life in all its fullness' that Jesus promised to those who follow him.[2]

Don't misunderstand me. I am not suggesting that current Christians are wilfully trying to reduce the Christian faith to a pale caricature of what it is supposed to be. This is no plot devised in smoke-filled rooms. Rather it is the product of failing to grasp the implications of Christ following in everyday life. It seems to me that this has two major dimensions.

First, *the Christian faith is poorly understood by its adherents.* This is demonstrated in multiple ways. At the heart of the Christian message is a cross. It speaks of unmerited but transforming grace. When we want to congratulate ourselves on the morality of our lifestyle it reminds us that our friendship with God is not a product of our hard work and moral fortitude, but flows from the merciful sacrifice of Calvary. Though forever indebted to grace, most versions of Christianity quickly lapse into a modestly disguised form of legalism. Legalism makes grace less remarkable. It reduces grace to a backstop required only by those foolish enough to leave their salvation to their deathbed, thus being unable to prove that they always had what it takes to earn their way into God's kingdom by adherence to the stated norms of the church of the day.

The lapse of grace into legalism is not the only distortion. There are many others. Think for example of the way in which our mandate to be stewards of creation has been used to sanctify the exploitation of the world's resources. The creativity inherent in being image-bearers of a God who makes everything from nothing is often battered into a predictable conservatism.

Or consider the monotonous regularity with which eschatology morphs into escapism. Instead of the contours of the coming

kingdom of God reshaping the pattern of our present relationships, we sometimes allow debates about the end times to be exer-
cises in irrelevance.

And then there is our attitude to revelation. So often we allow
revelation to be confined to the past tense. Instead of participating
in God's radical plan to make all things new, many Christians fall
into the trap of championing the status quo, apparently confusing
it with the agenda of God. At heart there is a failure to understand
the broad and winsome contours of a genuinely Christian world
view. Christianity proclaims that there will be a new heaven and
a new earth. That hardly sounds like a crusade to keep things as
they are.

If the first failure is one of comprehension, the second is of experience.

Prior to Pentecost, the product of the disciples' efforts was
pitiful. While Jesus both challenged and encouraged his disciples,
he rarely congratulated them. It was not that he was mean-spir-
ited – he was simply realistic and realized how much needed to
change. For all that, he never lost heart, not because he was confident that the disciples would eventually catch on, but because he
was aware that the coming of the Spirit at Pentecost would more
than compensate for their very obvious deficits. And he was right!

Post Pentecost, the disciples became a force to be reckoned
with. People listened when they spoke . . . more than that, they
were changed. Miracles took place, not so often that they became
routine, but sufficiently often for the disciples to be ever-hopeful
and expectant. Their message to the early converts remains valid
for today's disciples. We too must 'live by the Spirit' and 'keep in
step with the Spirit'.[3] Sadly too often the Spirit-empowered life is
in danger of becoming the self-propelled life. Instead of chanting
the word of the Lord that came to Zerubbabel, '"Not by might
nor by power, but by my Spirit," says the LORD Almighty', we
comfort ourselves that we are not as ignorant as they were, and
have the benefit of significantly greater reserves.[4] We tend not to
emphasize the difference between their outcomes and ours. Far
too many versions of faith operate without any obvious source of
divine power.

Though the major focus of this book will be on understanding
the big building blocks of a Christian world view, I hope that this
plea for a Spirit-enabled faith will not be overlooked. A better

understanding of Christianity without the addition of the Spirit's empowerment will prove to be inadequate.

Let me elaborate on why I think our inadequate understanding of the biblical message damages our witness.

Mind the gap

Most train stations have a sign urging patrons to 'mind the gap'. It is just a little step from the platform onto the train, but if it is mismanaged the consequence is serious. In a similar manner we might almost get the point of many of the main doctrines of the Christian faith. The problem is caused by the gap.

Let me be clear. While it is untrue to suggest that only those who obtain high distinctions in theology are adequately equipped to follow Jesus, sometimes the gap in our understanding produces unintended but negative consequences. Take the difference between law and grace. Viewing Christ following as an ethical mandate consisting of a lengthy list of 'do this' and 'don't do that' statements might give the impression that we hold the moral high ground and can claim to be virtuous. The downside is that it leaves us in a similar position to the Pharisees of old – and Jesus didn't seem to be especially fond of them.

Let me give you an idea of some of the gaps that I see. They make up the broad but crucial contours for a Christian world view. I will elaborate at chapter length on each in section B of the book, but hopefully this will whet your appetite to keep reading.

So when does the gap between a biblical world view and our own become a serious problem? Think of the consequences when we strike the wrong note with any of the following six . . .

When we sweat the 'how' of creation instead of the 'why' of creation

Steeped as we are in the scientific method of the last few centuries, our instinct on reading the opening chapters of Genesis is often to mutter a 'hardly likely' to its claim of a six-day creation. While we would acknowledge that the detail provided is scant, it is doubtful that anyone would suggest that the account should be prioritized for inclusion in the latest edition of the *Proceedings of the National Academy of Sciences*.

For some this becomes deeply problematic, and they either reject the Christian faith as a result, or they go to extraordinary lengths to try to establish that the Genesis creation account is in fact compatible with the discoveries of modern science. While they sometimes succeed in convincing themselves, that conviction rarely extends to those they attempt to persuade. An unfortunate impasse results. On the one side is a small group of devotees who believe that they have reconciled science and the Bible; on the other are a group who smugly chortle at what they consider to be an example of intellectual and scientific suicide. The latter quickly relegate the Genesis account to a waste basket of quaint but irrelevant myths from antiquity.

I would like to suggest that this is an exceptionally unfruitful approach and does a disservice to the biblical text, largely because it arbitrarily tries to force the Bible to answer questions of recent interest, rather than the truly significant questions the original authors set out to answer.

So what questions does Genesis answer? Here are a few . . . and don't miss how profound each is.

- Is there a God?
- Is this an accidental or intentional universe?
- What is God's relationship to the creation?
- Why is the world simultaneously wonderful and dreadful?
- What is the purpose of life?
- What responsibilities do humans have in the stewardship of this planet?
- What does it mean to be human?

Other chapters will explore these questions in depth, so I will not develop the argument here other than to suggest that an early step in clothing the emperor is to acknowledge that the Bible does not answer the question 'How was the world made?' in such a way as to render a scientific investigation of the question redundant.

Although the Bible does not focus on 'how' the world was made, it does answer a question most find more compelling – 'why' the world was made. When we focus on the question 'how', we usually land up in silliness, and parade around pretending we are wearing the clothing of contemporary science, while even a child can spot that in this sphere we are nudists. By contrast, when we focus on the 'why' question, we articulate answers of profound depth. They literally transform the way in which we see and understand the world. The answers we offer to the 'why' question are answers filled with hope and meaning. If accepted, they change the world for the good.

When we idealize or villainize humanity

Colliding truths are usually both true, albeit that they need some unpacking. Take these two. People are essentially noble and good. They can be trusted, indeed they are just a 'little lower than the angels' to quote the psalmist.[5] People are also villainous, cruel and depraved. If you ask, 'Can both of these contradictory descriptions be true?' the answer is yes. Genesis explains how.

On the one hand the Bible affirms that people are made in the image of God. This staggering truth is hard to take in. Theologians debate at length what is meant by the claim. The intention to create humanity in God's image is proclaimed in Genesis 1:26, with verse 27 signing off on the success of the project. As both men and women are made in the image of God, it is clear that the image has nothing to do with gender – a rather radical insight for a text written in a world where patriarchy dominated.

It is hard to overestimate the loftiness of the claim that humans are made in God's image. Implications that arise from it flow thick and fast. Although much of human history has been a reflection of our inability to live up to the creation mandate, the responsibility and privilege of being an image-bearer remains.

Being made in God's image is a statement about our identity – and the identity of every other human being. It affirms that we belong to God. The theologian Helmut Thielike expands on what Luther called the *dignitas aliena* (alien dignity) when he writes:

> The only question is whether I can see the whole person if I do not see him in his relationship to God and therefore as the bearer of an 'alien dignity'. If I am blind to this dimension, then I can only give the other person a partial dignity insofar as I estimate his importance 'for me' –

even if this includes far more than his mere functional importance for me! – but not insofar as I see his importance 'for God'.[6]

We only fully confer the worth each person deserves when we remember that all people are made in the image of God and therefore have inestimable value. Sadly this truth has been one that we have sometimes forgotten. When we fail to stand up for the rights of the marginalized and oppressed we imply that they are lesser humans. We close our eyes to their status as image-bearers, and in doing so, parade around like the naked emperor, pretending to stand for something beautiful, but actually revealing something quite different.

It is true to say that humans are made in the image of God. It is, however, an incomplete truth. When a partial truth masquerades as a complete truth it is in danger of becoming an untruth. A fuller account has to delve deeper into the creation story, and discovers in that narrative the explanation for the otherwise inexplicable cruelty and savagery shown by the human race. While humanity initially flourished in the Garden of Eden, the day came when they disobeyed the instruction to refrain from eating from the fruit of the tree of the knowledge of good and evil. While we could debate the deeper significance of that act, perhaps we can simplify many arguments by noting that in their quest to differentiate between good and evil, they staked their autonomy from God. After eating from that tree they hoped to decide what was good and what was not outside of any reference to God. This is the heart of human sin – the pull away from God, the desire for self-sufficiency – to know right and wrong without any need to refer back to God.[7]

Similarly, humanity is condemned for its attempt to build the tower of Babel – the account is found in Genesis 11. A superficial reading of the passage leaves most confused. Why is God so annoyed by this attempt to build a tower to reach heaven? Granted, it was a misguided quest. After all, this was the ancient world and any tower was unlikely to be more than a few storeys high – no doubt impressive to our ancestors, but paltry in comparison to the skyscrapers of today. The problem with the tower had nothing to do with its height, or its mistaken notion that heaven is up in the sky. The issue was the underlying attitude behind the project. At heart, the tower of Babel was an attempt to reach heaven unaided, and thus to render God obsolete.

The attempt to stake autonomy from God is the essence of the fall of humanity. We are made in God's image. When we try to dispense with the need for God, we sever ourselves from the One in whose image we are made. This is to shake the fist at God and to say that we no longer wish to be who we are – creatures made in God's image. It is the reason for the pervasive sadness that is never far from the surface of life. Something has gone awry. We no longer reflect the image of the God who made us. We have embarked on a misguided journey to create an alternate identity for ourselves. We are trying to become who we are not.

When grace is trivialized to legalism

In the light of humanity's decision to stake its autonomy from God, God could have accepted the insult and decided to have nothing more to do with our rebellious ancestors. Instead, God continues to strive with the human race, demonstrating a willingness to do whatever it takes to ensure that people come to their senses and reclaim their status as those who bear the image of the God who made them. The 'whatever it takes' turned out to be extremely costly. It took the form of the cross at Calvary.

Why did God do this? We should not answer too quickly, lest it imply that what God did was totally understandable and predictable. Actually, it was anything but. In trying to find an adequate word to describe it, theologians have settled upon a little word with an astonishing depth of meaning – that word is grace.

Ever since humanity deliberately defied God and severed the close relational tie they had previously enjoyed with their Creator, the universe has limped along awkwardly. To be sure, there have been moments of brilliance. As humans we should not think too highly of ourselves. Even our incomprehensible disobedience was not enough to totally ruin the good world that God made. The fingerprints of the goodness of God remain everywhere. But our rebellion has left deep scars. Things go wrong – sometimes devastatingly wrong.

When things go wrong and someone is clearly to blame, a common response is to ask what should happen to the person at fault. The Bible explores a few options.

Option one is the instinctive one. If someone does something wrong, punish them so severely that anyone tempted to follow their example will immediately eliminate the possibility from their mind. There is a troubling account found in Genesis 4:23,24. A man by the name of Lamech is injured by a younger man. While the detail provided is scant, we are told that in retaliation for this injury Lamech kills the younger man, thereafter boasting to his two wives, Adah and Zillah, of his feat. The implication of his victory song is clear. Do the slightest thing against me and I will obliterate you. It is a sure way to escalate conflict and to guarantee that any relational breakdown remains irreparable. With this model, the enemy remains enemy forever.

To soften this instinctive response, when the law was given to Moses, a system was put in place to limit retaliation to the extent of the offence. Put simply, the eye for eye (or tooth for tooth) principle was championed. Amongst other places, you find it in Exodus 21:23–27. It was a helpful advance. Rather than escalate violence, the eye for eye principle restricted it. It was a neat and tidy system. If someone broke your arm, you could break theirs. You could not, however, break their neck. That would be far more serious than the offence they had committed against you and would violate this tit for tat system.

While 'eye for eye' was better than Lamech's endless revenge, it had its limitations. Most notable was that it was powerless to reconcile warring parties. If someone broke your toe, and you carefully retaliated by breaking theirs, you might feel avenged for the wrong done against you, but it was unlikely that afterwards you would both hug and suggest drinks at the local pub. More likely you would continue to glare at the offender and growl, 'So don't ever do that again' before you both hobbled off, trying to mask the pain from your broken bones.

It took the brilliance of Jesus to suggest an alternate model. Now there is no doubting that at a certain level, Jesus' instruction sounds remarkably naïve. Perhaps you remember the drift of the argument in the Sermon on the Mount.[8] Rather than retaliating, Jesus suggests that we don't attempt to resist those who do evil against us. Jesus earths his teaching with a challenging example. If someone has just struck us on the right cheek, we should turn the left cheek to them. He goes on to suggest that instead of limiting love to our neighbour, we should extend it to our enemy as well.

At a certain level this sounds like madness. You can imagine what Lamech's response would have been – 'never in a thousand years' is the mild version! Yet, 2,000 years before Ghandi, Jesus recognized the power of non-retaliation. More than that, he recognized the transforming power of forgiveness. If we refuse to hold something against another, especially if we are perfectly entitled to be offended, we open the door through which the enemy can walk and become a friend. They do not have to fight the layers of our angry resentment before they can reach us. We are open to friendship with them, even while they are raging against us.

Why would we do this? The little word 'grace' springs to mind. As people who bear the image of the God who made us, we know that we are made for relationship with one another. If we close our heart to another, even if they have wronged us, we fall short of who we are made to be.

Opening our heart to those who reject us is a high-risk strategy. The cross of Calvary underlines this truth emphatically. Paradoxically, it is the very 'failure' of the approach that is its success. The mystery of the Christian faith is this. When we most reject the God who made us (and it is hard to imagine a greater 'we don't want you' than a crucifixion), we are the closest to re-entering into relationship with our Maker. Jesus' attitude and actions on the cross were so unexpected that the Roman centurion who had overseen his crucifixion was overwhelmed to the point that he was heard to exclaim, 'Surely this man was the Son of God'[9] What caused the change? We can't know for sure. Perhaps it was Jesus' plea, 'Father, forgive them, for they do not know what they are doing'.[10] Perhaps it was simply Jesus' trust and courage in the midst of extreme suffering. While our rebellion against God has marred the image we were created in, it is not so damaged as to be incapable of recognizing that through the cross, God invites us to find forgiveness and a restored relationship with our Creator. Why does God go to such extraordinary lengths to be in relationship with us? It is inexplicable, but that little word 'grace' is a start.

While this thumbnail sketch of grace is far from complete, at this introductory stage, I want simply to underline how sad it is when we allow this astonishing grace to morph into legalism. Too often we try to replace grace by a trite set of rules and regulations that suggest that being in relationship with God is about ticking whatever seem to be the really important moral boxes of our time. Depending on our context, that could mean anything from dressing in a certain way (usually making a virtue of the dreary), refraining from dancing, being shocked at the sexual struggles of others, having really boring Sundays, or opposing anything new. None of these has anything to do with grace, but they do leave us in charge of writing our own rules and appearing to win the right to a permanent audience with God as a result of our moral rectitude.

When the Trinity is about mathematical improbabilities instead of transforming community

Say the word 'Trinity' to the average Christian and their eyes glaze over as they prepare for a confusing explanation of how it is that God can appear to be three (Father, Son and Spirit) while actually being only one God. Most draw on imperfect analogies – it is like H_2O which is always H_2O but can be a solid (ice), liquid (water) or gas (steam). Others suggest it is like an egg which is made up of a shell, yolk and the albumen. And then there is Augustine's grammatical argument. God is the highest love, but in order to have love, there must be a lover, a loved, and the action of love. In order to be love, God must at the same time be the object, the subject and the verb, and thus have three parts. Yup – it's not too hard to understand why those eyes glaze over. It is inevitable when we treat the Trinity as a mathematical improbability which we have to justify and explain.

So how should we think of the Trinity – and does it matter?

The revealed God is triune. The mathematical complexity of demonstrating that one plus one plus one equals one has proved a theological red herring. The only God we can know is the God who is revealed and we can safely assume that God is as God is revealed – one essence in three persons. So we must work with what we know. The revealed God is never an isolated, lonely God, but comes to us in the rich relational life of Father, Son and Spirit. We are told that humans are made in the image of God, and we can argue that our life calling is to live up to the image in which we have been made. To image such a God would therefore presumably require a comparable rich communal life in the entity that we call church. At the very least, the triune God is a rebuke to excessive individualism, especially if it comes at the expense of the life of the community. That a strong stress on the individual, often at the expense of the communal, has been a characteristic of many churches should be of concern to us.[11]

It starts with an emphasis on individual salvation which is pivotal to the evangelical movement.[12] It continues on in the music of the movement which is often couched in the language of lovers, 'Jesus, I love you', 'Jesus, you are mine' and the like. This is not really in accord with the prayer Jesus taught his followers, which begins not with the 'my' word but with the 'our' word – 'Our Father in heaven'.[13] Now, a warm intimate relationship with our Father is entirely appropriate, but when it is emphasized at the expense of our communal life, something is amiss.

In Ephesians 3 Paul reminds us of two conditions that help the church to partially comprehend the width, length, height and depth of Christ's love for us. The first is that 'Christ may dwell in your hearts through faith' so that we would be 'rooted and established in love' which naturally leads to the second, which is of us being 'together with all the saints' in the communal quest to discover the love that 'surpasses knowledge'.[14] All this is a world away from the drift towards what Alan Jamieson calls 'churchless faith'.[15] The problem with churchless faith is that 'together with all the saints' simply disappears. When we discover God, we quickly find that this God is triune. We cannot enter into a one-on-one relationship with a God who although one, is three. We are immediately thrust into the community of Father, Son and Spirit.

This is not to suggest that the self disappears in community. Again, the triune nature of God helps us avoid this potential trap. The Father is not the Son, the Son is not the Spirit, the Spirit is not the Father. Rather than the disappearance of the self, the self is most truly self in relationship, in community. Outside of community, the self cannot image the God whose likeness it is invited to reflect.

We clothe the emperor when we grasp that relationship with the triune God thrusts us into transforming community life. There are no solitary Christians. We belong to God and so we belong to each other.

When stewardship of the world becomes exploitation, and resisting change is assumed to be virtuous

The opening chapters of the Bible paint an exciting picture of the task facing the human race. Having been made in the image of their Creator, they are to be stewards of God's creation, ensuring that they build a world where every plant and creature can be fruitful and multiply. One of the stunning portraits in Genesis 2 is found in verses 19 to 20. God invites Adam to name the birds and animals. The scene captures the imagination. God actively brings each bird and animal to Adam to see what he would name them. The Creator of all does not interfere in this process, for we are told that whatever name Adam selected, that was its name.

Think of the importance of names. A poorly chosen name can prove a heavy burden. Some nicknames are specifically chosen for their cruelty. We often become what we are named. I was born a few weeks early, a significantly underweight and vulnerable infant. But my parents named me Brian, which means strong. I like to think that they were right, and that in spite of initial appearances, this was my invitation to be who I could be – someone with some resilient strength. Names in the Bible are often changed, Abram, Sarai, Jacob and Simon being some examples of those whose original name was considered by God to not adequately reflect the call and potential of their life.

If names are so significant, the responsibility of naming creation should not be underestimated. Surely this was a task that could only be performed by one who was an image-bearer of the Creator – for great creativity is required to name appropriately. God's was the first creation, but in delegating the task of naming to image-bearers, God assigned humanity the task of building a world with a suitable name – one that reflects all the potential inherent in the original creation. The concept gives me goose bumps. Such an incredible and exciting responsibility. Imagine being caught up in a story where the main theme line is 'building a world with a better name'.

Building a world with a better name – such a lofty mandate – but in our current world, where the emperor strides naked, our experienced reality is that names are allowed to divide (name any ethnic group, and the name causes angst or ridicule in another), and some names have been allowed to disappear, some species now extinct because of our neglect of the creation mandate. Sadly, the church often parades naked because of a misguided attempt to safeguard the status quo, with conservative agendas being allowed to trump most calls for innovation. Many recent calls for change have been motivated by a desire to build a world with a better name, but have often been hushed into silence by people of faith who have failed to grasp the dynamic implications of their original directive.

To re-clothe the emperor, those who are committed to following Jesus the Christ will be willing to ponder and then act upon their delegated responsibility to find new and better names for a world where so many names jar and bring out the worst in us.

When eschatology becomes escapism instead of enticing invitation

Part of the reason for Christ followers abandoning their creation mandate has been their embrace of an inadequate and flawed eschatology. Much of our thinking about 'end times' has been reduced to unseemly debates about millennialism. Though most churches no longer require you to affirm whether you are pre-mill, post-mill or a-mill (and indeed, the fascination with millennialism has disappeared in many circles), an apocalyptic escapism is never far from the surface. In crassly reductionist terms – the world and everything in it is to be destroyed, so why bother to build a word with a better name if destruction is simply around the corner? In one rather extreme example of bad theology, a pastor is alleged to have urged his congregation to do all they could to degrade the environment, claiming that the chaos caused by pollution and global warming would hasten the return of Christ. While it would be unfair to suggest that such views are typical, an emphasis on the destruction of the present planet is unlikely to see a flurry of activity to ensure its wellbeing.

A closer examination of the biblical text suggests that what we actually await is the creation of a new heaven and a new earth. The title 'a new earth' is suggestive. It is the retention of the word 'earth' that is so especially interesting. Whatever the future holds, the concept of the 'earth' does not disappear. It will indeed be renewed – a new earth – but it will not be so discontinuous from the old that a new name is required. It is still earth.

Indeed, in John's vision in Revelation 21 he sees the merging of the realms of heaven and earth as the new Jerusalem comes down out of heaven to the new earth, so that the cry in verse 3 becomes 'Look! God's dwelling-place is now among the people, and he will dwell with them.' Perhaps this is why Jesus urged us to pray 'your kingdom come, your will be done, on earth as it is in heaven', to cite Matthew 6:10. Just as God's will is carried out in heaven, so should it be carried out on the earth. If we want to know how we should act on earth, we should therefore ask, 'How is this done in heaven?' Rather than the standard of heaven being an inaccessible one delayed until the end of all things, Jesus instructs his followers to pray for the strength to implement that agenda in the present. There is nothing escapist about this.

Stanley Grenz and John Franke have suggested that we view eschatology as our orienting motif in theological construction.[16] By this they mean that we should allow our convictions about the nature of our future reality to shape and direct, indeed to orientate, our present actions. Rather than eschatology becoming about escapism, it then shapes our current agenda. What will ultimately be, radically impacts what we back and support in the now. In 1 Corinthians 13:13 Paul reminds us that the three things that remain forever are faith, hope and love, with love being the greatest. What projects should we enthusiastically endorse in this present age? Those that flow from and reflect faith, hope and love, for they will remain forever.

To clothe the emperor, a willingness to allow our future reality to shape present reality could see Christ followers marching to a significantly different tune. It will require great courage, but projects birthed from faith, hope and love reflect the values of the new heaven and the new earth.

While these six 'gaps' clearly matter, if we are to reverse the gap between what we believe and how faith is played out in the world, a few additional matters need attention. There is the question of the role of the Bible and how we interpret it. Then there is the tricky question of culture. Is Christianity successful because it has adapted to numerous cultural settings spanning two millennia – or has that been its undoing? We will deal with these questions in the remaining chapters of section A.

One key question, then, remains for this opening chapter. This book's title is *The Big Picture: Building Blocks of a Christian World View*. What does the subtitle mean? What do we mean by a world view (or worldview), and more specifically, a Christian world view? And why are we looking for building blocks, rather than some bold summary statements of the Christian world view?

But what do you mean by 'world view'?

A person's world view is the overall perspective from which they see and interpret the world. For some this is a clearly thought-through perspective, arrived at after much philosophical thought and reflection. For others it is more intuitive – they might struggle to articulate what their world view is, but sense when aspects of it are violated. When someone complains, 'It's not fair!' they are usually telling you something about their world view. Why isn't it fair? Their objection presumably reflects that fairness is something that their world view leads them to expect, or else why bother to comment on its absence.

James Sire, whose work on understanding a Christian world view has been widely appreciated, suggests that 'A worldview is a commitment, a fundamental orientation of the heart, that can be expressed as a story or in a set of presuppositions (assumptions which may be true, partially true or entirely false) that we hold (consciously or subconsciously, consistently or inconsistently) about the basic constitution of reality, and that provides a foundation on which we live and move and have our being.'[17] He suggests that to arrive at an understanding of a person or group's world view we should ask eight key questions.

1. What is the prime reality – the really real?
2. What is the nature of external reality – that is, the world around us? For example, is the world chaotic or orderly; is the world real to the extent that we have a relationship with it or does it exist independently (objectively) apart from us?
3. What is a human being? Is the answer a machine, or a god, or a person made in the image of God, or a naked ape, or an accidental collection of chemicals – the list could go on.

4. What happens to a person at death? Should we expect extinction, transformation to a higher state, reincarnation, judgement and a decision about where eternity will be spent or some other option?
5. Why is it possible to know anything at all?
6. How do we know what is right and wrong? Indeed, is there such a thing as right and wrong?
7. What is the meaning of human history, presupposing there is a meaning?
8. What personal, life-orienting core commitments are consistent with this world view?[18]

Sire's list is really helpful if we wish to understand and evaluate the world view of those who do not embrace the Christian faith. The role of this book, however, is to help those who follow Jesus the Christ to think through the contours of the world view they implicitly embraced when they made the decision to embark upon the journey of Christ following.

I speak of the contours of a Christian world view because this is no straitjacket that Christ followers have to be squeezed into. The broad lines of our faith give zones in which we operate and roam, and creativity is to be expected from those who are made in the image of the God who made everything from nothing. The Bible is the text from which we source our ideas, and its pages are filled with the stories of people who responded to God in the messiness of their lives. Some managed to do so faithfully, others less so, but each gives us a clue to the kind of way our allegiance to the triune God can be worked out. Ah, but now I am starting to move into the material for our next chapter . . .

An interview with Ian Stackhouse

At the end of each chapter I ask a significant Christian thinker to respond to some of the ideas just explored. The first interview is with Ian Stackhouse, who is the pastoral leader of Guildford Baptist Church in the UK, and the author of several books, including *Primitive Piety*.[19]

1. *Ian, in your book* Primitive Piety *you lament that most churches embrace a suburban piety which is essentially bland and polite. You suggest that biblical faith is a lot more radical. Can you unpack some of your concerns?*
   I guess my concerns relate to the fact that biblical faith takes place at the extremes: sin and grace; dying and rising; praise and lament. Yes, there are ordinary times, and settled existence, but so much of the biblical narrative has an edge to it. Suburban living, however, almost by definition, seems to me to be an exercise in eradicating those extremes for something more manageable, to the point that what we have left by way of faith looks suspiciously more like modern consumer living than it does gospel. Take the way we programme our churches for instance, or the way we approach ministry as an attempt to fix things. In so many ways our busyness and our stock answers are ways of avoiding the darker, more perplexing aspects of our spiritual journey. And although I can sympathize with the instinct to want to do this, and am tempted myself to keep things safe, what it means in the end is one massive spiritual impoverishment.

2. *So would it be true to say you think the emperor is naked, and if so, what are the key reasons?*
   Yes, there are many times when I come away from things thinking that the emperor has no clothes, and I think the main reason has to do with lack of courage. A bit like the fable itself, so many of our Christian leaders, it seems to me, are so concerned to make the gospel appealing to the crowds that we seem to have forgotten that the genius of our faith lies precisely in its rugged orthodoxy, as well as its hiddenness. Whether we will be able to get back to this, back to a more honest gospel and a more authentic community, is a moot point. Until we find the courage to deal with our rank successism, as one person put it, and its accompanying idealism, which to me is a big part of the problem – the way we idealize the church as some kind of corporate hospitality – then I don't see how it will happen. Indeed, I suspect that it will take someone from somewhere else in Christendom, some little boy in the crowd who is not enamoured by the glamour of our consumer Christianity, to point out that the emperor has no clothes!

3. **Primitive Piety** *suggests that we should celebrate the oddity of the*
   gospel and the eccentricity of saints. What are you getting at?
   I think what I am getting at is the strangeness of everything. I
   think we have tended to flatten the gospel and sanitized our
   saints, to the point that we have stripped away the mystery.
   When I think about it, all the people who have influenced me
   most in my life have not been straightforward characters. If
   they had been, I dare say I would not have been attracted to
   them. It was their eccentricity, and by that I mean their unal-
   loyed passion for God, that was their genius. And although
   this meant they were a little uncomfortable to live with, it is
   precisely that sense of unpredictability that made them so
   much like Jesus. Unless of course we think Jesus to be simply a
   nice person! As I read the Gospels, yes, I observe a Jesus 'meek
   and mild', but I also have to reckon on a Jesus 'mean and wild':
   someone who lambasts hypocrites; who snorts in the presence
   of a dead body; who feels gut-wrenching compassion over the
   plight of the common people. All I am saying in *Primitive Piety*
   is 'let's have that kind of piety in our churches' rather than the
   saccharine, sentimental stuff that seems to prevail in so much
   of our contemporary Christianity, certainly here and in North
   America.

4. *What aspect of Christian faith do you think is most commonly misun-*
   derstood, and why?
   Without a doubt, for me it is the biblical doctrine of sin that is
   the most misunderstood aspect of Christian faith – most definitely. Our culture portrays sin in very repressive terms, as the
   doctrine that we need to jettison if we are to see our humanity
   flourish – hence, all the self-esteem books that are on sale in
   places like Waterstones. But for me it is quite the opposite.
   For sure, preachers can overcook the rottenness of the human
   heart, and leave Christians feeling thoroughly miserable about
   themselves. But handled properly a Christian understanding of
   our fallenness can be the most liberating doctrine imaginable.
   When I heard a preacher tell me about sin, or to put it more
   specifically, when I heard the message of the cross, from which
   I deduced that sin was indeed a problem, I didn't come away
   feeling terrible about myself. Not at all. Rather, I felt a huge

sense of relief that at last here was someone who had the guts to be honest with me about the condition of my heart, because only by facing the worst about myself is it possible to know the grace that Jesus brings. I am not sure our culture is up for such honesty.

5. *And the question I ask everyone . . .What do people really, really need to know about God?*
I spoke to a group of sixth formers recently about the things I have learnt now that I have turned 50. Some of it was a bit tongue in cheek to be honest, but towards the end of my talk I got serious and started talking about matters to do with God. The first thing I wanted to say was something that the Jewish philosopher Martin Buber argued, namely that what lies at centre of the universe is not an 'It' but a 'Thou'. In other words, we live in a personal universe. And what I then wanted them to know, as I want my congregation to know, is that this 'Thou' is not some tyrant just waiting for us to step out of line so he can catch us out – sadly, this is often how he is portrayed – but rather a God of outrageous grace: a prodigal father, no less, who runs towards us with open arms, puts a robe around us, sandals on our feet, and a ring on our finger. For me, everything flows from this revelation: worship, prayer, holiness, mission, social justice . . . everything. It is of course the revelation of Jesus Christ that I am talking about, and once we get hold of that, anything is possible.

To ponder and discuss

Each chapter of this book finishes with some questions for reflection and discussion. Ideas are best fleshed out in conversation with others, so perhaps you would like to host or join a conversation. Each chapter has about the right amount of material for a small group to study and discuss at a single sitting.

• Do you identify with any of the six gaps listed? To recap . . . Do you (or those in your circle)
1) Sweat the 'how' of creation rather than the 'why' of creation?

2) Idealize or villainize humanity?

3) Trivialize grace into legalism?

4) Regard the Trinity as a mathematical improbability?

5) Allow stewardship to become exploitation and assume the status quo to be the Christian default position?

6) Allow eschatology to become about escapism instead of enticing invitation?

- If you have quickly answered 'no' to each, challenge your answer.
- What difference would it make if you thought about these issues differently?

2.

Beyond Proof Texts: Knowing and Living the Story

I remember the sermon well. The preacher of the day was lamenting that many Christians claim a far greater allegiance to the Bible than their lives demonstrate. He told of a famous Bible teacher who at a large inspirational conference asked the crowd to wave their Bibles in the air if they believed God speaks through the Bible. The crowd readily complied. He then urged them to wave it in the air if they believed that what the Bible teaches is true. The vast majority waved their Bibles enthusiastically. 'Ah,' he then said, 'but some only believe parts of the Bible. I want to see who in this crowd believes the Bible from cover to cover.' Almost everyone waved their Bible vigorously. 'And now,' said the preacher, 'wave your Bible in the air if you not only believe it from cover to cover but have also read it from cover to cover.' Almost every hand was lowered.

The exercise demonstrated two things – first, that this was an honest audience willing to admit to inconsistencies, and secondly, that their emotional attachment to the Bible was far greater than their actual engagement with it. It is not unlike having a greatly loved elderly aunt, but rarely visiting her.

One reason that the emperor appears naked is that many Christians profess a deep commitment to the Bible that is in no way matched by their knowledge of its content, meaning or relevance. They bristle at the suggestion that any part of the Bible is not totally accurate, and might belong to churches that require their members to confirm their belief in its inerrancy, but when the most important reality check takes place, they are found to be ignorant of the teaching of large portions of the book they so readily defend. To the outsider, it seems a little strange.

In this chapter I would like to explore why the Bible is so important in constructing contours for a Christian world view, and how we should go about interpreting it. While each of these are huge questions in their own right, perhaps like Goldilocks we can explore them at a depth that is not too hot, nor too cold, but just right.

Why does the Bible matter?

Recently I was speaking to the senior pastor of a very large church and he told me that when he quotes passages from Scripture he no longer prefaces them with 'the Bible says' but instead cites the particular biblical author who makes the claim. Thus if quoting from the first Gospel he may say, 'According to Matthew, Jesus said . . .', or if it is a Pauline sentiment, he might express it, 'When writing to the Ephesians, Paul claims that . . .' It is not that he is averse to quoting from the Bible. To the contrary, he is noted for the depth of his biblical knowledge, but as he went on to say, 'I've noticed that when I say, "The Bible says" the mood of many hardens and shifts to "Are you trying to say we can't question anything you now say, because the Bible says it?" I think it is something about this postmodern era. You pull an authoritarian sounding trump card and people stop listening. By contrast, if I say, "Paul says" people seem to feel, "OK, so that is what Paul says. Let me see if I agree with him or not." In short, they keep listening.'

It is an interesting perspective and one which I have been pondering since the conversation. Christians, or certainly those of the evangelical variety (of whom I consider myself one), make bold claims for the Bible. Depending on the circles in which you move, you are likely to hear that the Bible is inspired, that it is authoritative, perhaps that it is inerrant. You might be urged to affirm the verbal, plenary inspiration of Scripture. You may have been told that not only is the Bible an inspired text but that it continues to be a Spirit-illuminated text, one through which God speaks to believers (and sometimes, also to those who do not believe). You are almost certain to have been informed that it is the final arbiter in all matters of faith and conduct, the authoritative source to which we appeal when we have any reason to doubt the veracity of any claim about God.

Even if you don't claim to understand each of the terms used, you will quickly realize that Christians believe that the Bible is in a category of its own. Certainly it is a holy book, but we actually claim far more than that. If pressed, we say that we must remain agnostic about all statements about God unless they can be evaluated in the light of what has been revealed to us in the Bible. And if it has not been revealed, at best the claim is of secondary importance, as all that is needed for our salvation and to instruct us to be faithful followers of Jesus is found in Scripture.

Clearly these are lofty claims, and in an anti-authoritarian age we might wonder why we persist in making them. What is at stake that we attach such high importance to the Bible?

When it comes to the crunch, it probably boils down to one key question. How can we speak about God and what God is like and what God has done in the world, unless we have some source of authority for our claims? While we can speculate about what God is like, the reality is that if 10,000 people were asked to describe God, we are likely to arrive at around ten thousand different conclusions. Even if that is a slight exaggeration (there could be more overlap than I suggest), we could never be sure which of these competing portrayals of God was accurate. Unless there have been some definitive 'God turned up' moments, where we are confident that God was present and that we have captured the essence of what was revealed at those times, we are working in the dark, speculating about a divine being who may or may not exist.

The claim that the Bible is God-inspired breaks this impasse. When we say that the Bible is inspired, we proclaim our conviction that we have been able to accurately preserve certain key revelatory events – times when God turned up in such a way that they continue to be definitive for our understanding of the supreme deity. This is not to suggest that God has only turned up in the events outlined in the Bible (for God's activity in the world is in no way limited to the events described in the Bible), but that via a process of Spirit-guided inspiration, certain revelatory events have been preserved in such a way that the church can for all time proclaim with confidence, 'This is what God is like, and this inspired recording of these events enables us to make these statements with conviction.' In short, without an inspired Bible, all claims and statements about God are, at best, speculative.

But how should we interpret the Bible?

Though most agree that the Bible is foundational for any understanding of Christianity, many feel daunted by the task of interpreting its message. Most theological colleges offer a subject called hermeneutics which explores appropriate ways to interpret the Bible, recognizing that biblical literature is made up of many different genres.

Almost half is narrative, and in the Bible we find story after story where God turned up – most commonly in a crisis situation. These were often complex and messy, and it is dangerous to assume that simply because God's presence was noted (and usually made the decisive difference) that we can construct a blueprint from the event and claim that God will always act in this manner. While it can be difficult to extract definitive truths from narrative passages (it can be tricky to differentiate between what is being permanently affirmed and what God was willing to leave unchallenged in unusual and non-representative circumstances), they serve as a helpful corrective to some of the more inflexible conclusions we might otherwise reach when we read passages which give a more straightforward account of what is acceptable and what is not. Narrative accounts help to soften such interpretations, as they remind us of the many exceptions we find in Scripture. So, for example, should we tell the truth? Zechariah 8:16, Psalm 5:6, Proverbs 12:19, Ephesians 4:15,25 (to cite a few), all suggest that this is a question with an obvious answer – yes. But Exodus 1 relays the story of the Hebrew midwives Shiphrah and Puah who both lied to Pharaoh in order to protect Hebrew babies from slaughter, and are rewarded by God for their deceitful courage. The narrative account helps to qualify and add nuance to what might otherwise appear to be a straightforward question.

Other passages are best described as wisdom literature, and are often written in a poetic style. Clearly you interpret poetry a little differently to a historical account of something. While this sounds reasonably obvious, on occasion the principle has been ignored, at times with devastating consequences. Those familiar with history might remember that in the early seventeenth century Galileo Galilei ran into strong opposition from the Roman Catholic Church when he suggested that the earth revolved around the sun. While Galileo argued that the psalmist's contention that God 'set the earth on its foundations; it can never be moved' (Ps. 104:5) was meant to be interpreted as poetry written from the perspective of the observer, the church leaders disagreed – which suggests that Galileo was not only a smarter scientist than they were, but also a better theologian. Tragically, poor theology had a consequence, and Galileo lived out his days under house arrest. Hermeneutics sometimes really matters.

Yet other passages of Scripture are written as law, others as history, other parts are apocalyptic literature, and so we could go on. The point is that to interpret a passage you should understand its genre. To treat poetry or apocalyptic as history is to invite a serious misreading of the passage.

This much is not really controversial. More perplexing is what we are to make of passages that at first reading appear to affirm something that we would consider to be ethically unacceptable. This is becoming a real issue in our day, as many of the New Atheists now accuse Christianity of being a faith that is both intellectually vacuous and morally suspect.[1] Rather than viewing the Bible as good news for all, they argue that it is an ethically dubious text which supports patriarchy, the use of force and other oppressive ways of structuring the world.

It is not too hard to see how this conclusion can be reached. If we are honest there are some Bible passages that feel uncomfortable. Take 1 Samuel 18:22–30 where David is told that in return for 100 Philistine foreskins he can marry the king's daughter. Perpetual overachiever that he is, David returns with 200. I don't know about you, but my instinct on reading that story is not an immediate, 'Gosh, I can't wait to preach about that!' If you don't agree, imagine for a moment what it would have felt like if you were the 10-year-old son of one of those 200 Philistine soldiers.

Visualize finding not just your father's body, but your father's body mutilated in this way. What would you think of the God of the Israelites at that moment?

So what are we to make of the really difficult passages? The answer has to be 'Yes, these are real stories. They are stories about broken people struggling and often not succeeding in finding a way forward in a fallen world. It is often a story about people choosing between bad and worse. But for all that, these are stories about God turning up and meeting with people, sometimes in the most appalling life circumstances.'

To help us to steer our way through these usually good but sometimes troubling stories, it helps to note some profoundly decisive passages in Scripture that help to orientate us to the way we should think about the biblical text and speak about it. These orienting passages help us to bring out the great truths of Scripture that we need to emphasize again and again.

So what are orienting, or line in the sand passages? They are passages that give us a clear portrait of where the larger picture is heading . . . the vision that can sometimes be buried in the messiness of the unfolding story. John 3:16 is an obvious one: 'For God so loved the world' (and that world includes Philistines) 'that he gave his one and only Son, that whoever believes in him shall not perish but have eternal life.'

To suggest that orienting passages have a special function is not to imply that other passages are not inspired, or that they should not be in Scripture. It is simply to argue that when faced with multiple different possible interpretations of a text, orienting passages help us to select which kinds of answers might be valid, and which are likely to miss the mark. So, for example, John 3:16 prevents us reading the book of Joshua and concluding that God hates Canaanites, and is indifferent to their deaths. Rather, John 3:16 helps us to note passages such as Genesis 12:3 where God informs Abram that his election is not primarily for his own benefit, but so that 'all peoples on earth will be blessed through you'. In spite of the punishment meted out to the Canaanites, our orienting passages alert us to a greater truth. God is working towards a plan that has been shaped in love and is for the good of all who are willing to open their hearts to it.

Let me unpack fifteen orienting or line in the sand passages, saying why I think they provide contours that are consistent with a Christian world view.

The first fifteen: A line-up of orienting passages

You might of course wonder if there can be any valid rationale for choosing which should be line in the sand passages. Given that they do not come written in bold capitals, why should we attach such special importance to them?

First let me acknowledge that there is no magical formula I have used to arrive at my first fifteen (the image is from rugby, for those not accustomed to this sport). Some might suggest there should be a dozen, twenty, or far more. And we could debate at length why these fifteen and not some others. Rather than quibble about this particular selection, let's explore a little more why we need orienting passages.

Nicholas Wolterstorff's concept of 'control beliefs' is useful at this point.[2] Wolterstorff notes that certain beliefs, be they religious, philosophical, biblical or other, exercise 'control' over what can and will be believed. He writes, 'Everyone who weighs a theory has certain beliefs as to what constitutes an acceptable sort of theory on the matter under consideration. We all have these control beliefs.'[3] Control beliefs lead us to reject certain sorts of theories, while they are also instrumental in the theories we devise. He notes, 'We want theories that are consistent with our control beliefs. Or, to put it more stringently, we want theories that comport as well as possible with those beliefs.'[4] Rather than attempt to eliminate control beliefs, Wolterstorff argues that they should be acknowledged and embraced. Thus he suggests that in theology 'the belief-content of the theologian's authentic commitment ought all the while to be functioning also as control over his theory-devising and theory-weighing'.[5]

What does this all mean? Do you believe that God is love? It is a statement made very firmly in 1 John 4:8. For most Christians, 'God is love' acts as a control belief. Whatever happens in life, they view it through a lens that affirms that God is love, regardless of what the evidence might suggest. So even in the midst of great personal tragedy, most Christians affirm their control belief 'God is love'. It means that in spite of their personal circumstances, they will not entertain the possibility that what has happened points to a cruel, vindictive or impotent God. If someone were to suggest that this is where the evidence points, they would prob- ably counter, 'That's because we can't yet see the bigger picture of what God will do through this. Ultimately (and that might mean when we are on the other side of death) we will see how this all makes sense and helps to affirm that God is love.' In short, the control belief trumps all other possibilities, and we do not seri- ously consider them.

While some may suggest that this is whistling in the dark, and a form of escapism, all people operate from certain control beliefs. To abandon our control beliefs is to say that we have discovered that something is so different from what we have always imagined that we have to completely rethink and re-evaluate everything.

Our control beliefs, then, provide the lens through which we understand our life and its experiences. Thus even if we become seriously ill, or lose someone we love, or are retrenched from a job we value, we continue to believe that God is love, and that at some point in the future (even if only the future represented by eternity), God's love will be vindicated by some good achieved, even though it may not currently be clear to us.

Put differently then, these orienting passages serve as control beliefs because if they are not valid, our understanding of the Christian faith is so far from the mark that we would have to reconsider everything – including whether we wish to continue to identify with the label 'Christian'. It is a very serious thing to reject a control belief, and those who do usually adopt a radically different attitude to life. Indeed, they adopt an alternate world view.

Let's get to my fifteen orienting passages. They each suggest key components of control beliefs that operate for Christians, or some of the contours that shape a Christian world view.

Genesis 1:1 An opening: We are not alone

The opening words of the Bible profoundly shape our under- standing of reality. It takes just five words to change everything:

'In the beginning God created . . .' The Christian story starts with the conviction that God exists. This same God predates and initiates our story, this being done in an intentional act of creating out of nothing. Rather than finding ourselves alive in an accidental but terribly alone universe, these five words affirm a purposeful creation. Chapter 4 entitled 'The Universe: Accidental or Intentional' will unpack this in significantly greater detail, but our first fifteen would be incomplete if this motif was absent from our opening line-up. Likewise, we should not forget that this passage helps to orientate our understanding both of the Christian story and of reality. In an increasingly secular age, the tendency is to assume the absence or irrelevance of God. This passage warns us that any such opening gambit will lead us wildly astray. God's existence is the only reason for our own existence, and a failure to grasp this results in a radically different world view.

That God is able to create the world, and to do so from nothing, is a clear indicator of the power and intellect of the God we worship. It is no small thing to relate to such a God.

Genesis 1:26–28 An identity: We are made in the image of God

Genesis 1:26–28 informs us that humans are made in the image of God – *imago Dei* as they say in the Latin. No matter how imperfectly they do it, each person in some small measure reflects what God is like. In spite of the impact of the Fall – that terrible time when humanity shook the fist at God and rebelled against Eden's lone restriction – the human race continues to bear the image of the God who made them. Thus Genesis 9:6 (clearly a post-Fall passage), continues to ban murder, the justification being that each person has been made in the image of God. No one with such a lofty status can have their life terminated without there being serious consequences for the terminator. This is an important point, as some suggest that the fall downgrades the significance of humanity being *imago Dei*. Genesis 9:6 firmly disagrees.

Also significant is that both women and men are made *imago Dei*. In a world that often speculates about gender differences, this line in the sand passage firmly proclaims that in that which matters most, namely that we bear the image of the God who made us, men and women are identical. What separates the genders is trivial in comparison to what unites us. We are human because we have been made in God's image, and the opening chapter of the Bible affirms that this has nothing to do with gender.

Not only does our *imago Dei* status force us to be a little tongue in cheek when we talk about gender differences, it also requires us to rethink all class and cultural distinctions, indeed, all distinctions made on the basis of education, wealth, intellect, physical stature . . . the list could go on and on. All fade into insignificance in the light of the momentous truth that we are God's image-bearers. It renders ridiculous any notion that some people are inherently superior to others or that slavery and the oppression of certain people is acceptable because they are somehow lesser humans. It is impossible to overstate the dignity and value conferred on each human by their being created in the image of God. Our great challenge is to live in the light of our God-conferred identity, and to encourage others to do the same.

Genesis 2:19,20 A task: To build a world with a better name

As God's image-bearers, humans are given a task that only image-bearers could do, for it involves great creativity and insight. In a world where the animals and birds have not yet been named, Genesis 2:19,20 informs us that God assigned the responsibility of name allocation to Adam, watching on as he made his decisions. It is a stunning portrait and one which we will unpack more fully in chapter 8. Names help to shape the one named. In allocating the responsibility to name animals and birds to Adam, God is essentially saying, 'I made them, now you shape what they will become.' The fact that God is content to act as an onlooker whilst Adam performs this key task shows how seriously God views humanity's role in world-shaping. If we are to summarize what control belief we can glean from this line in the sand passage, it is that humans are called to build a world with a better name – but to do so with the awareness that God is watching as we do. God may not quickly override our decisions, but we are ultimately responsible to our Creator for the names we confer and the world we build.

Genesis 12:3 A responsibility: Blessed to bless

When Abram was chosen to be the father of the Jewish nation, a nation for whom God had a special plan, it would have been understandable if he had thought that his election was not dissimilar to winning the lottery. Abram was well aware that he had no special merits of his own, but might have thought that he could simply bask in the status of someone lucky enough to have been chosen by God. To ensure that there should be no misunderstanding, God informs Abram that he has been chosen so that 'all peoples on earth will be blessed through you' (Gen. 12:3). Election is not about privilege but responsibility. We are blessed to bless. It is a biblical truth with challenging implications, but if we are to build a Christian world view we must repeatedly affirm that every God-given blessing is for the greater good of all. A key question that those who operate from a Christian world view ask is, 'How are the blessings and gifts I (or we) have received overflowing to bless and enrich others?'

Genesis 50:20 A conviction: God can bring good even from evil

Those who live long enough almost always face some form of tragedy. Be it the death of someone greatly loved, a major disappointment or a searing injustice, few are exempt from the ravages of life. For some, these experiences are permanently disorienting. How should Christians respond when confronted by the unacceptable? The biblical account of Joseph provides some clues.

The family life of all three of Israel's patriarchs – Abraham, Isaac and Jacob – was deeply flawed. One could go so far as to suggest that the author was at pains to remind us that Israel's election was unrelated to her moral virtue (which is largely absent in the account), but reflects the grace and mercy of God. This is particularly apparent in the genuinely ugly account of Joseph's treatment by his brothers. Even for a family torn apart by favouritism and petty jealousy, their decision to murder Joseph was extreme. This is stopped only by the fortuitous arrival of slave traders who can remove Joseph from his brothers' lives, an added bonus being that the brothers are financially richer as a result. The story weaves its way through one disaster after another, before abruptly turning the corner with former prisoner Joseph suddenly elevated to being second only to Egypt's pharaoh. Joseph's prophetic gifting and business acumen are responsible for saving both the Egyptians and Hebrews at a time of widespread drought. It is a stunning turnaround of fortunes.

After the death of Joseph's father, Jacob, Joseph's brothers are convinced that he will seek revenge for the treatment they so cruelly imposed on him. To their astonishment Joseph declines the game of payback, commenting perhaps philosophically, or maybe as a reflection of his great faith, that what his brothers had intended for evil, God had worked for good. The sentiment is found in Genesis 50:20, another of our orienting passages, because it richly suggests the redemptive way God works in broken and fallen situations.

This is seen with even greater clarity at the cross of Christ. There is no doubt that Jesus' execution was a travesty of justice – an act of great savagery and barbarism. What is equally beyond dispute is that God brought great good out of it. Again we see the principle – what humans intend for evil, God is able to work for good. This underlying hopefulness at the heart of the Christian faith is liberating. Without for one moment flinching from the reality of the evil and sadness of the world, Christians can at the same time quietly put their trust in a God who will ultimately work all things for good. The journey may be long and circuitous, and in many instances may only be completed on the other side of death, but the quiet conviction is that God always has the last word. And God's last word is always redemptive, and good. Kindness, rather than malevolence and evil, is the abiding truth.

Exodus 1 An understanding: When the choice is between bad and worse

If read quickly it may not be immediately clear why I have selected Exodus 1 as another of our orienting passages.[6] It tells how two Hebrew midwives, Shiphrah and Puah, outwitted a despotic pharaoh. Instructed to kill all male Hebrew babies at birth, they fail to carry out the order, and when asked to account for this disobedience, tell an imaginative lie to Egypt's king. Hebrew women, they inform Pharaoh, are not like Egyptian women, and have their babies so quickly that the services of a midwife prove to be superfluous. Not being required at the birth of Hebrew babies, they do not have an opportunity to kill them.

Ethically the passage raises numerous questions. Although the women lie to Pharaoh, the passage paints Shiphrah and Puah as heroes. Exodus 1:20,21 explicitly informs us that God rewards these two women by giving them children of their own. Should we deduce from this that God is unconcerned about deceit?

The nature of the midwives lie is also troubling. They categorize Hebrew women as abnormal others, people who give birth differently to Egyptian women. It is always dangerous to stereotype a group of people as being 'other', for once we regard some groups of people as being different, the journey to abusing them can seem to be justified. The history of the Jewish race demonstrates this all too tragically. The Holocaust was partially possible because Jewish people were again portrayed as radically 'other'.

It also turns out to be an unsuccessful lie. Pharaoh accepts the midwives version of events, and so changes his tactics, now requiring Hebrew boys to be drowned at birth.

If Shiphrah and Puah are unsuccessful, stereotyping liars, why are they regarded as worthy of special mention and praise? Incidentally, note that their names are recorded for us, while Pharaoh's name is intentionally omitted, so that we forever remember him as 'Pharaoh who?'. Like having children of your own, having your name recorded and remembered was one of the great blessings of the ancient world. So to say it again, these unsuccessful, stereotyping liars are specially blessed. Why?

The answer is liberating. It shows that the Bible recognizes that we live in a world where we sometimes have to choose between bad and worse – put differently, a world where we sometimes face conflicting moral obligations. These midwives were obligated to tell the truth, but they were also obligated to save lives. They validly recognized that saving life mattered more than truth telling, and for their courage, they are rewarded. The Bible attributes their bravery to their correct view of God, Exodus 1:21 noting that they feared God more than the pharaoh. This is the right kind of fear, a fear that liberates us to do good, because we know that God is good.

I include Exodus 1 as an orienting passage because it moderates what might otherwise lapse into an inflexible and inhumane attitude to ethics. Circumstances do make a difference, and Exodus 1 reminds us that God understands and is not unmindful of the moral complexity which we sometimes face.

1 Chronicles 22:6–10 and 28:1–3 A value: The temple David didn't build (or, not such a bloodthirsty book)

Ever heard people mutter, 'But the Bible is such a bloodthirsty book'? On more than one occasion I have been asked to defend the moral vision of the Bible, and particularly that of the Old Testament. The issue is the many corpses scattered across its pages. A quick reading could leave the impression that God is very one-sided, caring about the Israelites but having little time for anyone else. While the loss of Hebrew lives on the battlefields of the Bible is seen as tragic, Canaanite, Philistine and Egyptian carcasses don't really seem to matter.

1 Chronicles 22:6–10 and 28:1–3 give a clearer insight into the heartbeat of God. In these passages David explains that God had forbidden him to build the temple because the warfare with which he was associated excluded him from the project. For its time, this is radically countercultural, especially as ancient kings routinely built temples to thank their gods for military victories.

These passages are fascinating. After all, David's many military victories are attributed to God's help. David would never have defeated the giant Goliath unless God had made it possible. Why does God now decline David's services as temple builder? We must conclude that whilst God agreed that the brokenness of David's time required tough military action, God was unwilling for warrior imagery to be associated with the temple. In short, God makes it clear that warfare is a tragic consequence of human evil, and that it will never have the last word. Isaiah 2:4 imagines a day when swords will be beaten into ploughshares, and spears into pruning hooks. This is what we should long for and work towards. Jesus reminds us in Matthew 5:9 that it is peacemakers, not peace breakers, who are the children of God. When placed in the impossible situation of having to choose between bad and worse, it is true that warfare was sometimes seen as the lesser evil, but to imagine that it is therefore God's ideal is to ignore the witness of the temple David didn't build.

Matthew 5:21–48 An investigation: Getting to the heart of the matter

Moral instructions in the Bible can either be read as blunt instruments to be slavishly obeyed without question or qualm, or as spring-boarding from an underlying moral vision which should be clearly understood if it is to be appropriately adapted and implemented in changing circumstances. Spending a little time with the teaching of Jesus makes it clear that he favoured the second approach.

In the Sermon on the Mount Jesus makes his famous 'It is written but I say' statements. He applies them to several areas, but we miss the spirit of the text if we limit their relevance to these zones. In Matthew 5 we are reminded that while murder, adultery and breaking oaths are clearly forbidden, we should be as appalled at anger, lust and words which hide rather than reveal our intent. Likewise, whilst the instruction to take an eye for an eye and a tooth for a tooth was useful in ensuring that revenge did not escalate out of control, Jesus suggests that the path of non-resistance might be more effective. Similarly, whilst few would quibble that we should love our neighbours, and would fully understand our hatred for our enemies, Jesus pushes us out of our comfort zone, expressly commanding love and prayer for our enemies and oppressors. Rather than stopping at the letter of the law, we are to dive a little more deeply into it to uncover its underlying heartbeat. Instead of this leading to a compromised and endlessly flexible moral code, the approach is uncomfortably stretching.

It is significant that Jesus prefaces this teaching with a declaration that he had not come to abolish the law, but to fulfil it. This is tested in John 8:1–11.

Confronted with a woman caught in the act of adultery, Jesus sidesteps the clear instruction of Leviticus 20:10 and Deuteronomy 22:22 that adulterers (both male and female) are to be killed. He will allow only the sinless to throw the first stone. As none in the crowd were audacious enough to claim an unblemished status, they all depart. Left alone with the woman, Jesus instructs her to change her behaviour, but fails to implement the death penalty prescribed by the law. Is this consistent with fulfilling the law? It appears that Jesus thought that it was. Punishment was not the underlying vision behind the law. Creating circumstances in which people flourish in relationship with God, with others and with creation, was. Anger, lust and manipulative words block the arrival of this world, just as do murder, adultery and failing to keep oaths. Jesus saw this clearly, and consistently dug a little more deeply to uncover the purpose behind the law. When 'It is written, but I say' helps to orientate our approach to the moral vision of the Bible, we are exploring the right territory, as it urges us to investigate more fully what is at stake behind each ethical conviction.

Mark 12:28–33 A summary: The Jesus Creed

It could be argued that the selection of fifteen orienting passages is indulgent, and that we should have settled for one. After all, Jesus was asked what the greatest commandment was, and surely his answer should trump all others. In Mark 12:28–33 we find what Scot McKnight insightfully calls 'The Jesus Creed'.[7] Stripped of all unnecessary additions, the Jesus Creed, after affirming the unity of God, instructs us to love God with all our heart, soul, mind and strength, and to love our neighbour as we love our own self. Combining the Shema (a Hebrew word for hear) of Deuteronomy 6:4 (which was recited by Jews every morning and evening), with Leviticus 19:18, it suggests that genuine love for God will always lead to and be linked to love for others.

Rather than faith being an escapist journey of disengagement with the issues of this world, a robust and holistic love for God – a love which engages our heart, soul, mind and strength – brings us face to face with every other human, and requires us to explore and enact whatever genuine love for them will mean. It is a tragedy that the church did not allow this simple orienting passage to interrogate the practice of slavery, the support of racism and the disregard of minorities. Such mistakes must not be repeated.

If we follow the Jesus Creed, we are likely to see a radical realignment of our energy, wealth and creative endeavour. The Jesus Creed is not so much a statement to be enthusiastically endorsed as a call to a radically reoriented obedience – an obedience which is litmus tested against love for God and love for the neighbour.

Romans 3:23 A dilemma: Actually, sin does matter

In a brief bad news statement, Paul informs us in Romans 3:23 that all have sinned and fall short of the glory of God. The 'all' announcement makes the statement pretty inclusive – it is indeed a mistake to assume that you or I are excluded from 'all'.

The Greek word Paul uses for sin in this verse (a variation of hamartia) is the one most commonly used in the New Testament and implies a missing of the target, or missing the mark. The verse makes this clear. The target from which all humans fall short is the glory of God. This naturally raises the question of why this should be our target. The answer is that we have been made in the image of God, and as such, have been made to reflect something of what God is like. Our failure to live up to our core identity is the essence of our sinfulness. Made for relationship with God and to reflect something of what God is like, we usually reflect something quite different. This is not a negligible quibble. If we fail to live up to the purpose for our creation, why should we remain alive? Paul notes this logical consequence in Romans 6:23 with his sobering statement, 'For the wages of sin is death'.

One of the most recurring themes in the Bible is that things are not as they are meant to be, and that this is a result of human sinfulness. We repeatedly fail to live out our identity as beings made *imago Dei*. This theme is so significant that we will unpack it at chapter length in chapter 5, 'Humanity: Tragedy or Triumph'. However, as part of our first fifteen, Romans 3:23 reminds us of the real dilemma caused by human sinfulness. No one is excluded from its reach, and we are all both sinners and sinned against. As a result, the world limps as a pale shadow of what it is meant to be. Optimism about the ability of politicians or people of goodwill to solve all the world's problems should therefore be muted. Outside of God's intervention, Utopia is never within reach.

Romans 5:8 The gospel: Christ died for us

Perhaps you have watched an artist at work. A few strokes here . . . a step back from the canvas and after some pondering, some additional lines are added. A form takes shape, the artist steps back again and suddenly, with an exasperated sigh, rips the canvas from the easel and throws it away. 'Not at all what I have in mind,' she explodes. It is a simple life principle. When things don't turn out the way we want, we get rid of them. It is therefore remarkable that when humanity went in the opposite direction to God's intention, God's response was not to destroy the human race, but to find a way to bring it back to its senses.

All analogies are imperfect. After all, the artist has only herself to blame for the portrait not turning out to her liking. Humanity's rebellion against God is in a different category. There was no flaw in God's creation – only one elementary instruction to obey to demonstrate that relationship with God was voluntary and not compelled. In choosing to eat from the fruit of the tree of the knowledge of good and evil, Adam and Eve were essentially renouncing relationship with God, for if unaided they could differentiate between right and wrong, they would no longer need to live in reliance upon God. At heart, original sin is staking independence from God.

Given this backdrop, the gospel message is truly astounding – while we were yet sinners, Christ died for us. We will unpack this more fully in chapter 6, 'Amazing Grace: A Cross-Shaped Reality', but for now it is enough to note Romans 5:8 (and comparable passages, such as 1 Corinthians 15:3,4: 'For what I received I passed on to you as of first importance: that Christ died for our sins according to the Scriptures, that he was buried, that he was raised on the third day according to the Scriptures'). They alert us to a fundamental dimension of a Christian world view. God is the One who reaches out to us. God does whatever it takes to bring us back into relationship.

A more modest version of this principle is found in Genesis 3:21. As it is almost a throwaway line, it is easy to miss its relevance. We are told that before banishing Adam and Eve from the Garden of Eden, God made clothes for them. The image is staggering. The Creator of all, whilst punishing the human race for their disobedience and sin, pauses to consider what they will need to survive in their post-paradise life. Suitable clothing, especially now that they are awkwardly aware of their nakedness, features high on the list. The need is met by the one who is meting out the punishment. It speaks of a God of compassionate justice. The goal of this judgement is not their destruction, but a path that will ultimately lead to reconciliation. Mindful of their need to survive in the intervening years, God in compassion clothes our fallen ancestors. Even while punishing, a plan for their survival is put in place.

1 Corinthians 13:13 A permanence: Three things that remain

In 1 Corinthians 13:13 Paul names three things that will always remain – faith, hope and love. Of these, he lists love as the greatest. The Jesus Creed sits comfortably with this.

The Corinthian correspondence is addressed to a confused, compromised and chaotic congregation. Impressed by spiritual gifts which seemed spectacular, they had to be instructed about what really mattered. In this important letter Paul reminds the Corinthians that although gifts of tongues, healing and prophecy had their place and led to significant adrenalin bursts, what endured was faith, hope and love.

When we use faith, hope and love as an orienting motif we remember to ask of each endeavour, 'Does this flow from faith? Does this flow from hope? Does this flow from love?' If we answer in the negative, we should remember that we are chasing after that which will not endure, and should therefore ask if a more permanent choice would not be preferable.

Some might push back and ask, 'But what does it mean to say that something flows from faith, or hope or love?' Sometimes answers are better understood when we imagine their opposite. When we give in to our fears, we are not operating from faith or hope. When we are unconcerned about the impact of our actions on others, we are not operating from love. When we allow trivia to fill our agenda, we have forgotten to hope for a better reality.

Galatians 3:28 An irrelevance: Goodbye to the old divides

Galatians 3:28 proclaims that our faith in Christ trumps the importance of what often seem to be such significant human divides. Let's hear its sentiment: 'There is neither Jew not Greek, slave nor free, male nor female, for you are all one in Christ Jesus.' At a certain level this seems hopelessly naïve. National pride and interest – especially when linked with religious difference – has sparked more wars than it is comfortable to remember. Over two hundred years after Wilberforce attempted to abolish slavery, we continue to face fresh outbreaks of its horrors. As for there being neither male nor female – well, it doesn't take long to bump into fresh versions of the gender war. Of course the careful reader might rejoin, 'But that is because we are not all in Christ' – a valid insight. Sadly, the history of the church demonstrates that the irrelevance of these divides has not always been appreciated by the community of faith. It is time for this to change, and pointing to Galatians 3:28 as an orienting text will help to facilitate this.

Those who are shaped by a Christian world view should refuse to think of people in narrow categories that inevitably divide. Being in Christ trumps all other realities. It unites across what otherwise might be irreconcilable differences.

With Galatians 3:28 in our first fifteen, we will guard against allowing matters of secondary importance taking centre stage. We should orientate ourselves to the greater truth. In Christ the stereotypes of the old order fade. A new reality can emerge, and those shaped by a Christian world view will encourage its birth.

Colossians 1:15–20 A reconciler: Christ, through whom all things are reconciled and hold together

These verses from the Colossian letter are stunning in their scope and range. They affirm the supremacy of Christ over all, proclaiming that in Christ 'all things hold together' (v. 17), having earlier pointed out that 'all things' includes things both in heaven and earth, things visible and invisible. The reverse is true. Outside of Christ all things sever and fall apart. Even more startling, these verses point us to the range of reconciliation achieved through Christ. We are told in verses 19 to 20 that 'God was pleased to have all his fulness dwell in him [Jesus], and through him to reconcile to himself all things, whether things on earth or things in heaven, by making peace through his blood, shed on the cross.'

We sometimes erroneously think that the reconciliation achieved by the cross of Christ is limited to individuals who respond to the offer of forgiveness provided by the cross. This passage suggests that God has something wider in mind. At the heart of a Christian world view is the conviction that reconciliation is not simply a one by one reconciliation between individual sinners and their

Creator (important though that is), but that ultimately Christ's death will lead to the reconciliation of all things. We can hope for a universe that is fully in harmony. The scope of the reconciliation will even impact realities which are currently invisible to us. Our risk is therefore to have too small a vision of the scope of God's reconciling agenda.

These verses help to orientate us in that they refuse to allow us to settle for any parochial interpretation of Scripture. They also alert us to the danger of an anthropocentric approach. Important though people are, the reconciled community is not limited to fallen humanity. This is a far larger song. It should alert us to our need to expand our horizons and to note the 'all things' that have been created by and through Christ.

Revelation 21:1–4 A vision: A new heaven and new earth

As the Bible draws towards its close, the author of the final book describes his vision of the future. It is a vision of 'a new heaven and a new earth' (v. 1), a reminder that while the old order may pass, the new is not so discontinuous from the old that the previous names of earth and heaven are meaningless. More stunning yet, as John sees the New Jerusalem coming down out of heaven, it appears that the previously divided spheres of earth and heaven now merge, for the cry becomes 'Look! God's dwelling-place is now among the people, and he will dwell with them' (v. 3, NIV 2011). In this new order, God will be with us and the time of tears, death and pain will have ended.

In many ways this closing portrait brings us back to the beginning. God met regularly with Adam and Eve in the first garden. Their desire to stake their independence from God set in motion a cascading chain of brokenness. This is now reversed. Heaven and earth, two spheres which previously seemed irreconcilably separate, are now united, God's presence no longer something we can only fleetingly be aware of, but now part of our settled, permanent reality. Understandably, John ends his book with a cry that has echoed through the ages 'Amen. Come, Lord Jesus' before his closing prayer 'The grace of the Lord Jesus be with God's people. Amen' (Rev. 22:20,21).

The hopefulness of this closing vision should impact us deeply. Hope helps to orientate us. It keeps us going in life's bleakest

moments. It reminds us that the last word is never the disappointment of today, but the certainty of the ultimate victory of God.

This, then, is my suggestion for the first fifteen. They are fifteen
passages that help us to navigate the many stories in the Bible.
They help to capture the bigger picture. They remind us of the
direction and movement of the story. They highlight the heartbeat of God. They help us to remember what really matters as we
contemplate the contours of a Christian world view.

An interview with Lloyd Pietersen

Dr Lloyd Pietersen is a noted theologian with special expertise in
the New Testament. He is the author of several books including
Reading the Bible after Christendom, published by Paternoster in
2011.

1. *What are some passages that are key to your understanding of the
   Bible?*
   I was struck by your use of fifteen 'line in the sand' passages
   and your reasons for choosing them. Most would be in my top
   fifteen too! But your question here is slightly different, I think.
   My fundamental understanding of the Bible is that it is essentially a witness to God and, as such, it continually witnesses to
   a God in relation. God in relation to Godself, to humanity and,
   as the opening verses of the Bible so eloquently demonstrate, to
   the whole of creation. But testimony, by definition, invites interrogation and that is why, in my view, the Bible's primary form
   is narrative rather than a series of propositional statements. So,
   for me, a key passage is 1 Corinthians 10:1–14. In this passage
   Paul, remarkably, writing to predominantly Gentile Christians
   in Corinth, invites them to regard the Israelites as 'our forefa-
   thers'. In other words, Gentile Christians are now caught up
   into the story of Israel and thus into the ongoing narrative of
   God's relationship with humanity. In this way we are invited to
   engage with the text's witness to God. The Bible is essentially
   an invitation to put ourselves into the story – and the key result
   is to equip us to avoid idolatry and thus truly to image God (1
   Cor. 10:14).

Bearing in mind this key passage's invitation to put ourselves into the story, I have to mention secondly the book of Job which I still regard as probably the most significant book in the Bible. Job suffers unbelievable tragedy and yet maintains his innocence throughout. For most of the book, apart from the Prologue, God is both silent and absent. Finally, after 37 chapters, God speaks and Job, having finally heard and seen God, no longer needs to engage in groaning and lamentation. Nowhere does the book resolve the question as to why there is so much suffering in the world – certainly God's speeches do not address this – but we are invited in the midst of the most profound questions concerning human suffering to continue to address our complaint to God until he is finally seen and heard. Lament thus becomes a key mode in our address to God concerning the immense suffering in the world. Finally, and in keeping with my comments on 1 Corinthians 10, I have to add the famous 2 Timothy 3:16,17, not because of its contribution to any 'doctrine of Scripture' for which it is most commonly cited, but because it so clearly states that Scripture, via its teaching, reproof and correction, trains us to do justice and equips us to engage in every good work. In the words of Micah 6:8 we discover through our dependent relationship with God what it means to do justice and to love kindness.

2. *In* Reading the Bible after Christendom *you suggest that the early church lived out their faith from the margins of society and that the New Testament should be read with that lens rather than with a lens assuming power and influence. Unpack how this might impact our reading of the Bible today.*
   For the majority of the Christian period, the church has enjoyed enormous influence and privilege. This was not the case in its earliest period when Christians were a minority sect with generally little influence in society at large. Tacitus, for example, describes them as a class of people loathed for their vices. Many Christians in the West lament the increasing marginalization of the church, but I see this as an opportunity to recover readings of the text consonant with the environment in which the New Testament was first produced. For example, I provide a reading of the Parable of the Pounds in Luke 19:11–27 which subverts

a popular understanding that this is about using wealth to create wealth. I suggest that reading from the perspective of the margins alerts us, for example, to the prophetic denouncement of wealth in the teachings of Jesus and the poetic subversion of power in the parables of Jesus.

3. *What do you understand by Christendom?*
Christendom has been the controlling societal model in Europe where society is construed as consisting of both a secular arm (civil government) and a religious arm (the church) but both arms are united in their adherence to the Christian faith. The assumption is that all citizens are Christians by birth and Christianity is defended by legal sanctions to restrain heresy, immorality and schism. The ecclesiastical system itself is hierarchical, male-dominated and based on a diocesan and parish arrangement. Of course Christendom is being increasingly eroded by the rise in secularization but, nevertheless, there is still the concept of the state church, be it Roman Catholic, Orthodox, Anglican or Lutheran, accompanied by the baptism of infants constituting membership of that church.

4. *What do you think were some of the most common misreadings of the Bible during the Christendom era?*
I think the most fundamental misreading of the Bible has been to treat the Israelite monarchy as normative for Christianity. With the church so aligned with the state, it was all too easy to equate this with the combination of kingship and religion in ancient Israel. In this way the Old Testament was construed as the model for statecraft, the letters of Paul provided the model for Christian discipleship construed as primarily an individual's private relationship with God, and the prime purpose of the incarnation was the death of Jesus for our salvation. The imitation of the life of Jesus was seen as a special monastic calling and not something for ordinary Christians to aspire to. With the kingship model primary, God is seen primarily as the omnipotent, benign despot and Christ is conceived primarily as King of kings. This of course is not to say that the Bible does not provide such pictures of God, but in Christendom this was the controlling metaphor and the picture of Christ as King, rather

than, say, as Suffering Servant, leads too easily to the equation of Christianity with wealth, status and power. Furthermore, the Israelite monarchy with its state religion provided a model for war and conquest. In this way the Deuteronomist's fundamental suspicion of kingship (encapsulated in 1 Samuel 8:4–7) was ignored and Jesus' critique of wealth and power marginalized.

5. *And the question I ask everyone: What do we really, really need to know about God?*
That God is indeed love, but that this love is manifested in wild, unsettling holiness.

To ponder and discuss

- If you were invited to expand the list of orienting passages from fifteen to eighteen, which additional three passages would you choose, and why?
- If you were forced to reduce the list from fifteen to twelve, which would you drop – or would you refuse to obey orders?
- The interplay between loving God, loving self and loving the neighbour is rich. How does the one feed the other?
- Think of some friends who are not yet Christ followers. Which of these orienting passages are they most likely to respond to, and why? Likewise, which are they most likely to react against, and why?

3.

Culture as Friend, Culture as Foe

The 15 August 1988 cover of Time magazine is a mosaic of the face of Jesus built from portraits of Christ popular during different centuries. Each artist has captured a different aspect, highlighting something that was felt to be important during their lifetime. Some give a hint of Jesus the sufferer, others of Jesus the mystic, or king, or warrior, or judge, or . . . well, each suggests a slightly different story. It is a reminder that the account of Jesus has been read in many different cultural and historical contexts and that to some extent what we understand about Jesus and highlight from his life is shaped by our setting.

It is perplexing to explore the relationship between Christianity and culture. Has the Christian faith thrived because it has proved to be extremely flexible and able to adapt to a wide range of historical and cultural contexts? If so, could it be that there is no such thing as a genuine Christian world view, but simply a range of world views that provide a religious version of the prevailing culture? These might be softened with a light coating of Christian jargon to give the appearance of continuity with versions of faith from the past. Clearly if this is the case, our attempt to explore some of the significant building blocks of a Christian world view will prove fruitless.

One of the classic studies in this field is H. Richard Niebuhr's 1951 publication *Christ and Culture*.[1] It continues to shape the way in which we think about the topic, even though the context in which Niebuhr wrote has now changed so significantly.

Niebuhr identifies five ways in which Christianity has responded to its relationship to culture. He speaks of:

1) Christ against culture, where the sacred and profane are seen in opposition to each other, and where the response is to withdraw from worldly matters. While this might appear to lead to a pure version of faith, it usually leads to an otherworldly spirituality that has minimal impact on the world.

2) The Christ of culture, where the sacred is discovered in culture, the danger being that the sacred and profane merge, so that in the end a genuine awareness of the sacred is lost. Its proponents are very much at home in their culture, sometimes to the point of compromising on Christian essentials.

3) Christ above culture notes that some compartmentalize the sacred and the profane. Christ is for the churchly sphere, culture for the realm of business. The overall system is usually a little too neat to be authentic.

4) Christ and culture in paradox acknowledges the corrupt nature of culture, but recognizes that it is our embedding context from which we cannot be removed. We live in a time of struggle between faith and unbelief, and have the promise of life but still wait for its fulfilment. There is thus always a dualist tension with which to grapple.

5) Christ the transformer of culture proposes that all is permeated by the immanent presence of God in the world, and that rather than reject or assimilate to our culture, we should work to transform it.

While Niebuhr is sometimes criticized for an inadequate doctrine of creation, incarnation and the church, as well as for thinking of culture too statically, his influential typology alerts us to some of the pitfalls as we explore this area. In this chapter I plan to explore the impact of culture on any understanding of a Christian world view. I will argue that culture can be both a vehicle through which the Spirit of God can speak to us and guide us, but that just as easily it can be the sphere of the demonic, one which could seduce us into following false gods and idols. Discerning the difference between the two is not always as easy as we might hope, but I will provide some guidelines that can assist us.

One quick additional point. People sometimes argue that culture relativizes everything. Suggesting that there is no actual truth to be found anywhere, they maintain that our cultural starting point determines if we see promise or threat in any proposition. In addition, our culture may render some questions irrelevant. Lesslie Newbigin wisely cautions against attaching too much significance to such views, insightfully commenting: 'The argument about cultural remoteness is really a denial of the fundamental unity of the human race.'[2] Because all humans are created in the image of God, life's more significant questions are relevant regardless of our cultural grouping, albeit that our culture might see us frame these questions in a slightly different way.

The risk of naivety

The first risk to avoid is the assumption that we are not impacted by our culture, and that we have a 'pure' understanding of the biblical message. Mark Strom has suggested that 'evangelicalism works largely by maintaining the myth that it is not a cultural, historical and social phenomenon: "We simply believe the truth."'[3] While we could argue that such naivety, although quaint, is essentially harmless, the argument is not convincing. Take for example our willingness to uncritically read models of Western individualism into the biblical text, or our tendency to assume that models of capitalism are above biblical critique. Indeed, any rapid extrapolation from the world of the Bible into our own world is fraught with danger as the ancient Near Eastern world, in which the biblical story is located, operated from a very different view of the world from that which now dominates in the Western world.

Let me unpack this a little. Consider the impact of Western individualism on our understanding of the Bible. I have often heard preachers suggest that each member of the congregation substitute their name for 'the world' in John 3:16. So instead of reading, 'For God so loved the world . . .' it becomes 'For God so loved Brian (or Sam, Megan, Ruth) . . .' While the emotional impact of this might be great, it is easy to overlook that Jesus was making an inclusive statement, one which would have surprised the original readers who usually assumed that God's concern was primarily directed towards the Jews. The impact of this expansive statement on the extent of God's love is dramatically reduced when we narrow the scope from 'loved the world' (not just the Jews) to 'loved me'.

Likewise I have often heard preachers suggest that instead of starting the Lord's Prayer with the words Jesus suggested 'Our Father in heaven . . .' we personalize this with 'My Father in heaven . . .' Again, our culture blinds us to the danger of altering the script in this way. It is very nice to remember that God loves me and is my Father, but the text alerts me to the fact that this love has a wider address. If I forget this, I am soon likely to think that churchless faith is as valid as any other – after all, why this emphasis on community if faith is about me, myself and I? Indeed it can be argued that the emphasis on individualism and personal fulfilment, currently so rampant in Western society (and rapidly being exported to the majority world), is one of the key reasons we find it so hard to spot that one of the key themes in the Bible is the call to be part of a reconciled community. The scope of this reconciliation is cosmic. It includes being reconciled to God, to people from all tribes and cultures as well as to creation, for as Paul notes in Colossians 1:17, 'in him [Jesus] all things hold together'. This is not therefore a community where everything revolves around me ('my Father') but one in which I have the privilege of being a reconciled part of something so much bigger than me. The gospel frees me from a lonely egoism, but cultural readings of Scripture might trap me again within individualism's suffocating confines.

However, it is important to be nuanced in our approach. While individualism is often at conflict with a Christian world view, there are aspects which are compatible. Thus the Hebrew Bible predicted that a day would dawn when the then famous proverb would be renounced, 'The parents have eaten sour grapes, and the children's teeth are set on edge' (NIV 2011). Both Jeremiah 31:29,30 and Ezekiel 18:2–4 repudiate the saying, making it clear that there is a limit to how much we can dwarf individual identity and responsibility in community, or as Ezekiel 18:4b puts it 'The one who sins is the one who will die' (NIV 2011). Jesus was happy to assure us that even the hairs on our head are counted, surely an affirmation of our individual value and worth.[4] Our awareness of the importance of this has been heightened by our culture's emphasis on the importance of each individual. In other words, if asked if our culture's emphasis on the individual is divine or demonic, it is not possible to answer in one word. There are many shades and subtle emphases that need to come to the fore.

Let us then first look at the way in which culture might trip us up and prove a foe to us, before taking a more positive turn, and exploring ways in which we might hear the voice of God speaking through culture.

Culture as foe

God is always at work in the world, and it is therefore realistic to expect that at times a change in culture will reflect the fruit of God's activity in our cultural context. It is equally true that there are forces of evil at work in the world, and the consequence is that our cultural setting sometimes reflects the victory not of God, but of the demonic. At times the church has struggled to differentiate between the two, and consequently parades around like the naked emperor, unaware that in certain areas it is a herald not of life, but of death. A robust world view shaped by the broad contours of the Christian faith is needed if we are to critique our culture, not as naysayers who instinctively reject everything, but equally not as slaves of the latest cultural fad or fancy. An essential tool in doing this is to identify those things that our culture deeply values, and which shapes its direction. We could go as far as to call these the 'idols' of our time and setting, in that as our culture so greatly values them, it is likely to drive us to devote our time, energy and enthusiasm to their pursuit. Not every 'idol' has to be totally evil, though any which claims a greater allegiance than Christ represents a threat to genuine Christ following.

Examples of cultural idols from church history

When we review the past 2,000 years of church history, some idols quickly leap into view. Here are two examples.

Idol 1: The quest for power, by military means if necessary

The early church was often persecuted, and the idea that it would one day be a powerful force able to impact the fortunes of kings and emperors would have seemed in the 'too hard to believe' category for the first few generations of believers. That changed rapidly after the conversion of the Roman emperor Constantine in 312. By 380 the previously persecuted church basked in its now privileged status as the state church of the Roman Empire, a status decreed in that year by the Edict of Thessalonica.

How radically that was to impact the church was demonstrated shortly afterwards in one of the most fascinating examples of church-state conflict – a conflict which saw the power of the church enormously enhanced.

In 390 a charioteer in Thessalonica was accused of homosexual behaviour. The governor of the district had him imprisoned, but the people of the area, who enjoyed his charioteering skills, demanded his release. The governor refused, leading to an uprising in which the governor was killed and the arrested man set free. Incensed on hearing this, Emperor Theodosius, who had been instrumental in having Christianity decreed as the official religion of the Roman Empire, ordered that the residents of the area be punished. At a chariot race in Thessalonica, Theodosius's soldiers trapped those attending inside, and within three hours had slaughtered around seven thousand people.

Ambrose, the Bishop of Milan, was appalled at this indiscriminate slaughter, and in the name of the church called on Theodosius to repent. Initially Theodosius refused, and consequently Ambrose would not give him communion. Theodosius stayed away from church for a while, but his commitment to the faith made this situation untenable. He reluctantly accepted Ambrose's terms for reconciliation, which included the promotion of a law which required a delay of thirty days before any death sentence passed would be enforced. In front of a crowded congregation, Theodosius took off his imperial robes and asked for forgiveness of his sins. Ambrose initially declined to offer this, but after Theodosius had repeatedly requested it, at a church service on Christmas day Ambrose gave Theodosius the sacrament.

Shelley comments on the significance of this: 'It required unusual courage to humiliate a Byzantine emperor. Ambrose had hit upon the weapon – the threat of excommunication – which the Western church would soon use again and again to humble princes.'[5] The emperor could frighten people into obedience with the sword, but the church could determine their eternal destiny. This made the church more powerful than the emperor.

In this instance is appears that Ambrose was justified in calling the emperor to account. However, the power gained by the church from this encounter was considerable. It was a power that was often abused. For example, consider how forced conversions helped to ensure the 'Christianization' of one area after another. There have been some terrible atrocities. At the Massacre of Verden in 782, Charlemagne had 4,500 Saxons killed when they rebelled against their enforced conversion from Germanic paganism to Roman Catholicism. We could also consider the abuses of the Crusades or the torture administered during the Spanish Inquisition. Each is a sobering reminder that it can be a very small step from being a power holder to a power abuser, and that the justification for the abuse of power is often given in the name of God.

In a world where 'might was right', recognized representatives of the Christian faith often embraced the cultural idol of power in an unquestioning manner. It proved all too easy for the church to gloss over the biblical account of Nathan's confrontation of David for his abuse of his position in organizing the death of Uriah the Hittite.[6] Embracing the cultural assumption that power should be accorded unquestioning respect, the church often glossed over the risk of the demonic that so easily entraps power holders.

Idol 2: The quest for the quiet, ordered life, rather than the just life

A less obvious but very real idol has been the assumption that a peaceful and orderly life is more commendable than a life committed to the quest for justice, and all the unsettling questions that such a quest inevitably unleashes. The status quo, rather than the pursuit of a new heaven and new earth, often proves seductive. Consider this verse from Cecil F. Alexander's 1848 hymn, 'All things bright and beautiful': 'The rich man in his castle, The poor man at his gate, He made them high or lowly, And ordered their estate.'[7] Mercifully, most hymnals now omit this verse, but it gives a troubling snapshot of a nineteenth-century assumption. Apparently the establishment was God-ordained.

My own experience of growing up in apartheid South Africa provides evidence that this idol might not be restricted to the churches long distant past. The warm, passionately pious Baptist church I attended was deeply divided about how to respond to the evil of apartheid. Many did not believe it was an evil – others saw more clearly. For those who did see the evil before them, there was an additional dilemma. On far more occasions than I care to remember the opening verses of Romans 13 were unpacked to us. Verse 1 tells us to submit to the governing authorities while verse 2 instructs 'whoever rebels against the authority is rebelling against what God has instituted' (NIV 2011). So what were we to do in the light of the tyranny that confronted us? The guidance from the pulpit was 'do nothing' – for we were to submit to what God had instituted. I was just a teenager at the time, but even then I realized this stance to be a bizarre and immoral escapism. I am so grateful that in that church there were those who understood the ethos and feel of Scripture so deeply that they raised their voices and lives in dissent to the irresponsible nonsense we were being fed. If we draw from the categories we discussed in chapter 2, they knew that there are orienting passages in the Bible, passages which draw lines in the sand from which we must not deviate. Would apartheid ever build a world with a better name? Did it flow from faith – or from hope – or from love? How then could we remain silent in the face of such evil?

Although there were those who allowed themselves to be guided by the bigger picture provided by Scripture, far too many were lulled into complacency. They assumed that God was the author of the status quo, and that it should therefore not be seriously questioned. It also happened to be in their short-term interest to settle for such an assumption, and so we look back on that era and see too many unclothed emperors inviting others to convert to an equally compliant lifestyle. The nakedness of that era is now all too apparent.

Idols that often trap the church in the Western world

Hindsight offers 20/20 vision. It is easy to tut-tut over the short-comings of a previous era, but more difficult to spot the idols of one's own time and culture. We are accustomed to accept that some aspects of our culture need to be jettisoned if we are to claim to be Christian, but often the willingness to discard our cultural entrapment extends only to the more obviously defec-tive elements. Every culture needs to be critiqued in the light of the gospel. Indeed, of every culture we should ask, 'What are its idols?' Most cultures have some things which are regarded as especially precious, and it is here that Christ followers can easily be tripped up. Some things are so commonplace in our culture that we don't think to question their consistency with Christianity.

Let's examine three obvious idols of the Western world. It is all too easy for our faith to forge an uneasy alliance with them. These are money, sex and power.

Money

A delightful but unsettling story from the fifteenth century recounts that a monk from a small village visited Rome to purchase a silver chalice to use in the church where he served.[8] On his way home he linked up with a group of merchants both for company and safety. When night fell, he spoke about his journey and showed them the chalice he had purchased. Being merchants, they quickly asked what it had cost him, and when they heard the price they were amazed, for they realized that he had purchased it for well below its actual value. They congratulated him on his coup, and were delighted to think that such a modest and unworldly monk should have made so astute a purchase.

The monk, who had not realized the actual worth of the chalice, was stunned. In the morning he announced to the merchants that he was going to return to Rome. The merchants laughed. 'Are you going back to buy more from the man who sold you this so cheaply?' they asked, thinking they had converted the monk to their capitalist ways. 'Oh no,' replied the monk, looking aghast. 'I am going back to pay the man who sold me the chalice the amount that it is worth . . .'

This is a wonderfully countercultural story. I have told it to many groups and usually get them to discuss if they think the monk did the right thing. They rarely reach agreement, but tellingly, they all agree that the twist wasn't anticipated. We should ask why. Should it really be so surprising that someone should be committed to pay the actual value of something, rather than to pocket the proceeds offered by an extraordinary bargain? Surely it is surprising only if you accept the morality and normality of pushing for the lowest price that will be accepted.

Linked closely to materialism is consumerism. We want money to enable us to purchase and consume at will. Rampant consumerism is placing great strain on the world's resources, and its rate of growth is not sustainable. Jonathan Wilson perceptively writes: 'Let's move beyond the familiar, ineffective "we are consumers" and "we consume a disproportionate share of resources." Here is a deeper and more deadly truth: *we are being consumed.*'[9]

It is not surprising that most religions have a negative attitude to both materialism and consumerism, and it would therefore be easy to assume that this is an idol to which those within the church will not bow the knee. After all, James 5:1–6 has strong words to say against those who hoard wealth for their own benefit, while Jesus counselled that it is impossible to serve both God and money.[10] As a result of this, most Christians are able to avoid a crass enslavement to materialism, and many give generously. However, the assumption of what constitutes a normal and acceptable lifestyle tends to be shaped by the broader society. Obedience to Jesus' instruction to accumulate riches in heaven rather than on earth proves difficult when you live in a society that attaches so much importance to financial security, and is paranoid at the possibility of living so long that one might exhaust the savings made for retirement. Likewise, we live in an employment environment that tends to favour offering employees short-term contracts rather than being locked in to long-term commitments. A consequence is that it is difficult to foster a sense of calling to a vocation. Work becomes a means to earn a living, rather than part of the way we seek to answer God's call to build a world with a better name. Christians can easily search through job advertisements in the hope of finding better working conditions, rather than a more effective way in which to serve God and the world.[11]

Sex

Many of Jesus' statements challenge and sometimes disturb us. Take his claim that 'At the resurrection people will neither marry nor be given in marriage; they will be like the angels in heaven.'[12] Though not explicitly stated, it seems reasonable to assume that this implies that heaven will be a sex free zone.[13] This radically relativizes the importance of sex, a relativization that those saturated in Western culture find very hard to accept.

You see it in on both sides of the current debate about gay marriage.[14] Those who are scandalized that Christians could contemplate the validity of gay sexual relationships don't question whether they are attaching too much importance to sex – is it really so important, if sex is one of those things that will pass away? Likewise those who consider it an outrageous injustice to deny gay people a context in which to express their sexual orientation also fail to question if they are attaching too much importance to sex. Again, if sex is one of those things that will pass away, is it really unthinkable to suggest that it is more appropriate for some to remain sexually inactive? If this is hard to read, ask if it is not because in our sexually obsessed society we have accepted the myth that sex is life's greatest joy. If we believe it is, we are bowing the knee to one of the idols of our age.

Even as I write this I am starting to imagine the kinds of comments that these statements might elicit. This is not neutral territory for most of us, which is why this is an area that is likely to trip us up. The fact that our Lord embraced singleness and a celibate lifestyle is an inconvenient truth in an era where an exploration of our sexuality is often classified as one of life's nobler journeys. The biblical witness, while never prudish, gives little encouragement to those who would attach too much importance to sexual discovery and gratification.

What is more important in the biblical account is the willingness to enter into faithful, life-serving, covenantal relationships. In the end it is not about my sexual desires being met, but the kind of community that the relationships I enter into, builds. I'll say more about this in chapter 7, 'Because the Three are One: Trinity and Community'.

Power

While the church has far less influence and power than it did in the Middle Ages, we should not conclude that in this post-Christian era it is immune to power struggles. They emerge in many different forms, but perhaps most clearly in our thinking about leadership. The words 'leader' and 'leadership' are actually used very rarely in the New Testament – yet the topic dominates the discussion of most denominational leaders. Graham Hill has insightfully suggested that it is more biblical to think in terms of servantship than leadership and has called for 'four movements of radical servantship'. These are the movement from:

- leadership to outwardly focused servantship
- shallowness to dynamic theological reflection
- theories to courageous practices
- forgetfulness to transforming memory[15]

In the same book, Lance Ford writes, 'Leadership has become the number one subject among those who are called as servants in Jesus's church. I do not believe it is an overstatement to call it an addiction, an all-out obsession' and a little later on laments, 'In our search for identity we have fashioned and formed out identities as leaders – all the while Jesus and the writers of the New Testament clung to the identity of *servant* of the Lord.'[16]

Implicit in the critique is the awareness that the quest for leadership is often a search for power and the ability to control and shape a group's agenda. Whilst the rationale for this is often stated in lofty terms, when we dig a little deeper, all too often we find a compulsive need to be in charge. It is hard to be following Jesus and to be calling the shots at the same time. The lure of the limelight is seductive and the desire to do whatever I want can prove a powerful temptation. This reflects all too clearly the culture of our time where 'No one tells me what to do' is viewed as a commendable mantra. Followership is an essential ingredient of discipleship. True, it is Jesus we follow, but when we answer the call to leadership we should regularly check that it is Jesus at the front of the pack, and not our own wishes and tiny ambitions.[17]

Culture as friend

We have just explored the negative territory of false idols whose dangers are often rendered invisible by our cultural bias. Culture can also be a friend of a Christian world view, helping it to appreciate more deeply aspects of the biblical message which might be glossed over in another cultural setting. Let's investigate some of the more hopeful aspects of our present time. I plan to do this by exploring the postmodern turn in Western (and some non-Western) society.[18] While it is common to cite the shift to the postmodern as a threat to the gospel,[19] there are many aspects that should be embraced.

Tony Jones in his book on youth ministry explores ten values that are highly prized by a younger generation.[20] He suggests that youth greatly value the:

- experiential
- spiritual
- altruistic
- creative
- communal
- environmental
- global
- holistic
- authentic
- relational

What is striking is how consistent these values are with the Christian faith. After all, the Bible is not interested in theoretical truth, but in wisdom that works itself out in the actual experiences of individuals and communities. It is also clearly a book committed to the reality and vitality of the spiritual; in Christ's sacrifice we see the ultimate model of altruism; the opening chapter of the Bible introduces the creative God who makes everything from nothing, and so we can go on down the list.

In some ways a post-Christian generation is closer to a Christian world view than those who grew up with the remnants of Christendom. Consider the world view of those shaped by the baby boomer era. As a primary school-age boomer, I remember the local insurance company giving schoolchildren in my city a ruler imprinted with the inspirational message, 'Knowledge is power'. We could use that ruler to underline our class reader which was entitled 'New Worlds to Conquer'. It is not hard to understand those values:

- The head ruled. Knowledge would open all doors.

- The goal of knowledge was the attaining of power. Presumably, therefore, power was a desirable good.
- Consistent with those values, our 'New Worlds to Conquer' reader never questioned our colonial past (as previously mentioned, I grew up in apartheid South Africa), assumed the environment existed for our exploitation, and never contemplated that conquest might not be life's noblest goal.

So this is the irony. A boomer generation raised with the remnants of a supposedly Christian world view was actually operating from a world view that was essentially opposed to the ethos of the Christian gospel, while a postmodern and supposedly post-Christian younger generation are embracing values which largely fall within the contours of a Christian world view. We should celebrate the contemporary turn towards concern for the environment, a commitment to authenticity and transparency and an insistence that a holistic lifestyle, rather than a race to the top of the company ladder, should guide our progress through our career pathway.

Not that we should be naïve. I am fully aware that it takes more than the overlap of some values to classify someone or a group as being Christian. But isn't a key missiological principle (perhaps even principle number one) that one examines a culture and its values for both lines of continuity and discontinuity with the Christian gospel? Where there are more lines of continuity than discontinuity, one faces a simpler missiological task.

Not that Jones only mentions the positives when he talks of postmodern youth. He also suggests that they are committed to pluralism and view most things as being relative. Likewise, it is a generation filled with contradictions.

The communal focus of Gen Next is clear. But it is also accompanied by a strong individualism. The two often make uneasy companions. And the reality is that while some find themselves part of a community of significance, loneliness is a curse of our age. Even those who find community rarely find it for the long haul. Life is fragmented. Communities are transitory.

Likewise it is true that Gen Next is altruistic. It is also narcissistic. Again, the two form an uneasy alliance. One can imagine the image of the helix, where the one spirals away from the other.

These dimensions complicate our cultural analysis. Being 'not far from the kingdom of God' is not enough if a rampant individualism and a determination to do things my way and on my terms prevents a bowing of the knee to Jesus. Add to this the innate suspicion of this generation towards authority. Whilst this has many positives, an unfortunate spin-off is that it makes unquestioned obedience to Jesus seem less than ideal. As a result, it is likely to prove impossible to find a culturally friendly way to live out the lordship of Jesus. We are thus back to our paradoxical dilemma. Never a culture or a generation closer to the kingdom of God. Never a culture or a generation further from the kingdom of God. It is as though the helix sweeps around, almost touches and then spins away from Christ and his kingdom.

There is, of course, nothing new in finding signs of God's kingdom outside of religious communities rather than within them. Jesus was scathing in his comments on the religious leaders of his day. Matthew chapter 23 makes for rather depressing reading, especially with Jesus' repeated refrain that the Pharisees were hypocrites and blind guides. It was not an isolated conversation. Matthew 21:23 records a conversation Jesus had with the religious leaders of his day, and verse 31 notes Jesus' startling claim that tax collectors and prostitutes were entering the kingdom of God ahead of the bastions of the religious community. When we analyze contemporary culture for signs of continuity and discontinuity with a Christian world view, we should not forget to embark on a constructively critical cultural analysis of church communities, which often function as discrete subcultural groupings. At times they are encouraging signs of light and hope to the wider community, but at other times, as in Jesus' day, there are more signs of hope when one looks beyond the walls of the church. This is a troubling truth, but it is not a new truth.

What then should we conclude? Probably that we should approach every culture, including church subcultures, with both openness and suspicion. At times we will find signs of God's presence in unexpected places. If Jesus was willing to cast the hated Samaritan as hero and role model in the realm of compassion and humanity, we should be prepared for some pleasant surprises as we analyse our own time and culture, and find within its contours not just the demonic but also the divine.

An interview with Andrew Picard

Formerly the director of student life at Laidlaw College, Andrew Picard now teaches Applied Theology at Carey Baptist College, Auckland, New Zealand.

1. *Andrew, do you think there are multiple versions of the Christian faith, each shaped to fit with a particular culture and time, or do you think there are some constants that remain?*
Try as we may, we cannot boil the pure gospel out of cultural expressions. Whilst this may seem unsettling, it is a reflection of the kind of God we worship. God is not a dormant deity or a set of abstract ideas for us to study; God is the living God and his gospel is good news not good ideas. The good news is that the Creator God comes to us, in our particular cultures, and reveals himself as Lord through the Son and in the Spirit. This lordship is universal, but it is expressed in diverse ways in different cultures, and this has always been the case. In the first century, Jewish Christians were very different from Cretan Christians, but they worshipped the same God. God does not destroy human culture and supplant it with divine culture. Instead, through the humanity of the Son and the power of the Spirit, God works within the creation, and human culture, to redeem and perfect created realities which God declared 'very good' in the beginning. In the biblical story, images of the promised end celebrate and affirm diverse cultural advances that have happened throughout time and have contributed to the perfecting of creation.

2. *Which aspects of Western culture do you think are most likely to trip us up as we try to figure out what it means to be Christ followers?*
Individualism and consumerism are huge issues in Western culture, and they define us as masters of our universe. Freedom in consumerism is defined as freedom from relationships. The freedom of online shopping is the ability to shop without intrusions, whilst Facebook offers light friendships and the mechanisms to block, hide or unfriend any space invaders or burden-makers. Relationships are designed to be easy to enter and easy to exit, without any heavy burdens or demands. In

employment, loyalty between employee and employer is no longer sought nor rewarded. Individuals are free and on the move, from suburb to suburb, job to job, relationship to relationship, product to product, and freedom is measured by the flexibility and agility to be on the move. Those without power cannot keep pace. They are trapped in undesirable neighbourhoods, bogged down in queues and filling out forms; they are stuck in a mobile world. Stripped of community bonds, individuals in consumerism must relentlessly make and remake themselves into desirable products. This is a compulsory task, as the individual is responsible for their own social acceptance. Consumerism's definitions of freedom stand in opposition to the gospel's vision of freedom; we are set free in relationship to God for relationship with God, others and the creation.

3. *Do we live in a world that more closely reflects Christian values than it did 100 years ago? What are we getting right?*
Many Christians wring their hands at the loss of Christian values and wonder how we will sing the Lord's song in a strange land. Undoubtedly, the assumptions of personal morality 100 years ago were more closely aligned with Christian values than today. In the past, Christianity was closer to the centre of society and had an influential public voice. Today, Christianity is on the margins of society and is regarded as one 'spiritual' voice among many. Speaking from the margins requires a different skill than speaking from the centre, and the church must learn to speak with less power, and less predictability. Whilst wistful of the past, we must also remember that the church of yesterday uncritically participated in the colonial oppression of indigenous and minority cultures. Many indigenous communities, people with disabilities, migrants and women were the recipients of systemic oppression and violence under the assumptions of an ordered society. The rise of globalization and freedom movements has seen the growth of otherness and difference which is much more aligned with the gospel's vision of a rich plurality of difference flourishing in Christ's new community. As a result, contemporary communities are both much more difficult, and much more interesting.

4. *Any comments on different understandings of Christianity that you see in the majority world as opposed to the Western world?*

I am struck by the faith of Christians from the majority world. They find praying, believing and sacrificing much easier than I do. This exposes my own shortcomings as well as the influence of Western culture. Western culture is a very technological and rationalistic culture. With God given a protracted leave of absence, and heaven and hell cut out long ago, most Westerners, whether believers or non-believers, live as functional atheists. Faith, prayer and sacrifice do not come easily in the rationalistic culture of the West; they are radically countercultural actions. Secure in our wealth and insurances, Westerners sense little need for God and easily forget that paradise is yet to come. By comparison, many Christian migrants have faced harrowing situations, and they have a lot to teach Western Christians about faith, perseverance, hope and prayer. Unfortunately, their gifts are not always well received. Western churches often offer conditional hospitality to include strangers in their unchanged prevailing order. By retaining mastery over the community as sovereign hosts, Western churches, often unwittingly, ensure that strangers remain strangers whose gifts are not received. However, the gospel destabilizes our settled notions of hosts and guests as Jesus comes to host us as friends who belong together in his new community.

5. *And the question I ask everyone: What do we really, really need to know about God?*

What we really need to know about God has been revealed to us in his Son by the power of the Spirit; God has given himself to be known in his Son by his Spirit. I had a wise mentor who kept reminding me of Herbert Butterfield's [Regius Professor of History and Vice-Chancellor of Cambridge University] principle: 'Hold to Christ, and for the rest be totally uncommitted.' This is important when we think about culture. Niebuhr's famous book *Christ and Culture* sets Christ and culture in separate categories, whereas I would want to argue for Christ *as* culture. In him, through the enabling of God's Spirit, we see the firstfruits of creation being set free from its bondage to decay, we see true humanity as God intended, and the flourishing of true human culture. Christ's culture is the eschatological culture of the kingdom of God where God's will is done on earth as it is in heaven. Christians are called to know Christ, and his kingdom culture, so that we might imaginatively and courageously live the world's true future, today. As John's vision reminds us, 'The kingdom of the world has become the kingdom of our Lord and of his [Messiah], and he will reign for ever and ever' (Rev. 11:15).

To ponder and discuss

- The chapter identifies three current cultural idols – money, sex and power. Identify some others. What risks do they pose to authentic Christ following, and how can they be overcome?
- The chapter affirms that cultural changes sometimes reflect the activity of God in the world. List some positive cultural changes that you think are consistent with a Christian world view.
- If you are a part of a church community, do you think it acts more as a ghetto of escape from the world, or as a launching pad for incarnation and mission?
- What image does Christianity have in your society, and why?

Section B:

Big Building Blocks
of the Christian's Faith

4.

The Universe: Accidental or Intentional

A basic divide

Two sociology lectures from my undergraduate days remain etched in my memory. In the first, the lecturer introduced us to the possibility that we did not really exist, but that what we perceived to be reality might be a figment of our imagination. He challenged the class to disprove the thesis. We set about it enthusiastically. Someone claimed that they knew they were real because of their ability to accurately predict actual states of affair. 'When I get home, my bed will be unmade, just as I left it, and as I already know this, it must exist.'

'Not at all,' our lecturer replied. 'You just think that you will see an unmade bed. It doesn't mean that it is real.'

'I know I am real,' another posited, 'because I just pinched the person next to me, and ouch, it hurt when he punched me back.'

Unimpressed, our lecturer replied, 'No, you didn't pinch him, and no, he didn't punch you back; you just thought he did.'

On and on it went. No matter what we suggested, we were told it was illusionary. I suspect the lecturer was coming around to Descartes's maxim 'I think, therefore I am', but the bell terminating the lecture rang before we reached this point. As our bare-footed lecturer (this was the seventies) left the room, he tripped over one of the steps, and kicked his toe. He hollered out in pain, only to be greeted with a cry of: 'Don't worry! You didn't really kick your toe. You only thought you did.'

The incident has stuck with me because it highlights an important truth. While we may not be able to carefully articulate how we know we exist, we know that we do. This leads us to the inevitable question: 'Why?' After all, it would be more reasonable to assume that there would be no existence, human or otherwise. The existence of matter, and even more so the presence of living and thinking matter, leaves a mystery to be solved. 'Why?' Nothingness would make perfect sense, even though there would be no one to make sense of it. But we do not live in the realm of nothingness. We exist, and we know that we exist.

In trying to answer the 'Why do we exist?' question, answers usually fall into one of two broad categories.

There are those who suggest that existence is essentially purposeless, there being no intrinsic meaning or significance to it. Life is viewed as an essentially random outcome of improbable statistical odds. While these long odds have come together in such a way that it gives the impression of an orderly and carefully designed world, this is not the case. Random chance, rather than intentional purpose, lies at the heart of the universe we inhabit.

Alternate explanations focus on a purposeful creation, overseen by a Creator. In this view, life has the appearance of being designed precisely because it has been.

While there are many nuances in the debate, they essentially boil down to one of these two options – random chance or intentional and intelligent design.

The answer one gives to the 'So why do I exist?' question significantly impacts one's understanding of life and radically shapes one's world view. I saw this all too clearly in the second sociology lecture that remains at the forefront of my memory.

Our second lecturer boldly proclaimed her atheism. 'This is an accidental universe,' she opined over and over again. 'Because it is accidental, don't let anyone ever fool you into believing that life has any "oughts". Ought presupposes reason and purpose. But there is none. We are alive as a result of random chance and are therefore obligated to no one. Indeed, you are not even obligated to stay alive. As you didn't ask to be born, and as there is no fundamental underlying purpose to life, staying alive should not be considered to be a "moral" category. If you are enjoying life, wonderful – enjoy it. But if not, why not commit suicide? Suicide is the ultimate "stuff you" to the meaninglessness of life. Rather than representing moral cowardice, it represents cool logic and courage.'

Being the class we were, and knowing our lecturer to be unhappy with her lot in life, someone asked the inevitable question: 'So why are you still alive? Why haven't you committed suicide?'

I remember the haunting reply: 'A very good question. I haven't yet found the courage. Perhaps one day I will.'

It is hard to imagine any more fundamental world view divide than that which flows from our view of the origin and purpose of life. If this is an accidental universe, then talk about meaning and purpose is artificial. We can, of course, choose to select a meaning or purpose for ourselves, but this is in the entirely optional basket. At root we are constantly confronted with a simple conviction that there is no essential purpose or meaning to life other than any meaning we voluntarily adopt – but such an adoption is at best akin to selecting the booby prize at a competition. It would have been nice if there really was some meaning, but as there isn't, we can attempt to build significance for ourselves. One person might choose to do this by being the greatest cricketer of all time, another might be a generous philanthropist, while yet another might opt for fame by being a mass murderer. In the end it makes little difference, for there is no actual reason for any of us being alive in the first place.

The alternate view, which argues that life has the appearance of design and intentionality precisely because it is designed and intentional, moves in a very different direction. Rather than deciding if they should try to construct a meaning for life, holders of this world view attempt to discover the purpose behind the creation. As it is reasonable to assume that a Creator creates for a purpose, discovering this purpose is a logical quest. Meaning is then not self-created, but accepted as being conferred by the Creator. Put differently, holders of this world view believe there is a reason they were born. This reason cannot be limited to a purely mechanical explanation of how they came to be born, but is linked to their part in a larger story. Finding their place within that story becomes a valid life journey.

The Bible's version of creation introduces a rich range of motifs that help to answer the 'So why do I exist?' question. Before we explore some of these, it is as well to tackle the 'how' versus the 'why' question, especially as the failure to distinguish between these questions often causes confusion.

How versus why

An interest in 'how' something happened is different to an interest in 'why' something happened.

The 'how' question is technical. Often we ask 'how' something was done so that we can duplicate it. Getting the recipe for a tasty dish is the first step to impress the guests at our dinner party with comparable fare. Or we might ask 'how' someone built their kitchen cabinets to assess if the tasks required fall within our skill range.

Knowing how something is done takes away the sense of mystery. When we know 'how', we no longer need to gape in wonder saying, 'That's incredible!' To the contrary, we can smugly claim that we know how it's done and decide if we are also able to do it – given that knowing how something is done does not automatically confer the ability to do it.

The 'why' question is different, and probes purpose and intention. It is usually open to the possibility of persuasion. If my teenage son can give an adequate reason why he should be exempt from his household chores this weekend, I might be willing to substitute for him – though I'll grant that the likelihood is small! Likewise if my doctor tells me why I should lose weight, I might be willing to attempt it – though strong and emotive reasons would be required.

If the answer to the 'why' question is sufficiently convincing, it might be followed by a 'how' question. If my doctor makes a compelling case for why I should lose weight, I am likely to follow up with some 'how' queries. But not every 'why' needs to be followed by a 'how', as 'why' is primarily about understanding motivation, rather than duplicating the feat.

The relevance of this becomes clear when we contrast the outcome from sweating over the 'how' of creation, rather than the 'why' of creation.

Those who rank 'how' questions highly and opt for a 'face value' reading of the biblical creation accounts are likely to spend significant amounts of energy trying to understand how God created the universe in a very short span of time, and that by simply saying that it should happen. The questions follow some predictable paths. Should the Genesis account be understood literally?

If it should, does it really mean that the world was created in six days of twenty-four hours? Should the genealogies in the Bible be considered exhaustive? If so, the logical conclusion is that the world is around six thousand years old. Presumably that means either the vast majority of scientists are wrong in their estimate of the earth's age, or the Bible is wrong. If we work from the assumption that the Bible cannot be wrong (in a literal sense), the only possibility is that most scientists are wrong. The battle lines are drawn, and you probably know them well. The science versus religion debate quickly becomes ugly, with both sides questioning the gullibility and intelligence of the other.

The problem with the 'how' question when attached to the creation account (some would say 'accounts', and contrast the Genesis 1 and Genesis 2 version) is two-fold.

First, it is relative late comer in the sphere of questions. The Genesis account has been around for thousands of years. For most of that time there has been little interest in the scientific interrogation of the text, and where that interest has existed, the scientific tools to systematically examine the text have been missing. Indeed, for most of the time there has been little interest in science as we know it today. Whoever the author of Genesis was, they were not schooled in the scientific method of the last two centuries. The models and assumptions of this world did not drive their description of creation. Consequently, those who look to the text to answer these essentially recent questions require the biblical text to answer queries that were not at the forefront of the author's mind. The answers are therefore likely to disappoint, and it should not surprise us that the debate continues to leave a trail of confusion and muddle.[1]

The second issue with an obsession over the 'how' of creation is that 'how' is often asked to empower us and to demystify the object we are querying. In the unlikely event that I ever fully understand how God made the world, I might be tempted to shout out, 'So that is how God did it' rather than to stand in worshipful awe of the Creator of all.

When applied to creation, the 'how' question might prove too hard to answer. By contrast, the 'why' question is quickly fruitful. If I ask, 'Why is there life on this planet?' the answer is that a Creator God considered this to be good. What is more, when I explore the biblical text, the 'why' question is answered at an expansive level. Rather than the clipped answer provided to the 'how' question (God said it and it came about), in one way or another the answer to the 'why' question is developed in each of the Bible's sixty-six books.

This is not to suggest that the 'how' question is irrelevant. Theologians have often spoken of the two books of God – the book of nature, and the Bible. In their own way, each points to God. Trying to answer the 'How was the world made?' question should lead to a sense of wonder and awe as we become aware of the complexity of the universe. Psalm 19:1 rightly notes that the 'heavens declare the glory of God'. The study of science should eventually strengthen, not weaken, faith.

However, my point remains and although simple, is important. The Bible does not attempt to answer the 'how' question. Rather, it gives us insight into the motivation and purpose of the Creator. The stories of creation offer lenses through which we should understand reality. True, at times there are tension points. For example, if the world is indeed billions of years old and death and decay precede the arrival of the first humans, in what sense are humans responsible for the Fall, and did they arrive on a perfect planet? Intriguing though such questions are, in developing a Christian world view it is probably better to dive deeply into the biblical stories to get a clear sense of what they are affirming.[2] Rather than quibble with a scientific chronology, we should get to the heartbeat of what we are being told about ourselves and the world in which we live.

Let's explore this a little more.

So why are we alive?

The question about the purposefulness of life is a deeply personal one. Potentially it is very threatening. In life's easy days, times when I can eat, drink and be merry, the question can be pushed into the too hard basket. Why ruin today by agonizing over questions that might prove unanswerable?

This quickly changes when darker seasons dawn. If faced with a prolonged illness, or an incapacitating depression that simply will not lift, or when I am forced to watch the prolonged pain and struggle of someone I deeply care for, I need to know if there is any fundamental reason to keep going. What if I conclude that sometimes the dice of life rolls for you, sometimes against, and if it is against, there might be nothing you can do about it except perhaps to terminate it all.

For those who embrace a world view consistent with that found in the biblical narrative, answers to life's more difficult times are provided. There is a story with an overall purpose, a plot line, and an ability to account for contradictions and complexities.

The opening portrait in the biblical account of creation is one where a creative God decides to bring about something that did not previously exist, and in doing so builds something to which a satisfied 'and it was good' evaluation, can be ascribed. This reaches a new height after the creation of Adam and Eve. After this creation, the author of Genesis informs us that 'God saw all that he had made, and it was very good.'[3] We are therefore not simply looking at a good creation, but one which is very good. Is such an enthusiastic assessment justified?

In considering your answer, think of the portrait of the world painted in the opening chapters of Genesis. It is a deeply relational world. The setting is an idyllic garden, filled with fruit-bearing trees, each well-watered by the river which ran through it.

This garden is visited regularly by the God who made it, and who communicates with the original couple as they go about their task of representing God (or being the image or icon of God) to the rest of the created order. Animals and birds are not anonymous objects in this garden, for each has been named by the first human created. The diet appears to have been vegetarian, meaning that no living creature had to fear being eaten by another. Indeed, it seems that death had no part in the original scheme of things. Work was, however, necessary, but this was not the work of a later post-Fall era, for at this stage, labour represented creative tending of the good world that God had made. It was pleasurable.

Clothing was unnecessary, and Adam and Eve formed and occupied the first nudist colony, being completely at ease with the bodies God had given them. We are not told whether these bodies were short or tall, fat or thin, hairy or bald, clear-skinned or spotted, and the absence of this information perhaps indicates its irrelevance in a world where shame caused by unfavourable comparison was not a feature.

The first human was made from the dust of the earth and the breath of God. There is something deeply poetic about this. Frailty and majestic otherness reside together in Adam. He is indeed the dust of the earth, but he is also made from the breath of God. As if to emphasize this, a tree placed in the very centre of the garden bears fruit which the original couple are forbidden to eat. Perhaps if the tree had been located at the outskirts of the garden it could have been overlooked. Many don't wander to the borders of their property, but how can you ignore something at the very centre? Its message was clear. As image-bearers, obedience to the God who made them was not compelled, but invited. They were always free to choose the other, for how could they be like God if they had no capacity for independent action? The choice to obey was always theirs, and the centrally located tree was a constant reminder that another option was within their grasp.

Not that the temptation to disobey was strong. The picture painted in Genesis 1 and 2 is of death-defying vegetarian nudists – a delightful community where all are known, named and comfortable with their existence. Innocence dominates, and there are no sour experiences to cause any troubled dreams. No doubt each night's sleep was simply a pleasant interlude before the start of another day in paradise.

Those familiar with narrative theory will recognize the classic plot-like structure. We begin with the ideal, but a threat is never far from the surface. In Genesis chapter 3 this emerges with force. The simple existence of the tree of the knowledge of good and evil had not launched Adam and Eve into rebellion, but this changes when a crafty serpent suggests that a desire to restrict rather than kindliness lay behind God's instruction that they leave this fruit untasted. The temptation is succumbed to, and the narrative theme shifts from paradise to paradise lost.

And what losses they are. On eating the fruit, the eyes of Adam and Eve are opened in such a way that what they see no longer delights, but brings a sense of shame – a realization of nakedness. For the first time, the body is viewed negatively. Not only do they feel a need to hide their bodies behind clothes made from fig leaves, they now wish to hide their very selves from the God who made them. As God walks through the garden searching for them a question is needed, 'Where are you?' The portrait is poignant. Adam and Eve are no longer innocents rushing to a caring parent, but guilty rebels, aware they have done something of magnitude. The instinct to embrace has been replaced by a gulf of alienation.

The severed human-divine relationship is quickly replicated in a strained husband-wife relationship. When asked if their clothing and hiding indicates that they have eaten from the forbidden fruit, Adam decides that attack is the best form of defence. Genesis 3:12 records his reply, 'The woman you put here with me – she gave me some fruit from the tree, and I ate it.' In other words, 'God, this is your fault. You made the woman (did I ask you for her?) and now she has led me astray. Clearly the two of you are to blame . . .'

Eve adopts a similar strategy, though she suggests that the fault should be placed at the serpent's door.

Would the outcome have been different if the instinct of our ancestors had been to cry out, 'I and I only am to blame. Lord, have mercy'? We cannot know, for clearly this was not their response.

A different order dawns. The door of paradise is closed, work becomes difficult and joyless, childbirth is painful and dangerous, male-female relationships change and become about desire and dominance.

Not that grace is absent even from this first portrait of disobedience. Aware that Adam and Eve are about to enter a hostile new order, God clothes them in something more substantial than fig leaves. They exit the garden clothed in the skin of animals. Though punishing them for their rebellion, God is committed to their survival. The cost is great. Death has entered the world, and Adam and Eve are protected from the elements by the animals that have died on their behalf. A theme of substitution is introduced. The animals they named are now victims of our ancestors' disobedience.

If the Bible is a story with plot and purpose, it passes through the usual three stages that undergird most narratives. After the opening stage where the scene is set and life is portrayed in its ideal form, we move rapidly into stage two, which in most narratives is where a problem is introduced and developed. Hopes of easy resolution are explored but invariably turn out to be ineffective, and the complexity of the problem grows with each aborted attempt at a solution.

The Bible is no exception to this classic structure, and the lengthy second stage explores the impact of human sin, and attempts to resolve it. One crisis follows another. God chooses a nation and gives it laws to abide by. This nation is to be a light to all others, and to point them to the path that leads to peace with God, the neighbour and creation. However, the chosen nation, Israel, rather than adhere to the law they have been given, routinely abandons it. Punishment follows to varying degrees, and often leads to a temporary repentance and a fresh compliance, but the change is never long-lived. The drama grows until God sends his own Son to point people back to a path of obedience and relationship. Rather than changing everything, it leads to a yet greater act of rebellion against God. The human race crucifies God's Son, Jesus. At this stage it seems as though this narrative is a tragedy. Rather than the problem being resolved, it has escalated dramatically with the human race adding to its shortfall the execution of the Son of their Creator.

This, then, is a narrative without the usual third stage, that of resolution. Except . . . Except that as in the greatest narratives, when we have given up in despair, the impossible suddenly becomes possible. The crucified Jesus conquers death (the terrible consequence of the first rebellion), and returns to commission his followers to continue his mission in the world. This will not be an unaccompanied journey, for although Jesus will return to his Father, he will ensure that his followers are empowered by the Holy Spirit to do what would otherwise prove impossible. Great adventures lie ahead, and to date, 2,000 years of church history have followed. Whilst following the Spirit's leading in the mission of transforming the world, Christ followers engage in tasks that need to be done, but also face an inner journey. As offspring of the first Adam, they discover within their own being a similar bent towards rebellion and evil. While the consequence of this bent was removed through the crucifixion and resurrection of Jesus, the pull towards it remains. Part of the significance of their journey is not just about what they do, but who they become as they grapple with the evil within.

This story has more than a single twist. There is actually a double resolution. Breathtaking a resolution though the resurrection is, it is not quite the last word. Jesus will return to this world and a time of reckoning will follow. Those who have responded to the invitation to follow him will be invited into a new order, a new heaven and a new earth, where each of these realms is somehow merged and a paradise, greater than the first and without its vulnerability, begins. It is a beautifully bookended story. Paradise, paradise lost, paradise restored – but magnified.

This concise plot summary has seen us run ahead. Let's allow some of the earlier portraits from the biblical account to impact us a little more . . .

Expelled from the garden, Adam and Eve conceive two boys. We are told little of their childhood and are hurried forward to their adulthood where the one, Cain, kills the other, Abel. Lest we had been inclined to think that their parents' rebellion had been a temporary blip and God's response a significant overreaction, this account alerts us to the brooding evil resident in the human race. Like his parents before him, when confronted with his sin, Cain's initial response is to deny responsibility. God asks 'Where is your brother Abel?' 'I don't know,' is the lie Cain responds with, following it up with a somewhat aggressive counter question (again following the attack is the best form of defence model): 'Am I my brother's keeper?'[4]

Not fooled by the denial, Genesis 4:12 notes that God condemns Cain to a future where the earth will be unresponsive to his efforts to cultivate it. He is told he will be a restless wanderer on the earth. Cain had previously been one who 'worked the soil',[5] so the punishment represents both the loss of his livelihood and his place of belonging. A 'restless wanderer on the earth' is a haunting summary of the depth of Cain's alienation. Cain's fear is tangible and he is convinced he will soon be killed. God's grace again bubbles forth. As God clothed Cain's parents after their disobedience, he now 'clothes' Cain with a mark to protect him. The mark alerts any would be attacker that if they harm Cain, a fate seven times worse would befall them.

And so the accounts continue. Humanity's descent into evil is unchecked. The crisis point is reached during the time of Noah, when the evil on the earth had grown to such an extent that 'The LORD was grieved that he had made man on the earth, and his heart was filled with pain' – to quote the sobering summary of Genesis 6:6. The portrait is clear. God is not detached from his creation but experiences sorrow as a result of human sin. It matters to God how the world fares. Be it Adam's rebellion, Cain's murder of his brother, or the evil of the people in Noah's time, the biblical account is lucid. Evil is never ignored or glossed over. Judgement follows in the form of a flood which destroys all except those protected within Noah's ark. The portrait is again of punishment within protective boundaries. A remnant survives, and a new start it made. Surprisingly, God makes a covenant with those who have survived the flood that all earthly life will never again be destroyed by some natural catastrophe, the covenant sign of a rainbow given as a reminder of God's pledge.

Why am I narrating this summary of the biblical account? We are trying to answer the 'So why are we alive?' question. The Bible's answer is that we find ourselves in the middle of a story of great significance. There is a part for us to play. We can resist our role. The tree of the knowledge of good and evil reminds us that the possibility of choosing against what God desires has always been present – for those who image what God is like cannot do that if they are deprived of real choice. But for those who respond to the invitation to serve as Christ's followers in the world, a journey of real adventure awaits.

So what difference does this make?

Depending on your inclination and imagination, you might respond to this highly summarized recollection of the biblical narrative with a 'Very interesting, but frankly, so what?' or an 'Ah-ha, I think I see where this leads'. Let me spell out some of the implications of finding ourselves within a story with these broad parameters. First let's unpack what this account reveals about the God who created us.

The God portrait

As any story develops, your understanding and insight into the characters grows. The first and most important character in the biblical account of creation is clearly God. Though we might be tempted to think that the biblical narrative is all about us, it is primarily about God. The Bible's opening statement affirms the existence of God with the simple statement 'In the beginning God . . .' and then indicates what this from the beginning God does, namely, 'created'. The opening data 'In the beginning God created' thus sets the direction for all our understanding of the purpose and direction of life. Take God out of the picture, and there is no start to the story and therefore no story to tell.

To build a Christian world view, it is therefore critical to ask about the nature and character of the God who intentionally creates this planet. Here is a list of a dozen qualities that quickly spring out of the early chapters of the Bible. You might well have spotted others. The God revealed is:

- creative
- powerful
- intentional
- relational
- observant
- involved
- confronting
- emotional
- protective
- just
- merciful
- persistent

Let's unpack each briefly.

Creative

Genesis 1:2 informs us of a time when 'the earth was formless and empty, darkness was over the surface of the deep, and the Spirit of God was hovering over the waters'. By the end of the chapter we read of an orderly universe filled with sun, moon and stars, and of the earth, now filled with oceans and dry land, plants, fish, birds, animals and humans. The narrative moves from empty darkness, to a very good creation, all in the space of a single chapter. You would have to be very unobservant not to note that a transforming but orderly creativity has been behind this dramatic change. The

God introduced to us is thus one who can make something tangible and meaningful from nothing. Note that it is not creative chaos that is designed, but an ordered universe, where everything has its place. So the different spheres of sky, sea and land are created, and each is filled appropriately. 'This belongs here' is the sense given as fish occupy the oceans and birds the sky. A purposeful creation rather than random experimentation is thus portrayed.

Powerful

If creativity was required to build a universe from empty darkness, so was power. The Genesis account is content to inform us that to create the universe, God simply issued an instruction (such as in Genesis 1:3 'Let there be light') and the order was fulfilled. To state desire was enough to see it accomplished. This presupposes unimaginable power. This is the God who is powerful enough to will a universe into being. The request is stated, the request is fulfilled. No detail is given on how this happens. The point is that God's power is such that what is willed, happens.

This could be a terrifying thing. If an all-powerful being desired to inflict pain and suffering, we would be defenceless in the face of the onslaught. However, God's power is always linked to good intention. The Creator desires to build a world which can be described as good, and very good. God's power turns out to be the power to put divine love into practice. Hope, rather than fear, is thus the theme of the universe.

Intentional

As God sets about an orderly creation, it is clear that purpose and intention guides each move. The spheres of sky, sea and land are created to be filled. Humans are made to manage the creation, and God's verdict that what was made was good presupposes some standard in God's mind against which something could be evaluated as being not good. God's decision to rest on the seventh day implies that what was intended had come about, and that rest was now in order. Adam and Eve were instructed not to eat from the fruit of the tree of the knowledge of good and evil, implying an agenda that could be complied with or violated. In other words, this creation was not a random outcome of 'nothing better to do on a rather dull day', but flowed from an intentional, powerful, creative God who had a good outcome in mind.

Relational

The creation account makes it clear that God desires to relate to the humans created. God watches as Adam names the birds and animals. God notices Adam's loneliness prior to the creation of Eve, and addresses the shortfall. It appears that God regularly met with Adam and Eve in the Garden of Eden, and is quick to spot their absence when they hid after their rebellious disobedience. All this speaks of a God who communicates and relates. This is, then, no *'Deus absconditus'* who creates but remains hidden and unknowable, but rather a God intimately involved in the day to day affairs of this planet.

Observant

God relates to Adam and Eve, and immediately notes any change in their condition. When they hide, God spots their absence. When Cain kills Abel, God is conscious of what has taken place. As evil grows in the world during the time of Noah, Genesis 6:5 informs us that 'The LORD saw how great man's wickedness on the earth had become'. God also notices a pleasing exception to this trend, Genesis 6:8 noting, 'But Noah found favour in the eyes of the LORD.' There are different ways to make this point. Theologians speak of the omniscience of God – in other words, God is all-knowing. For our purposes, it is enough to note that the creative, powerful, intentional, relational God is also observant, and sees and knows what goes on in this planet.

Involved

God not only sees everything, but acts upon it. This is not to suggest that no freedom is allowed. When Adam names the birds and animals, God is content to occupy the position of observer, and does not interfere in the process. Not interfering is not the same as not being involved. The evil on the earth is allowed to grow to the point where it is clear that the human race has no intention of sorting it out. At this point God intervenes with a flood. The portrait is thus of a God who keeps an eye on creation, allows a significant measure of freedom, but intervenes when required. This is, therefore, not an abandoned planet, nor is it one that allows no room to move.

Confronting

When awkward things happen, we have a choice to pretend that all is as it should be, or of confronting what has taken place. The Genesis account makes it clear that God does not gloss over wrongdoing, but confronts it directly – think of God's probing questions after Adam and Eve hide in the garden, and the appropriate consequences that follow.

Of course some may ask, 'But were they appropriate? Isn't that a lot of fuss over a piece of fruit – forbidden or otherwise?' However, God is not so concerned about what has happened as about what this act reveals. In Genesis 3:5 the serpent tempting Eve promised that if she ate the forbidden fruit, she would 'be like God, knowing good and evil'. At a certain level, the decision to eat the fruit could be made to sound noble. What is wrong with a desire to differentiate between good and evil? The twist is in the first statement, 'you will be like God'. True, as image-bearers, Adam and Eve were already in many ways like God. But this was a promise of more. At its heart, this temptation was to be like God so as to no longer need God. Instead of God serving as the point of reference for ethical decisions, Adam and Eve hoped to make such decisions unaided. It would then be a short step to declare God redundant. The deeply relational God was being informed by those who bore the divine image that considerably less relationship was desirable.[6]

A world in which God and humans are not in relationship cannot be paradise, so God immediately confronts what has happened. It is not an isolated incident. When Cain kills Abel, God immediately challenges Cain. When evil grows on the earth, God sends a flood, whilst sparing a remnant to ensure the continuance of life on the planet. The picture is consistent. When things go wrong, God does not ignore what has occurred. Evil is confronted. It is never brushed under the carpet.

Emotional

While confronting evil, God's disposition is not detached and unconcerned. Hear the pathos in Genesis 6:5,6: 'The LORD saw how great man's wickedness on the earth had become, and that every inclination of the thoughts of his heart was only evil all the time. The LORD was grieved that he had made man on the earth, and his heart was filled with pain.' Some depictions of God portray a detached first mover – the One who got the universe underway, but who is essentially unconcerned with how it fares. Genesis will have none of this. A Christian world view points to a God whose heart can be filled with pain, a God impacted by creation. We can push this too far, and imply that God's emotions are entirely contingent on our obedience. This is deeply problematic as it would suggest that humans control God's emotions. Rather than push things to the level of the absurd, we should note the intent of the anthropomorphism. God cares and is not coolly detached from the affairs of this planet.

Protective

Whilst God refuses to gloss over evil, and is willing to administer punishment, it is done in a way that protects and opens a path for the journey ahead. While banished from the garden, Adam and Eve depart clothed in the skin of animals killed for their benefit. Cain is punished for the murder of his brother, but embarks on his punishment protected by a mark especially provided. The flood terminates the life of most on the planet, but God has ensured that a small remnant are spared to repopulate the earth and to give it another chance. Judgement has a restorative intent.

Just

God's actions are always just. Adam and Eve did rebel against God. Cain did kill Abel. The people of Noah's time did 'only evil all the time'.[7] There is no incident where we scratch our heads and say, 'Now, why did God treat them like that?' The wrongdoing is named and addressed.

Merciful

The clothing of Adam and Eve, Cain's mark of protection, and the preservation of a remnant in Noah's time all point to a deeper quality of God. It is clear that God is quick to protect and limit the impact of judgement, and that the actual judgement is always just, but beneath that another word begs to be birthed. This God is merciful. Why do Adam and Eve rebel while in paradise? Why does Cain kill Abel? Why does the human race do 'only evil all the time'? We should not give an answer too quickly, for the provision of an answer implies that there is a justification for their behaviour. Like the noted Dutch theologian, G.C. Berkhouwer, we must quietly adopt as our refrain, 'sin is inexplicable', for any other answer diminishes its seriousness by attempting to rationalize it.[8] If we rationalize sin, we downplay the depth of God's mercy, for we start to imply that mercy was justifiable. Instead we should allow these early narrative accounts in Genesis to delight and amaze us. This God shows mercy when none is called for. God is merciful not because we deserve it, but because mercy gushes forth as a reflex response.

Persistent

If God's mercy is remarkable, think of our Creator's persistence. It becomes more and more obvious as we dive into the biblical narrative. It is not only in the early chapters of the Bible that we encounter a God who refuses to abandon creation. This is a refrain through all of Scripture. God never gives up, but persistently reaches out. The relational God refuses to accept that alienation and separation can be the last word. This reaches a climax with the sending of Jesus to this planet. It dramatically speaks of the persistence of God. Augustine of Hippo famously wrote, 'You have made us for yourself, O Lord, and our hearts are restless until they rest in you.' Strangely, a further dimension is true. God's own heart appears to be restless until reconciliation has been achieved. The maker of all persistently reaches out until our alienation is ended.

And what about loving and wise?

As you read through these dozen qualities of God revealed in the opening chapters of Genesis, you might be asking, but isn't God love? And isn't God wise? Why have they not been mentioned? These are fair questions. Perhaps the best way to think of them is to ask, 'But what does it mean to say that God is love or that God is wise?' All of Scripture helps to provide the answer, but these opening chapters provide twelve snapshots that help to develop our understanding of the love and wisdom of God. So the God who is creative, powerful, intentional, relational, observant, involved, confronting, emotional, protective, just, merciful and persistent, is all these things because ultimately God is wise and God is love. This is what God is love means. God is love and God is wise in a way which is creative, powerful, intentional, relational . . . well, you know, the list of twelve. Each of these portraits of God draws us to the powerful conclusion that this God of infinite wisdom loves us. It is an overwhelming truth.

If God is like this, then image-bearers should be . . .

This chapter started by exploring two alternate options, life originating as a result of random chance, or as an intentional and purposeful act of creation. A Christian world view clearly points to the second option. However, more content must be given to this. The early narratives of Scripture provide an explanation for the story we find ourselves in. We are made to be image-bearers or representatives of the God who created us. And if this God is creative, powerful, intentional, relational, observant, involved, confronting, emotional, protective, just, merciful and persistent, in some measure, humans must be too.

Rather than despair that my origin is accidental and essentially meaningless, a Christian world view points to a purposeful story in which I have a role to play. It is a story of paradise, paradise lost and paradise in the process of being reclaimed. As we wait for the reclaiming, there is work for us to do. That work is shaped by who we are called to be in the story. While there is a person-specific component to this (my particular role in the story), all humans are called to reflect something of the image of the God who created us. We too should be creative, involved, just, persistent and so on. We will unpack this a little more in our next chapter.

An interview with Nicola Hoggard-Creegan

Dr Nicola Hoggard Creegan is a noted theologian with a special interest in the interface between science and theology. She has published several books, including *Animal Suffering and the Problem of Evil*[9] and is a senior lecturer in the school of theology, mission and ministry at Laidlaw College, Auckland, New Zealand.

1. *The chapter glossed over the evolution/creation questions pretty quickly. Are there some aspects to this debate that you think we should consider more carefully?*
   Yes I do! You are careful to distinguish your account from a six-day creationist story, but you appear to be taking the rest of the story more or less literally – first people (created how?), first sons, first choice, first death, and so on. Maybe you don't intend this but that is how it appears. Your account also distinguishes sharply between the 'how' and 'why' questions, but I would say they are much more densely intertwined than that. The 'how' of evolution has been a threatening account precisely because it gives an account in which no 'why' is needed.
   We live in a world where the evolutionary account has been with us for 150 years. Although I would suggest the mechanisms of evolution are now undergoing paradigm changes – and becoming more compatible with faith – the facts of this progression only grow stronger every day. In my opinion we cannot speak of death being new with humanity. We cannot speak of all evil and death entering the world through humanity.
   The creation myth does gives us hints of a threshold being crossed and I would agree that that is significant and remains so. But unless we respect the 'how' that science has pursued we cannot really expect the contemporary world to heed us.
   Death, for instance: where do we go with that? Death, disease and suffering along with some degree of aggression pre-dated

the coming of humanity – at least these exist today in our cousins and penetrate the mammalian line to an extent that we can make these statements with almost certainty. I think there is much scope for creative theological attention to this threshold. In what ways are we free? Why do we fear death? What does dominion mean, and so on?

2. *You have a special interest in the relationship between science and faith. Why do you think it matters?*
   Well, I think it matters for a number of reasons. The first is that the 'why' and 'how' of a story are intertwined, as I mentioned above. The second reason is apologetic. We cannot continue to ignore science because too many people feel they must choose between faith and rationality. It speaks ill of the creation God has made to blatantly deny or ignore those who have studied the laws of God in nature. Third, it also matters for the problem of evil. The old Fall story made humans the provenance of all evil in the world. What an incredible burden that was to carry. But it was a neat and effective theodicy. We must now grapple with the problem of evil in a renewed way. Fourth, there is much theological work to do. Traditional Fall accounts were tied to very transactional interpretations of atonements. Breaking the old Fall narrative opens us up to more holistic understandings of atonement and purpose. Fifth, nature is an important part of revelation. God's truth is present in science, and we must enter into the community of interpreters of science and play a part in that, rather than withdrawing into sectarian fundamentalism. Finally, the other reason that science matters is that it is a source of inspiration. There are in nature dense levels of order and beauty and these are 'seen' in part through the eyes of science.

3. *Which images from the creation account keep coming back to you, and why?*
   The creation account is very beautiful; the separations, the hovering of the Spirit over the waters of the deep, the suggestions of the tohu va bohu (without form and void) – and with them deep dissonances keep coming back to me. Striking also is the way in which God speaks and all comes into being,

because we, made in the image of God, also speak and bring things into being. The breath of God breathing life into clay is striking, as is the creation of life that bears new life. We still don't really know what life is or how it began, but we all recognize life and distinguish life from non-life. The so-called curses are descriptive of the human condition – that food will be hard to produce – the wheat and the thorns will always be with us; and that there will always be a dominating of women by men. I think both of these are manifestations of evil that need to be resisted. Feminism is therefore a bit like farming. I have come to note the tension between Abel and Cain, perhaps reflecting the early transition to agriculture. And then I note also the way in which the garden scene is resonant with the Song of Songs, with the wilderness temptations, and with Gethsemane. That some texts inter-textually make their presence felt by stealth has always intrigued me because truth is often like that – whispered and hidden and tacit and always deeper than we suspect.

4. *Is it possible that we all have a part in a larger story, or is this wishful thinking?*
   Absolutely! The Hebrew Scriptures are replete with characters of little worth and status who do great things for God – women waiting long for a child, a man vomited out of the mouth of a whale, Davids who slay Goliaths, a despised brother who comes to rule Egypt and so on. The weak come to rule the strong and life comes out of death. In other words, the Scriptures tell us that faithfulness is more important than the apparent cultural necessity for wealth and status. For most of us we are tempted to feel as though we have no place, and very little voice in a world of political power and celebrities. But if we follow the God of Jesus and Spirit then out of darkness and death and discouragement will come new life, the only life that matters. So yes, we are all a part of a larger story. Sometimes we might get little glimpses of that story, and sometimes we don't see it but have to believe by faith that it is there. After all, we all know that the story can only be seen by the ending. That is why stories are so powerful. The ending can make a difference to how everything is understood.

This is why reading biblical stories to children is important. But also important is a whole heroic literature, seemingly removed from the Bible, in which the little person, the insignificant person, comes to have an important part of the drama. These stories unveil heaven, showing us that in a world of mimetic rivalry only these hidden dynamics of weakness overpowering strength really matter.

5. *And the question I ask everyone: What do we really, really need to know about God?*

We really, really need to know that God is love. This is a lifetime's work, however. There are so many ways in which the love of God is misrepresented. [Anglican theologian and philosopher of religion] Sarah Coakley makes the point that to know the God of Father, Son and Holy Spirit is to participate in the life of a trinity that includes a cross. Love and the cross are all a part and parcel of the same God. We need to know that God is subject, and can be known only by interaction. When we describe God or theologize too much about God we run the risk of veering very far from the truth of the God who loves and befriends. If God is subject we too are subjects, and animals, many of them, are also subjects. The turning of subjects into objects is a danger of our rationalistic mechanistic world and we need to resist it in every way possible. That means that our communities of faith and deep prayer lives are crucial to knowing God. I don't think we really, really need to have a perfect doctrine of the Trinity, but we need to know that the ineffable Creator God has become human in Christ and that Christ is the image of God. It helps also to know that the Spirit is the One by whose power these polarities are overcome, and that the Spirit can take us deep into the heart of God.

To ponder and discuss

- Why do you think some people focus more on the 'how' of creation than the 'why' of creation? Do you think it matters?
- What images strike you from the early chapters of the Bible? Are they still relevant today?

- The chapter discusses a dozen qualities of God that spring out of the early chapters of Genesis. Can you spot any others? Which do you find the most inspiring, and why?
- So which do you think it is – an accidental or an intentional planet, and why?

5.

Humanity: Tragedy and Triumph

A story

In my view, Sam was one of the nicest members of our congregation.[1] He was enthusiastic, affirming and willing to get involved in any project the church undertook. His wife Jo was equally endearing and they had a 10-year-old son who was outgoing, confident and happy. Sam's faith was evident, and he spoke about it freely. There was only one thing that puzzled me. Whenever we had communion at church, Sam didn't participate. Others might not have noticed, but it was clear to me. As pastor, I sat at the communion table and watched as the bread and wine was passed around. Without exception, when the tray carrying the elements reached Sam he would pass it on without taking either the bread or one of the tiny cups carrying the grape juice, which substituted for wine. Initially I thought it might be the result of a tender conscience. Perhaps he and Jo had argued before the service and he felt he should make things up before partaking of holy things. But it soon became clear that this was a pattern.

So I asked him, 'Sam, why don't you ever take communion?'

'Ah, you've noticed,' he replied. 'Well, I guess I better tell you. You've known me for a couple of years, and you've met me during the happiest period in my life. But it hasn't always been like this. You probably don't know, but I was married before. The marriage was a disaster, and it wasn't her fault – it was mine. I don't know why . . . I mean I really, really don't know why . . . but I was unbelievably cruel to her. No – not physically violent, I've never been a violent man – but emotionally cruel, really cruel. I sensed her vulnerability, and it brought out a bully in me. I destroyed ever iota of self-confidence that she had. In the end she had a complete breakdown. Friends advised her to leave me, and somehow she found the strength to do that. But she has never really recovered. It's fifteen years later, and she is still a pale shadow of the person she was before I wrecked her life.'

He paused. He was struggling to speak. 'So you ask me why I don't take communion. I know who I am. I know what I am capable of. And I can never forgive myself for what I did to another human being. Take communion – I will never be worthy of that . . .'

Striking and sad though this story is, in a certain sense it is everyone's story. On our better days we do things of which we are proud and go to bed content and satisfied. But not every day is a better day. We disappoint and confuse ourselves. It might be a temper tantrum, or an act of pure selfishness. Lust might dominate the landscape. Or we might lack the courage we need in a testing situation. We are not the giant of our dreams. The apostle Paul spoke of a universal human dilemma when he wrote, 'I do not understand what I do. For what I want to do I do not do, but what I hate I do.'[2]

A Christian world view is quickly confronted by the puzzle of our humanity. On the one hand we are, to cite the psalmist, just a little lower than the angels.[3] On the other, 'all have sinned and fall short of the glory of God' to quote Paul.[4] Let's explore this paradox and unpack its implications.

'[F]earfully and wonderfully made' but 'There is no-one righteous'[5]

To be human is undoubtedly a wonderful thing. Genesis 1:26,27 announces that people are made in the image of God. In Psalm 139:13,14, David writes, 'For you created my inmost being; you knit me together in my mother's womb. I praise you because I am fearfully and wonderfully made . . .' 'Fearfully and wonderfully made' – the description is both suggestive and moving. While God declared all other aspects of his creation to be good, the creation of Adam and Eve was proclaimed to be very good.[6] The task set for humans was lofty. As image-bearers of the God who made them, they were to represent God in the world and to be stewards of God's good creation.

We are, however, quickly confronted by a shadow side. Humans promptly showed themselves to be capable of rebellion and evil. Fratricide is committed in the very first family, as Cain kills his brother, Abel. The book of Genesis tells not just of the origins of the human race but from Genesis 11 picks up on the formation of the Hebrew people. Called to be a light to the nations, Genesis recounts the story of the patriarchs of this nation. They are scandal-filled accounts. Rather than recalling scenarios of idyllic family life, we read of the ugliness surrounding the birth of Ishmael, of the divisive favouritism in the family life of Isaac and Rebekah and of the chaotic relationships between Jacob's twelve sons – to say nothing of the squabbles between his four wives. There is incest, rape, the sale of a family member into slavery, as well as a host of other petty jealousies and much bitterness. 'Fearfully and wonderfully made' seems an excessively generous assessment of our ancestors. We have to think in terms of paradox. Honour and shame dwell together, with neither ever far from the surface. A survey of the history of the world quickly highlights our capacity to show cruelty to others. But we also uncover a story of love, kindness and creativity. How then does a Christian world view shape our understanding of what it means to be human? Perhaps we can start by briefly noting some alternates to a Christian world view.

Alternate world views

Whilst Christians affirm that being made in the image of God is the key to understanding our humanity, alternate world views exist. Whilst we won't discuss these in any depth, note some of the possibilities. Some think of humans as:

- *Machines*: In this view the focus is on what people can do. People are regarded as means to an end rather than as an end in themselves. Whilst most companies would deny they treat employees in this way, when we objectively analyze their behaviour, they often do. Employees are valued on the basis of what they produce or what they contribute to the company. If they are no longer able to do this, they have no value to their employer. Their ability to produce, or lack thereof, trumps all other considerations, although this might be masked by a slow process of terminating their employment.

- *Animals*: Although humans have a greater brain capacity than animals, we share much of our DNA with animal and plant species. Proponents of this view usually feel that we make too much of the differences between humans and animals, and that our anthropic view of the world is often at the expense of other species and the environment. Behavioural psychologists note that the stimulus-response mechanism in animals can usually be generalized to humans, enabling human behaviour to be shaped and conditioned in much the same way as in animals. Many behavioural change programmes are based on a system of reward (and sometimes punishment). Changed behaviour, rather than reflecting a change of heart, results from a shaped and conditioned response. Taken to an extreme, our actions are not seen to reflect a moral centre within, but a predicable response to the range of stimuli we have experienced.

- *Sexual beings*: Freud regarded sexuality as the basic framework of our humanity, although his understanding of what was sexual was very broad. He suggested that three forces shape each person. We are id, ego and superego . . . the id constantly trying to fulfil its basic drives and urges, whilst the ego and superego serve to regulate or redirect the urges of the id into socially acceptable behaviours. Though Freudianism is well past its heyday, sexual imagery and titillation undergird many aspects of contemporary life – be it marketing, entertainment, or the clothes we wear. Its emphasis highlights that for many, our sexuality is the essence of who we are.

- *Economic beings*: While Marxism with its dialectical materialism is the most advanced formulation of this theory, at a more popular level we can see that people are often dominated by economic forces. Much behaviour can be regulated with the promise of a pay rise, and the bottom line is usually understood to be a financial equation. Where we live, how we fill our waking hours and how much time we spend with our children are all hugely impacted by economic considerations. When asked, 'If you had all the money you could ever use, what would you do differently?' most are able to provide a lengthy answer, suggesting that financial factors significantly impact our behaviour.

- *Pawns*: In this largely cynical view of life, forces of blind chance are seen to determine our destiny. Where we are born and the social standing of our parents hugely impacts our life prospects. We are helpless pawns in a game which is being played for no obvious reason. It is a short step from this view of life to theories of absurdity and despair.
- *Free beings*: Taking a different approach to the view that we are pawns, holders of this perspective believe that when adequate education, nutrition and care is provided, people are free to make choices that can lead to happiness and wellbeing. Most government is modelled from these assumptions, and funding the right projects is often seen as a key to building a better world.

Clearly there are some elements of truth in each of these views. When pushed to an extreme, most appear exaggerated and absurd, but the danger is that we ignore the kernels of truth that they highlight.

What, then, marks an anthropology as being distinctly Christian? A Christian world view would include at least seven elements, affirming that:

- We are created beings, not creatures of chance. We were made through a conscious, purposeful act of God. Perhaps nothing is more fundamental to a Christian world view than this.
- Having been made in the image of God, we possess what theologian Helmut Thielicke calls an 'alien dignity', that is a dignity that is conferred upon us from outside, a dignity given by God. Speaking of the implications of this, Karen Lebacqz writes:

Precisely because it is 'alien' to me, it cannot be given away by me or taken away by others. It is both alien and inalienable. It is indelible, a mark put on us by God's love that permeates our being to the core. Since the alien dignity of humans depends only on God's love, and since God's love is constant and enduring, so is the dignity of each person.[7]

- Because our value has been conferred upon us by our Creator, our meaning lies outside of ourselves and in relationship with God. Deep in the human heart is the quest for 'home'. Whilst people often struggle to articulate what this means, it is linked to our sense that there is 'something more' in life, and that we find this only when relationship with God is restored.
- We have an eternal dimension. While we are created at a point of time, we are creatures made for eternity, and part of our humanity is reflected in our taking this dimension seriously. While the present matters, our being creatures of eternity is reflected in our near-instinctive orientation to the future. Unlike the animals, the 'what next' question is never far from our minds.
- We are physical beings, and our bodily wellbeing is of concern to God. Because we are unified beings, hunger and pain can affect our spiritual condition. While Christians would argue that we are more than animals, we are also not less than animals. Basic needs for food and protection are a key part of our humanity, albeit that they are needs shared with the animal kingdom. Just as we look out for our own welfare, we should look out for the welfare of others, for our humanity is not detached from our physicality.
- We are made for community and to be in relationship with other people. The first 'not good' in the Bible is God's comment that 'It is not good for the man to be alone.'[8] For most of human history we have intuitively grasped this, but the excessive individualism in Western society means that an important corrective is now needed.
- We are image-bearers of the God who made us, and although the image has been tarnished by the Fall, being image-bearers remains intrinsic to our humanity. It confers both our identity and points to our life task of representing God in the world.

It is this seventh element of being an image-bearer that we are now in a position to explore.

What does it mean to be made in the image of God?

Why were we made in God's image, and what does this mean?
These are questions that have sparked more than a little debate
amongst theologians, so perhaps we should start with what is
beyond dispute.

The creation of the first humans in God's image is immediately linked to their responsibility to provide oversight of God's
good creation.[9] They were to be God's representatives in ruling
over what had been made, and the stewardship motif helps us
to understand one key aspect of what it means to be an image-
bearer. Peter Enns has written:

> . . . although what 'image of God' means in its fullest biblical witness
> may be open to discussion, in Genesis it does not refer to a soul or a
> psychological or spiritual quality that separates humans from animals.
> It refers to humanity's role of ruling God's creation as God's represent-
> ative. We see this played out in the ancient Near Eastern world, where
> kings were divine image bearers, appointed representatives of God
> on earth. This concept is further reflected in kings' placing statues of
> themselves (images) in distant parts of their kingdom so they could
> remind their subjects of their 'presence'. Further, idols were images
> of gods placed in ancient temples as a way of having a distant god
> present with the worshipers.[10]

Ruling over creation did not confer limitless power on Adam and
Eve. The rule was to be in God's name or as God's representative.
They were to be accountable.

Whilst most have agreed that as God's image-bearers humans
have a special responsibility in the world, this is not necessarily
the limit of what it means to be made in God's image. Many see
the image in structural terms, arguing that the properties which
constitute us as humans represent the image of God in us.[11] In
other words, the image is not limited to what we must do (represent God) but also who we are at an ontological level. If the image
is linked to properties we possess, the issue immediately becomes
– which properties?

Some suggest it is our rationality – the fact that we are thinking
animals. Problems are quickly apparent. Does that mean that those

who lose their rationality as a result of an accident or the ravages of dementia, or those who are born facing significant intellectual challenges, are not made in the image of God? In addition, if the image was tarnished by the fall of humanity, in what way was our rationality impacted? If anything, our intellectual heritage has become more, not less, impressive. The question then becomes, how can we be both fallen and yet so clearly possess this sign of our essential humanness?

Others suggest that the image of God is reflected in our moral capacity or our openness to the spiritual. Whilst these views have some merit, it is unlikely that we can link the image to a specific human quality. The issue always becomes, 'But what about humans who do not have that capacity?' If moral sensitivity is a criterion, do we exclude psychopaths or sociopaths from our defi- nition of humans? If spiritual sensitivity is the key, what are we to make of the many people who seem completely disinterested in this dimension of life?

There are real risks in linking the image to a particular aspect of our humanity. Part of being human is our vulnerability. What we possess today we may lose tomorrow. I vividly remember a discussion with a mother whose 23-year-old son James[12] had been severely brain damaged in a car accident shortly after graduating as a lawyer. His memory had been reduced to his name and an oft-repeated statement, 'Jesus loves me.'

'Who is he now?' she asked me. 'Where has he gone? He looks just the same, and every day when he wakes, I think he is back with us. But then I speak to him, and he's not there.'

Did James cease to be human the day he lost his ability to remember, that dreadful day when his IQ plunged from the upper to the lower extreme? Yet this same James is able to remember a key truth. As he now says over and over, 'Jesus loves me.' Could it be that as this and his name are the only things he remembers, he is more of an image-bearer than before? This is not a question to answer too quickly.

Some argue that the image should not be understood as an aspect of our essential human nature, but rather as signifying our standing before God. This standing was lost by Adam at the Fall, but is restored to us by Christ. This helps to shift the focus from anthropology to Christology. Christ is the bearer and restorer of the divine image. Put slightly differently, if we want to know what it means to be human, we should not look at other humans, even those in the Mother Teresa and Nelson Mandela category. The image of God and human nature is best understood through studying Jesus, not other fallen people. In his humanity, Jesus reflects what all humans should be like.

While few would dispute that Jesus is the ultimate representative of what it means to be human, suggesting that the image was completely lost at the Fall is perhaps too gloomy. After all, in Genesis 9:6 the murder of other human beings is forbidden on the grounds that they are made in the image of God. Likewise, James 3:9 laments that we use the tongue both to praise God and to curse people 'who have been made in God's likeness'. These are post-Fall passages, but the writers continue to point to the intrinsic value of all humans as image-bearers.

A way forward could be to see the image as something comprehensively tarnished at the Fall, but capable of restoration. This restoration begins as a result of our standing in Christ, and in the process of our sanctification it is progressively restored, albeit that the full restoration will only be complete in the life to come. Theologian Daniel Migliore expresses this well when he writes, 'Being created in the image of God is not a state or condition but a movement with a goal: human beings are restless for a fulfilment of life not yet realized.'[13] In other words, I move towards living up to the image in which I have been made.

While we have not come up with a tight definition of what it means to be made in the image of God, this is not necessarily a bad thing. Watertight definitions sometimes remove a sense of mystery, and stop us from exploring areas that could prove fruitful. There are, however, a number of things which have been highlighted by our study. Pulling them together we can say that:

• The image of God is universal within the human race. Prohibitions of murder (as in Genesis 9:6) and cursing (as per James 3:9,10) are post-Fall restrictions forbidden on the basis that the other (the person we might murder or curse) is also an image-bearer. They apply to all people.
• While tarnished, the image of God has not been lost by the Fall. We could consider the Genesis 9:6 and James 3:9,10 passages

again. While a range of punishments are imposed as a result of the Fall (such as work and childbirth becoming difficult), the removal of the image is not one of them.

- The image is not more present in one person than another because they have greater intellect, reasoning powers, moral sensitivity or the like. Likewise, the image should not be correlated with any variable. Being made in God's image is not limited to certain conditions or situations. There is no suggestion that a person is made in the image of God provided that, and only provided that, they are – and here we would add the variable we consider important – intelligent, of a certain race, above five foot three, and so on.

- The image refers to that in our make-up which enables us to fulfil our destiny. Our goal is to love and obey God, to live in harmonious community with others and to steward creation. As image-bearers, who in Christ are in right standing before God, we can be who we have been made to be, albeit that living up to the image is a journey that will only be completed in the life to come.

A raft of implications quickly flows from this.

- We belong to God. While being image-bearers reminds us that some of God's attributes belong to us, more significantly we are reminded that we belong to God. It is God's image we bear. The question 'who am I' cannot be answered outside of a reflection upon whose image I bear.

- Jesus is the only true image-bearer. To know what it means to be human, I should look to the model given by his life, and pattern myself on him.

- We are properly human only when we are related to God.

- Being an image-bearer confers a task – the stewardship of this planet. There is therefore goodness in learning and work, and in striving to do the best we can.

- People are always valuable as the image is universally present in all. Human life is viewed as sacred even after the Fall. We should not forget this the next time we encounter a homeless person, or ponder the plight of refugees. All people matter, and prejudice and discrimination are inconsistent with image bearing.

- Because the image is universal, all people have points of sensitivity to spiritual things. Even those who appear to be the most disinterested have a God-created vacuum that can only be filled when relationship with the God in whose image we are made is re-established.

Never less than humanists, but usually more

Many books on Christian world view spend a great deal of time talking about alternates to a Christian world view. One of these is usually humanism. Whilst we will not explore humanism in depth, I think some comments about it are important. This is partly because I have so often heard Christians say things like 'but that is humanism' as though some distasteful evil has just been admitted into the room. Sometimes the context is one in which a call is being made to compassionately care for another, and the renunciation of Christian responsibility ('that's humanism') sounds bizarre to those who hold to no religious faith, but assumed they could count on Christians for some support in the matter.

Humanism is capable of several definitions. On the one hand it is a technical term that refers to a cultural and intellectual movement of the Renaissance. It emphasized secular concerns as a result of the rediscovery and study of the literature, art, and civilization of ancient Greece and Rome. As such it tried to resurrect ancient wisdom that it felt had been overlooked as a result of the dominance of Christianity.

When not specifically linked to the Renaissance, humanism can mean a system of thought that rejects religious beliefs and centres on humans and their values, capacities and worth. The centre of study is humanity, not some external being who may or may not exist.

Even more broadly, humanism does not need to be linked to either an embrace or rejection of religious concerns, and can signify a focus on the interests, needs and welfare of humanity. With this as the focus, some Christians have been happy to call themselves Christian humanists, arguing that the Christian faith provides all the resources needed to live a fully human life, both at a personal level, and as members of human society.[14]

When Christians react against humanism they are usually anxious about those branches of humanism that wish to promote the human quest at the expense of spiritual matters. There are indeed many humanists who argue that a focus on religious concerns detracts from issues of human welfare, pointing to some tragic examples where human atrocities were supported by appeals to the Bible or Christian faith. For example, while Christians are rightly proud of William Wilberforce's pivotal role in the abolition of slavery, and validly point to his strong Christian faith which prompted his compassionate response, another story can be told. That story is of the opposition he encountered. This was often justified by appeals to the Bible, and particularly the Old Testament, where several passages were cited which on face value seemed to support slavery. So whilst a leading Christian was a key player in the abolition of slavery, some of his greatest opponents were Christians who based their opposition on their reading of the Bible. Some humanists would therefore ask, 'Would it not have been easier if we hadn't had to worry about the Bible, and simply operated out of our deep concern for the welfare of all people?'

Similar concerns are expressed about the role of religion in acting as a brake on scientific research which could potentially be for the benefit of humanity, or of implementing other changes which are seen to be humane and just. Be it the religious concerns surrounding stem cell research, or the ethical caution theologians display when discussing issues such as euthanasia or gay marriage, religious people are portrayed as slowing the progress of humanity. Not that religious people are the only ones who express caution about these potential changes, but what humanists resent is that when it comes to these issues, religious people appear to be unwilling to consider any evidence that does not accord with their pre-existing beliefs. As such it is almost impossible to get them to change their minds, regardless of the evidence produced.

Whilst this sometimes occurs, it is more often the result of a toxic version of the Christian faith, than of Christianity itself. In chapter 2 we explored fifteen orienting passages from the Bible that help us to assess if our interpretation of a particular passage is likely to be correct. We noted that moral instructions were not used as blunt instruments, and that Jesus was happy to say 'It is written, but I say unto you' as he went on to unpack a level of meaning in the law not previously appreciated. Theological construction is a dynamic exercise, and involves an ongoing discussion between the Bible, the traditional practice and understanding of the church, and the insights of contemporary culture. We should not dismiss humanism because some humanists have been unimpressed by the close-minded approach to life adopted by a small number of Christians, albeit that this group is sometimes very vocal.

I would argue that Christians are never less than humanists, but they should be more. Rather than detract from the human quest for meaning and significance, the belief in a God who has made all humans as image-bearers confers infinite dignity on each human person. How can a Christian have anything less than a deep and profound concern for the wellbeing of another image-bearer?

Christian humanists are also a little less naïve about the human propensity to evil. Many humanists believe in the innate goodness of all human beings. Christian humanists point out that this neglects an important part of the human story. The history of the world is a history of the cruelty of its people to each other. Without a clear category to help us understand the widespread nature of evil, we are at a loss to account for our dismal record. We also have no narrative to suggest a path towards reconciliation. Here again, then, a Christian version of humanism leads to a richer understanding of life, rather than the reduced understanding that comes when we try to rid humanism of a Christian framework.

In addition, to listen to 'rumours of another world' (to quote the memorable title of Philip Yancey's book),[15] rather than making us less alive and alert to the present world, makes us more observant to the threats and challenges it faces. After all, we are part of a planet that has been intentionally created; we are part of a larger story. Playing our part is therefore even more important than if this world was all there is, and it wasn't part of a wider narrative.

Some criticize humanists for their focus on humans, which is sometimes seen as being at the expense of plant and animal life, and the environment in general. If human concerns dominate, why worry about whales or dolphins? Again, Christians are more than humanists. Our ancient ancestor Adam was assigned the task of naming all birds and animals. Building a world with a better name was the very first human task. The stewardship of all of creation, rather than an anthropocentric absorption, is the first responsibility of image-bearers in a Christian world view. This will not be at the expense of human concerns, for in God's good creation all things cohere together and the wellbeing of one is not at the expense of another.

But what about the Fall?

I have argued that while the Fall tarnishes the image of God in all humans, it does not remove it. A Christian world view will always affirm two aspects of humanity. We are fearfully and wonderfully made, but we are also fallen creatures. It is important that we take both seriously. If I only believe in the goodness of people, I will be doomed to disappointment. The reality of the Fall permeates every area of life. This needs to be taken with the utmost serious-ness, and finds tangible expression when society provides prac-tical safeguards against human sinfulness.

Here is an example. As I have said, I grew up in South Africa during the apartheid era. In the 1980s the ruling Nationalist Party, who since 1948 had implemented their ideology of racial sepa-ration, declared a state of emergency. In the face of escalating violence, legislation was approved to permit what would other-wise be forbidden. Among other measures it allowed for deten-tion without trial. When challenged that the police might abuse this new power, the public were told to trust them, as they had the welfare of society at heart, and would only arrest people who were known to be troublemakers – even though there was not enough evidence to prove anything against them.

Although the Dutch Reformed Church was largely complicit in the apartheid regime, this trite denial of the risks inherent in this legislation provoked a response from them. 'How could the state ask its citizens to simply trust the police?' they asked. Were the police not merely human, and therefore impacted by the Fall? All fallen beings, if given unchecked power, are bound to abuse it. They urged (largely unsuccessfully) that more protections be put in place.

Back to our opening story.

Sam's horror at the evil he had seen within himself was real. With his former wife an emotionally destroyed invalid as a result of his cruelty, he needed no convincing that he had fallen far short of the image he was made to bear. What he found more difficult to accept was that forgiveness was possible. While Sam's story is a little more extreme than some, we all have our shadow self to deal with. How are we to deal with the shame that flows from being human? This is the question we address in our next chapter.

An interview with David Cohen

Dr David Cohen is the author of *Why O Lord? Praying Our Sorrows*.[16] He is the head of the department of Bible and Languages at Vose Seminary, Perth, where he specializes in Hebrew Bible.

1. *What is your understanding of what it means to be made in God's image?*
   Being made in God's image is not easy to define. However, it seems to me that two considerations are foundational to our thinking about the concept. First, Genesis 1:26 reminds us that humanity is not only described as being made in the image of God but also being made in the likeness of God. Both the Hebrew words used for 'image' and 'likeness' are difficult to define precisely but the second of the two seems to me to suggest a 'likeness' which emphasizes a humanity which acts like God. This walks hand in hand with the 'being' aspect expressed through the use of the word 'image'. In other words, a more complete expression of a humanity created in God's image encompasses both who a person is and what a person does.
   Second, Genesis 1 establishes God's relationship with creation as a whole and culminates in God's relationship with human-kind. But in Genesis 2 another facet of relationship is intro-duced. We discover that there is a sense of 'incompleteness' in the individual who, despite being created in God's image, is alone. Of course the remedy to this dilemma is not found in any of the animals. Rather, it is in the encounter with another human that this 'incompleteness' is rectified. As I consider the drama of the man and woman encountering each other I hear echoes of 'male and female' from Genesis 1:27. It suggests that

as we encounter the image of God in the 'other' we begin to perceive it more clearly in ourselves. It could be that the image of 'being' which the man encountered in the woman is further enhanced when humans become dynamic participants in God's creative action pictured in Genesis 3 as tilling and keeping the garden.

2. *We are often told about what was lost at the Fall. What wasn't lost?*
The term 'Fall' is an interesting one. Occurring much later in history, in the book of 4 Esdras, the term is overlayed onto Genesis 3. The focus on 'Fall', at least historically, has tended to place the spotlight firmly on the disobedience narrated in Genesis 3 and ruminations around the problem of sin. While this is a key issue in the narrative it can overshadow whatever was or wasn't lost; conversely, what might have been gained.

Taking my dual vision of the 'image of God' offered above ('being' and 'doing'), it seems to me that while neither of these qualities were totally lost, Genesis 3 does picture a humanity which, by personal volition, chooses to be less than what it was created to be. The marring of relationship, resulting from disobedience to the divine will, prematurely foists humans, who failed to maintain their divine potential, out of the garden into a world which has not yet reached it divine potential. Questions such as God's, 'Where are you?' and 'What have you done?' (Gen. 3) along with the 'Where is your brother?' (Gen. 4) are all indicative of a relational 'lostness'.

Despite the losses explicitly outlined in the narrative, a gain is present, albeit perhaps more implicit. The gain could be characterized as a challenge; finding the answers to God's questions, which are more existential than spatial. Perhaps it is in wresting with these questions, together with God, that we discover where we are (in relation to God and ourselves), what we have done (to God and others) and who and where our brothers and sisters are (in relation to ourselves). In reconnecting with God, ourselves and others in this way we begin to rediscover what it means to be truly human.

3. *Genesis is filled with stories of dysfunctional families. How could godly people like Abraham so often get it so wrong?*

   While the major characters of the Hebrew Bible might be popularly envisioned as paragons of faithfulness and morality, even a cursory reading of the text reveals both the very best and the very worst of human attitudes and behaviour. If relationship remains our key interpretive lens for the stories that unfold in the biblical narrative beyond Genesis 1 – 3, then the tensions which create dysfunctions in the families of Genesis may begin to make sense.

   Losing a clear sense of what it means to relate in healthy ways to God, oneself and others (an outcome of the events in Genesis 3) resulted in gaining existential questions. Hence, the quest to find what was lost could now begin. Though the various characters in Genesis and beyond set about answering those questions, the quest is not explicit. This is important to notice, because the existential questions are not always obvious in the lives of the narrative's characters. Nevertheless they do undergird questions of identity, purpose and, more broadly, meaning in life.

   The way back into relationship with God, oneself and others has always been a rocky pathway which inevitably involves taking wrong turns, making poor decisions and, at times, losing the pathway completely. But it is the pathway to recapturing a life which expresses the image of God in all that we are and do. This is a pathway that all the imperfect biblical characters and their families wanted to find. The most remarkable quality of the narratives in Genesis is not that frail human beings failed so many times and in so many ways but that God continued to prompt them to think about these significant existential questions and, in the meantime, continued to work out God's purposes in spite of human failure.

4. *Is our membership of the human race a cause for both pride and shame?*

   We live somewhere between the dust and the divine; sometimes closer to one or the other. Both biblical history specifically and human history generally illustrate how human beings constantly oscillate between these two extremes. Rarely, or perhaps never, are both qualities witnessed in isolation. Instead, together they bear witness to the quest for humankind to find our way back to God, ourselves and one another.

The temptation is to view human beings as either/or rather than both/and, setting up a dualism which is not so clear-cut in the biblical narratives. Both pride and shame, dust and divine together form who we are as human beings.

The tension for us between what we are proud of and what we are ashamed of in our humanity ought not to be viewed as an entrapping vortex that ends in a nihilistic abyss. Rather, the tension ought to be reflected on as a dynamic force, encouraging us to desire reconnection with the God who created us and, in so doing, birth a rediscovery of our true humanity, created in the image of God.

5. *And the question I ask everyone: What do we really, really need to know about God?*

God is relational at heart. The nature of God as a dynamic tri-unity animates this reality and, amazingly, initiates humankind into that animation as a created, living being. This invitation is to be and to do as *God would* in the midst of creation. While this invitation creates a world of potential and possibilities, it also presents enormous challenges which often, in turn, result in struggles.

While we are created and called to be like God we are, of course, *not God*. But, rather than disavowing the challenges and struggles, we are called to embrace them wholeheartedly. Through this embrace we might just discover that we cannot struggle alone. We need others on the journey with us and, ultimately, the presence of God in our lives to negotiate the journey successfully. Should we embark on such a journey, a truly profound discovery awaits us; while God's creating work began in Genesis it also *continues* to be at work creatively in us and through us bringing about God's purposes for all creation. This view of God reminds us that while lamenting over the very worst of humankind's actions, God has remained focused on restoring humanity and continuing the creative process begun in Genesis; never abandoning us to our own resources or condemning us to aloneness. This restoration narrative begins early on in the biblical account and culminates in the revelation of Godself in the person of Jesus Christ.

To ponder and discuss

- Do you think that some people are nice, and others not, or that we are all a mixture of good and evil? Does the question matter?
- What do you think distinguishes humans from the rest of creation? Can we make too much of the differences?
- What do you think it means to be 'never less than humanists, but usually more'?
- What would you say to Sam?

6.

Amazing Grace: A Cross-Shaped Reality

At a British conference on comparative religion, delegates were debating amongst themselves what was unique about Christianity. One suggested that it was Christmas – that God came and lived with us. Those more knowledgeable dismissed the idea, rightly pointing to some other religions' claim that the gods came and lived amongst humans. Someone else confidently asserted it was the belief in the resurrection. But that was refuted as other faiths have accounts of people returning to life. And so the discussion went on, with no obviously unique factor being highlighted. At this perplexing point, the famous novelist and apologist C.S. Lewis walked into the room, and hearing the question responded quickly: 'Oh, that's easy. It's grace.'[1]

As they thought about it, the delegates realized that Lewis (as usual) was right. In every other religion, you have to earn the approval of God. Christianity teaches that God loves and accepts us because of God's nature and character, not because of ours. Muslims have a code of law, Buddhists have an eight-fold path to follow, animist religions have sacrifices and rituals to perform. By contrast, Christianity teaches that we find the favour of God not by what we do, but by trusting in what Jesus did for us on the cross. That's why it is a faith about grace. It goes to the heart of what Christians believe.

At its simplest, grace affirms that we are not treated on the basis of our merits but on the basis of God's love and goodness. It is God's way of breaking the impasse in the relationship between people and God. The journey is tracked in the Bible. To answer the question, 'What happens when things go wrong and there is a major breakdown in relationship?' the Bible explores three options. Let's look at each in turn.

Three responses when things go wrong

A real dilemma in life is that 'stuff happens'. Things go wrong, and sometimes the consequences are devastating. This can be heightened by the knowledge that someone is clearly to blame. Recently I listened to a radio talk-back show discussing forgiveness. A woman phoned in and told the story of her daughter who had been killed by a drunk driver. Claire[2] had stopped at a red traffic light when a heavily intoxicated driver smashed into the back of her car, catapulting it into the stream of traffic passing through the green light. After months of unsuccessful treatment for her extensive injuries, Claire died. 'Forgive that drunk driver for what he did?' said the distraught woman. 'Never. I will never, ever forgive him.'

So what do we do when things go wrong and someone is to blame?

Option 1: Escalate the conflict

Genesis 4:23,24 records the almost instinctive human response. In this passage (which we have mentioned before) an exhilarated Lamech boasts to his two wives, Adah and Zillah, that he has killed a youth who wounded him. He smugly notes that whereas Cain was avenged seven times, if anyone acted against Lamech they would find that he enforced a seventy-seven-fold revenge.

While the passage provides us with very little detail, it would appear that a young man had acted as an aggressor and wounded Lamech. Lamech had killed him in return. As Lamech's strength and heartiness is apparent, it would seem that the wound he received was very minor in comparison to his vengeance.

The desire for 'revenge with interest' is a basic instinct. We are wired to defend our rights and if anyone tramples on them, we feel entitled to teach a lesson that will not be forgotten. While in reality it is often not possible for us to react in this fashion, many play out revenge in their fantasy life, finding in their imaginings some relief for the pain and rage that they feel.

When implemented, Lamech's model of reprisal is deeply damaging. An ever-escalating spiral of revenge is quickly in place. The originating event is often forgotten as new offences dominate the landscape. There is no way out – just endless retaliation with interest, which must then be returned with even greater interest. It is a deeply disturbing model, but one which is implemented far too often.

Option 2: Repay measure for measure

Perhaps because of the dangers inherent in Lamech's model, when the Law was given to Moses the extent of revenge was limited to the offence committed. Exodus 21:24 spells it out. If in a fight an eye is lost, you are entitled to knock out the other person's eye. If a tooth is dislodged, you can remove the offender's tooth. It is measure for measure . . . not a tooth more, nor a tooth less.

The benefits of this limitation are obvious. Instead of conflict galloping out of control, it is carefully managed and limited. Nothing is overlooked, but equally nothing is escalated. Once the offender's tooth or eye is removed the matter is settled, and life can return to normal – or as normal as it can be without an eye or tooth.

The principle has gained widespread acceptance, and reflects a fairly obvious, albeit simplistic, justice. A slightly more sophisticated version came in law to be known as, to quote the Latin, *lex talionis*, or the law of retaliation. Its undergirding principle is to apply equitable retribution, and is now usually understood to mean that reasonable compensation must be made for any offence committed. Most commonly this is understood in financial terms – so that whereas we are now unlikely to literally take an eye for an eye, we will endeavour to calculate the value of the eye and to ensure that the offender reimburses accordingly.

Option 3: Grace and forgiveness

Jesus, however, commands a different response. In the Sermon on the Mount he discusses the eye for eye instruction, and essentially rejects it. In Matthew 5:38,39,43,44 we read, 'You have heard that it was said, "Eye for eye, and tooth for tooth." But I tell you, Do not resist an evil person. If someone strikes you on the right cheek, turn to him the other also . . . You have heard that it was said, "Love your neighbour and hate your enemy." But I tell you: Love your enemies and pray for those who persecute you'. It is hard to imagine a response further removed from either that of Lamech or of *lex talionis*.

Indeed, Jesus seems keen to distance himself as fully as possible from Lamech-like responses. In Matthew 18:21 Peter asks Jesus if he should be willing to forgive his brother as many as seven times. In verse 22 Jesus replies, 'I tell you, not seven times, but seventy-seven times.' Whereas Lamech boasted of his policy of multiplying revenge seventy-seven times, Jesus suggests we do the exact opposite, and forgive that many times. The spirit of the text makes it perfectly clear that if a seventy-eighth occasion is needed, it should be indulged.

Jesus takes the discussion on retaliation to a completely new level. While the eye for eye principle might have prevented revenge spiralling out of control, it had significant limitations. As Calvin Miller has perceptively noted, 'Eye for eye, tooth for tooth. A just, satisfying and rapid way to a sightless, toothless world.'[3] Jesus envisioned something that was transformative. Instead of a tidy settling of debts he makes a radical new suggestion, and advocates a path of non-resistance and non-retaliation. The underlying hope is that this might leave the door open to the enemy becoming the friend. He advocates loving our enemy. After all, if we love the enemy, he ceases to be an enemy, for how can we consider someone we love an enemy? Although we are tarnished image-bearers, Jesus' teaching resonates deep within us. We are not so far from the Garden of Eden that we have ceased to long for a world of friends and true neighbours.

What Jesus is talking about is grace. It is not about ensuring that everyone gets the appropriate punishment for their deeds, but about finding a way to make enemies friends. That's the heartbeat of grace. It is never earned – and Jesus does not suggest that we love our enemies because they deserve it. To the contrary, our love is so unexpected that it disarms the recipient, and leaves them open to new possibilities.

This example from my childhood might seem a little superficial, but perhaps it makes the point. When I was a young child my parents took me to a wedding and the reception that followed afterwards. It was a very trying experience and seemed to drag on forever – one boring speech following another – sheer torture for an active 4-year-old. I became restless and noisy. My father started to threaten, 'Be quiet, or you'll catch it later.' I knew what he meant. This was not an era when smacking children was socially unacceptable. However, when you're 4, later is a long time away. I became more restless. My father became more threatening. Confident that there was a limit to what he could do in public, I ignored the warnings that came with increased frequency.

The reception eventually ended, and we trooped to the car. 'So do you want your punishment now or at home?' he snarled.

'At home,' I pleaded.

When we got home, he repeated the question, 'Do you want your punishment now, or after your bath?'

'After bath time,' I begged.

Bath time came and went. 'And do you want your punishment now or when you are in bed?'

'When I'm in bed,' I whimpered.

When in bed, my father came into the room: 'Now for your punishment,' he growled. And then to my amazement he threw me a chocolate bar and left the room.

To this day I still remember my sense of amazement. Over fifty years has gone by, and it still astonishes me. Fancy being rewarded instead of punished. It was a little encounter with grace – and it has proved unforgettable.

A parable about grace

Matthew 20:1–16 is a passage about grace. It is one of the less popular parables, probably because it flies in the face of our 'eye for eye, tooth for tooth' mentality. It is the parable of the workers in the vineyard. Let me quickly recap it.

The owner of a vineyard employs some people to work in it. Some are engaged at the start of the day (around 6 a.m.), others at midday and yet others when only an hour for work remained – about 5 p.m.

Those employed last get paid first. To everyone's delighted astonishment they get paid the rate for a full day's work. Aware of the kindness shown to those who had only worked for an hour, those contracted at midday come hopeful that they will be treated with comparable generosity. And indeed they can't complain, for although they only worked half a day, they get the rate for the whole. It was a little confusing, however, for clearly in comparison to those who had worked for an hour, their payment was not as munificent. Finally those who worked the full day get paid. To their dismay, they get paid the standard rate for the day. It was what they originally expected, but in the light of the largesse shown to the others, they feel cheated.

An aside is helpful at this point. Jesus was actually telling a story found in the Talmud.[4] It was first told at the funeral of a popular Jewish rabbi who died young. The mourners naturally asked, 'Why did such a good man die so young?' This story was originally told in answer to that question. There was, however, a small but very significant difference in its original form. The conclusion was different. When those who had worked the entire day asked why they were paid the same as those who worked the shorter time, they were told, 'Those who worked for an hour were indeed paid the same as those of you who worked for twelve. But did you not notice? In their hour they worked so hard that they picked as many grapes as you did in your twelve hours. It was therefore only fair to pay you all the same.'

In its context it answered the pastoral question of why the popular rabbi had died so young. He might have been young, but he had managed to cram so much life into his limited years, that he had accomplished as much as those who lived out their allotted three score and ten.

This is a classic 'eye for eye, tooth for tooth' understanding of life. Everything is carefully and neatly worked out. Everything balances. Grace is absent and would probably be considered unfair.

But Jesus astonished everyone by giving a different ending to the story. In Jesus' version there is no talk about those who worked for an hour doing as much as those who worked the twelve-hour shift. To the contrary, Jesus takes the focus off the workers and puts it onto the owner of the vineyard, who represents what God is like. In Matthew 20:15 the parable concludes with the owner asking those who had worked the long shift, '[A]re you envious because

I am generous?' That's grace. It is not what we deserve, but what God in love gives. C.S. Lewis was right. It is the unique feature of the Christian faith. Not that it is a feature we sit comfortably with. Few cite the parable of the workers in the vineyard as their favourite. Its logic is unsettling. We can follow it, but we often feel more at ease in a tit-for-tat world. That, of course, changes when we become aware that we are the one-hour workers and are the ones in need of grace.

So why do we need grace in the first place? What have we done that is so bad that we need a special display of favour?

Why is grace required?

Grace is required because, to quote the words of Paul in Romans 3:23, 'all have sinned and fall short of the glory of God'. So what is sin, and why does it matter?

John Stott has helpfully noted that the New Testament uses five Greek words for sin.[5]

- *Hamartia*, the most common term, depicts sin as the missing of a target. Because this is the most frequently used term, it is worth unpacking a little. The idea is not unlike that of archery, where instead of hitting the bullseye, you miss the board altogether. The target of our humanity is to reflect what it means to be made in the image of God. It is this idea that Paul refers to in Romans 3:23 when he says that 'all have sinned and fall short of the glory of God'. The target we have fallen short of is the glory of God. This is true of all humans. There are no exceptions. We are not who we have been made to be. If we are not who we have been made to be, how can we justify our continued existence? Though initially this understanding of sin may seem fairly soft (we have not lived up to our potential or purpose), when we think it through, we realize how devastating the claim is. We have failed to realize the reason for our existence. It is therefore only reasonable that the consequence (or wage) for *hamartia* should be, to cite Paul in Romans 6:23, death. Why should God continue to sustain us if we fail to meet the purpose of our creation? A termination of the experiment is totally understandable.

Things have not worked out as they were meant to. The target has been missed. A good reason to end things . . .

- *Adikia* is the least clearly defined of the terms for sin. In Greek mythology *Adikia* is the goddess of injustice, which she personifies. In the Bible adikia most commonly refers to sin as a form of injustice, usually towards another human being rather than towards God. Jesus uses the term in Luke 18:6 to describe the unjust judge while Luke in Acts 1:18 describes Judas Iscariot's wickedness with this term. *Adikia* can point to something being wrong or perverted within a person's character, or of a deed that violates law and justice.
- *Ponēria* points to evil of a particularly vicious or degenerate form. It refers to the intentional desire to do harm. Satan is often referred to as *ho ponēros*, the evil one.
- *Parabasis* indicates that a known boundary has been stepped across. The implication is that we are trespassing in territory we know to be forbidden, but have chosen to enter anyway.
- *Anomia* is lawlessness or the intentional disregard of a known law.

The range of meaning of these terms is significant. Most commonly, sin means that we have missed the purpose of our creation (*hamartia*), but it can also refer to injustice, intentionally harming another, trespassing into forbidden areas, or the deliberate disregard of known laws. We might not be guilty of every manifestation of sin, but we are all guilty of some. At the very least, as a consequence of the Fall, we fail to reflect the purpose of our creation and so fall short of being the image of the God who made us.

Our sin is serious because we are responsible for it. Part of our being image-bearers is our ability to make free decisions. While it is true that a range of circumstances always impacts every action we take, and at times we are less free than at others, in the end all humans are accountable. We do not consider caterpillars, cows or tulips responsible for their actions – but then nor do we claim that they were made in the image of God. Our sin – be it sin as missing the target of God's holiness, or sin as injustice or as breaching a known boundary – is always our responsibility. It is why Paul describes the outcome of our sin (death) as a wage – or something we have validly earned for what we have done.[6]

It is in this context that we begin to understand why grace is so amazing. We have validly earned our punishment. Why, then, are we offered life, not death? The answer lies not in our actions but in the grace of the God who forgives us.

Not that grace is without cost. We should not think that God decides that sin is essentially unimportant and can therefore be glossed over. To the contrary. Grace is a cross-shaped reality. Our forgiveness comes at the price of the crucifixion of Jesus. What is the logic of this justice?

A cross-shaped justice

The Bible portrays sin as an affront to God's holiness and as earning God's wrath. Because humans bear the image of God, our sinfulness is an insult to the holiness and purity of God. In a moral universe, God's natural response to evil is wrath. There would be no morality if God rewarded sin with praise, or more neutrally, simply ignored it. Glossing over evil might cause less trouble in the short term, but in the longer term it is not only fundamentally unjust, it leads to an untenable situation. We all know that wrong-doing ignored grows steadily. We would not live in a just or moral universe if sin was brushed under the carpet. The ostrich response of pretending evil is not real simply does not work.

The real issue is whether it is fair for someone other than the individual sinner to carry the penalty for sin. In short, if someone guilty of *hamartia*, *adikia*, *ponēria*, *parabasis* and *anomia* faces death as a wage of their sin, there would be few objections to the justice of this. It is the *lex talionis* principle of a proportionate response.

What is more perplexing is why in a Christian world view it is maintained that a deeper level of justice is served through the death of Christ on our behalf. And there is no doubt that the Bible teaches that Jesus' death on Calvary was for the forgiveness of our sin. Paul puts it bluntly in Romans 5:8: 'But God demonstrates his own love for us in this: While we were still sinners, Christ died for us.' How can Christ's death remove my sin?

Perhaps the most striking point to make from Romans 5:8 is that Paul is speaking of the logic and justice of love. As he notes, the cross is a demonstration of the love of God for us. Justice without love would simply call for the termination of the human experiment. Made to be image-bearers, we have rebelled against the God who made us. A just and fitting response would be the extinction of the human race, with a 'note to self' – 'Experiment seriously flawed. Do not repeat it.' A just and fitting response – but one which love cannot accept. The dilemma is therefore to find an appropriate response to sin which does not bypass the requirements of justice, but which can be embraced by the God who loves us.

The cross is God's solution.

You cannot look at the pain and suffering of the cross and imagine that sin is irrelevant or without consequence. And the biblical account goes to great pain to demonstrate that it is our sin that leads to this cruel execution of Jesus.

There are so many characters linked to the crucifixion that only the most deeply insensitive fail to realize that they are represented there. Our presence could be in the gullible crowd, so easily duped into demanding the crucifixion of Jesus; or in the religious leaders who congratulate themselves on defending the status quo by demanding this aspiring Messiah's death; or in Pilate, who consoled himself that he made a modest (but clearly unsuccessful) effort to abort the execution; or his wife, who ineffectually warns Pilate to have nothing to do with the death of Jesus; or in the soldiers, who were, after all, simply doing their job. Even if we do not identify with any of those directly implicated in the death of Jesus, the Bible makes it clear that a larger narrative was at play. It had been prophetically predicted 700 years earlier when Isaiah spoke words he could not fully have understood: 'But he was pierced for our transgressions, he was crushed for our iniquities; the punishment that brought us peace was upon him, and by his wounds we are healed.'[7]

After the crucifixion of Jesus, no one could possible claim that sin was glossed over. If you think that God bypasses evil, you clearly have no understanding of the horror of crucifixion.

But was it fair that Jesus was allowed to be our substitute? It depends on your definition of fair. If fair is tit for tat, eye for eye, perhaps not . . . Tit for tat requires the logic of my sin, my life.

But the justice of love requires a model for enemies to become friends. Tit for tat does not accomplish this. Only Jesus' death on the cross can do this. As we look on the crucified one, we are confronted with the truth that his death is a consequence of our sin. We realize that the death he dies is the death we should have died. The power of looking at one who has substituted for us is convicting. To truly look at the cross is to be overwhelmed. It is to repent – to be deeply, forcefully, gut-wrenchingly sorry for repeatedly shaking the fist at the One who made us and loves us. It is to find ourselves begging for forgiveness and committing to a life of obedience and of following the One who died on our behalf. This is the justice of love – it actually changes the situation. Tit for tat merely levels the slate. The loving justice of the cross makes enemies friends. This is a far deeper level of justice. It is justice that transforms.

Did we earn the loving justice of the cross? Of course not. This is grace, grace and grace again. It is wholly unmerited, but when embraced, it changes everything. And everything means everything . . .

Can costly grace lapse into cheap grace?

We spoke of the cross triggering a repentance deep enough to transform us. The Greek word for repentance, *metanoia*, refers in the New Testament to a sorrow and regret so deep that it leads to a change of heart, mind and lifestyle. It is sometimes compared to making a U-turn. In biblical terms, it is impossible to repent, and to carry on in exactly the same way as before.

What is to stop us taking grace for granted? In other words, is there a danger that we can accept the death of Jesus on our behalf lightly, without really seeing it as a call to repentance and change? It is alleged that in 1856 the German poet Heinrich Heine said on his deathbed, 'Of course God will forgive me; that's his job.' The German theologian Dietrich Bonhoeffer, writing before the start of World War Two, lamented that he saw everywhere in the Germany of his time what he called 'cheap grace', and in response made a call for costly grace – hence the title of his classic work *The Cost of Discipleship*.[8] It is a dilemma Paul contemplated when he asked and answered, 'What shall we say, then? Shall we go on sinning, so that grace may increase? By no means! We died to sin; how can we live in it any longer?'[9]

Any taking of grace for granted shows that we have not really experienced it. A genuine encounter with grace is always transformative.

The apostle Paul makes it clear that we are restored to a right relationship with God on the basis of God's grace, and not our works – consider his statement in Ephesians 2:8,9, 'For it is by grace you have been saved, through faith – and this not from yourselves, it is the gift of God – not by works, so that no-one can boast.' Given that this is the case, is there any place for rules and laws in a Christian world view? After all, there are many rules in the Bible – the Ten Commandments being an obvious example. Should we abandon these commands because our failure to keep them does not disqualify us from the presence of God?

Jesus gives a clue to an appropriate response when he says in Mark 2:27: 'The Sabbath was made for [people], not [people] for the Sabbath.' The rule was therefore to help us, not to trip us up. Given that God rested on the seventh day, the Sabbath rule is a gift that assists us reach our calling of being an image-bearer. What we think of as rules are often a means of grace. Imagine if we lived in a world where we actually kept the Ten Commandments. With killing forbidden, there would be no more war. If we adhered to laws of sexual purity, marriages would have a far greater chance of thriving, there would be no child prostitutes, no sexually transmitted diseases. If we kept the Sabbath, it would help us to keep our life in perspective and stop our unhealthy obsession with work.

To answer our question, can costly grace (and what can be more costly than the crucifixion of the Son of God?) become cheap grace, the answer is, 'Only if it was never understood.' Real repentance leads to genuine transformation. And every law of God is really the love of God packaged in a practical and life-affirming way.

About Sam . . .

In the last chapter I introduced you to Sam – who would not take communion. You will remember that I asked him, 'Sam, why don't you ever take communion?' – and his reply.

We spoke often after that. We spoke about grace . . . Not silly, cheap grace, but real, costly grace. Grace that takes the shape of a cross. And we spoke about metanoia – real, U-turn change. And we spoke about the God who not only forgives, but gives the Spirit to empower us to change.

It was the first Sunday of the month – the week we always had communion. I watched as the bread and wine approached Sam. I could sense his struggle. I willed him to reach out his hand and to take the bread and wine that spoke of the forgiveness that had been offered to him. I knew he wanted it. He almost took it. But not this month . . .

Another first Sunday of the month. Another communion service. Another almost. And this time it really was close. I actually saw his hand hover over the plate. He almost reached down and took some of the bread that spoke of the broken body of Jesus. But then he abruptly withdrew his hand, and passed the plate on.

Another first Sunday. Another communion service. Sam took the plate – held it – took the bread, took the small cup of grape juice that followed just after, ate and drank. Costly, costly grace – but grace received at last. And he has not looked back, but continues to allow God's loving justice to transform and change him.

An interview with Michael O'Neil

Dr Michael O'Neil is the director of research at Vose Seminary and the author of *Church as Moral Community*.[10]

1. *Is it excessive to suggest that all need grace? After all, some people seem to be genuinely nice.*
   Some people are genuinely nice and moral, and yet the idea that some of us are so inherently good that we do not require grace comes from an overly optimistic self-assessment, and an under-appreciation of the impact, penetration and depth of

sin in our own lives. Sin, in its biblical portrayal, is not simply external, nor simply our actions, nor simply that which characterizes other people.

In our heart of hearts we are aware that we do not live up to our own standards, let alone those of others and, most especially, those which God requires. Many centuries ago the prophet Jeremiah noted that 'The heart is deceitful above all things, and desperately wicked: who can know it?' (Jer. 17:9,10, KJV). When we ponder our own hearts we very quickly discover a quagmire of the most unlovely and disreputable feelings and motivations, intentions, commitments and attitudes.

All these are indicators of the penetration, presence and power of sin in our lives, sin which alienates us from God and renders us culpable before the blinding, blazing light of his holiness. If God were to deal with us in bare justice we would have nowhere to stand and nowhere to hide, no matter how apparently good we are. How desperately we need grace!

2. *Is grace fair, or is that the wrong question?*

I believe divine grace goes far beyond the boundaries of human justice, and especially beyond a watered-down concept like 'fairness'. There was nothing 'fair' about Jesus dying in our stead. He died, 'the just for the unjust' (1 Pet. 3:18, KJV). Saving grace is not 'fair': God justifies the *ungodly* (Rom. 4:5). Far from being 'fair', grace is a scandal! It is the completely undeserved favour and loving-kindness of God given to those without merit or claim.

Human justice is an attempt to regulate human relationships and actions according to a principle of equity. This *is* important and must not be diminished. It is, perhaps, the best human society can aim for in the conditions of an often very unjust world of competing interests and powers. But we must not confuse human concepts of justice and fairness with the reality of divine grace. Grace is what God has done for us in Christ in all its scandalous glory. Divine grace triumphs over human justice not by negating it, but by going beyond it and doing more than justice could ever imagine (see Jas 2:13). It is a divine *restorative justice*, justice operating on a higher plane and in a different mode.

3. *We are both sinners and sinned against. Should the fact that we are
   sinned against excuse us from responsibility for our later actions?*
   No. The fact that one has been the victim of another's evil can
   never be used as an excuse for one's own evil. Nor should
   we seek to justify ourselves on the basis of a previous wrong
   suffered. While it is true that some people have suffered the
   most egregious evil at the hands of others, they are and remain
   moral agents themselves, and will be held accountable for
   their own actions, just as those who did the initial evil will be
   accountable for theirs. To use our own suffering as an excuse
   for perpetrating additional wrong is to indulge the very worst
   aspects of our deceitful heart, to presume that we are exempt
   from the claims of justice, and to contribute to the escalation of
   violence, evil and retribution. We remain responsible for our
   own actions regardless of what has previously occurred and,
   according to Scripture, shall give an account at the final judgement for every word spoken and every deed done (Matt. 12:36;
   2 Cor. 5:10).

4. *Does grace transform us, or is that wishful thinking?*
   The gracious activity of God towards us does not cease with
   his pardon, for the Holy Spirit is 'God's empowering presence'
   given to us to transform our lives into the image of Jesus (2 Cor.
   3:17,18). Thus, grace is not only a gift but a calling and a responsibility.
   The promise of transformation is not wishful thinking but
   neither does grace function like Tinkerbell's fairy dust. Eugene
   Peterson likens grace to water. If we were to pass our hands
   through water it would run through our fingers and escape.
   We know it is too weak to hold us, and we cannot hold it.
   Nevertheless, if we can learn to relax in it, and like a swimmer
   to begin to make a series of strokes – simple repetitive actions
   – we will find that the water miraculously holds us and we
   begin to make progress. We are not holding the water; it is
   holding us.[11]
   Peterson's analogy helps us understand the mysterious interplay between grace and works, between God's will and our
   will. Transformation is not our work but God's work in us.
   Yet it does not occur without our participation. Our simple

repetitive actions –spiritual practices and habits such as participating in congregational life and worship, reading Scripture and learning to pray, humble service and generous kindness – become a *means of grace* by which the Holy Spirit works transformation more deeply into our being. This is how grace becomes a fruitful and transformative power in our lives. This is the kind of response that does not 'receive the grace of God in vain' (2 Cor. 6:1 ESV).

5. *And the question I ask everyone: What do people really, really need to know about God?*
   Just this: that God has come, God has made himself known to us and given himself to us, in the person of Jesus Christ. If you want to know God, look here. If you want to see God, look at Jesus Christ. Read the stories of Jesus, and hear the words of Jesus in the Gospels: these are windows through which we see what God is like and what God has said.
   The angel said to Joseph, 'His name shall be Immanuel, which means, God with us' (see Matthew 1:18–25). Jesus himself said, 'Whoever has seen me has seen the Father' (John 14:9 ESV). Turn to Jesus Christ and you are turning to God. Open your life to Jesus Christ and you open your life to God. Receive Jesus Christ and you receive God. This same Jesus has already opened his life to you, stretched out his arms on the cross to welcome you. Grace always comes first – and grace has already come: in Jesus Christ.

   And the Word became flesh and dwelt among us, (and we beheld his glory, the glory of the only begotten of the Father), *full of grace and truth*. . . . And from his fullness we have all received, *grace upon grace* (John 1:14,16; taken from KJV and ESV, italics mine).

To ponder and discuss

- While Lamech's response was excessive, is eye for eye really unreasonable?
- In practice, do you find it easier to operate with models of revenge, proportionate retaliation, or grace?

- Can you think of a time when you were shown grace instead of receiving what you deserved? How did it impact you?
- Explore the different meanings of the words the Bible uses for sin. How do they help us understand the nature of the Fall?
- Can we stop grace becoming cheap grace? Does it matter?

7.

Because the Three are One: Trinity and Community

Getting going

When people hear that you are about to speak on the Trinity, their eyes usually glaze over, and you sense that an internal conversation is progressing along the lines of 'Oh dear. Here we go again. Another exercise in improbable mathematics and unconvincing analogies. Does it actually matter?'

It is a question worth asking. Christianity finds itself in the awkward position of being an extension of the strongly monotheistic Jewish faith, which in its core prayer asserts '*Shema Yisrael, Adonai Eloheinu, Adonai Echad*', or to translate, 'Hear O Israel: The LORD our God, the LORD is one.' Known as the Shema and taken from Deuteronomy 6:4 (as we mentioned earlier), it doesn't create an expectancy that the one God we worship will be revealed to be three. In other words, the doctrine of the Trinity is not one the church always expected to arrive at, which makes it all the more fascinating that it has. Indeed, the Trinity has become accepted dogma largely because the evidence of what God is like can't easily be explained in any other way.

We can go further. Although the exercise is mind-stretching, it more than repays the effort, because 'Trinity' names who God is. Our knowledge of God is very limited until we appreciate that the God we worship and adore is triune. Is there a more basic word that can be spoken about someone than their name?

So what does the doctrine of the Trinity affirm? In essence, that God is one God in three divine persons, Father, Son and Holy Spirit. While the three persons are distinct, they are one substance or essence, the orthodox formula being 'three *hypostases* in one *ousia*' – to throw in the Greek words. The doctrine compels us to answer yes to each of these three questions. Is the Father God? Is the Son God? Is the Holy Spirit God? Yes, yes and yes again. However, the fact that the Father is God and the Son is God does not mean that the Father is the Son. To clarify, the Father is not the Son. The Son is not the Father. The Father is not the Spirit. The Spirit is not the Father. The Spirit is not the Son. The Son is not the Spirit. But the Spirit is God, and the Father is God and the Son is God. Well, you get the point . . .

The church came to its conclusion about the Trinity towards the end of the fourth century, though up until then debated a range of options that eventually saw it reach its final formulation. Exploring the implications of its conclusion has always been on the theological agenda, though it has galloped along with renewed energy and zeal in the last few decades.

Although the Bible does not contain any passage that expressly articulates the doctrine of the Trinity, it speaks about the activity of God in such a way that the reader is constantly pointed back to a God who has to be understood in Trinitarian terms. Put more bluntly, the Bible reveals a Father who does what only God can do. It reveals a Son who does what only God can do. And it reveals the Holy Spirit who does what only God can do. And the Bible is equally clear that we worship only one God. Paradoxical though it may seem, the conclusion to which we are drawn is that this one God exists in three persons. Or back to the formula, 'three *hypostases* in one *ousia*'.

In every action of God all three persons work together as one. This means that if you want to know what the Father thinks, you can ask the Son; if you want to know what the Son thinks, you can ask the Father. There is no tension or competition in the activities of the three persons of the Trinity. The Trinity is a communion of persons. Never think of God in solitary terms. God is never lonely for God is the perfect community of love – a love that is deeply relational. 'God is love' finds its first expression in the relationship between the three persons of the Trinity.

Classic errors to avoid

Before exploring the significance of the Trinity for a Christian world view, it is as well to outline some of the more common errors that have been identified when people speak of the Trinity. While it is not particularly inspiring to name mistakes, noting them puts us in a better position to develop a robust understanding of the Trinity, one that helps clothe the emperor. So here are some common traps that have tripped people up over the ages.

Modalism

Modalism views the three persons of the Trinity as different 'modes' of the Godhead. The Father, Son and Holy Spirit are not seen as distinct personalities, but different forms of God's self-revelation. It would be usual for a modalist to regard God as the Father in creation, the Son in redemption, and the Spirit in sanctification. In other words, God exists as Father, Son and Spirit at different points in time, but never as triune. Many analogies for the Trinity fall into the modalist trap. For example, in my teenage years my youth group leader encouraged me to think of the Trinity as being akin to H_2O, which at low temperatures has the form of ice, at room temperature is water and when the mercury rises beyond boiling point, becomes steam. Three forms (not quite persons, but it is only an analogy), but always one substance, H_2O. At the time I was impressed, and the example is a solid attempt, but in the end it falls over. At any one time H_2O exists as ice, water or steam. Sometimes it is solid, sometimes it is liquid, and sometimes it is steam. God is not sometimes Son, sometimes Father, and sometimes Spirit. God is eternally each, always at the same time. When the Son acts, the Father does not cease to be Father, as in this modalist error – well, actually modalism is labelled a heresy, but that seems a little harsh for a genuine effort to understand something that is more than a little complex. Perhaps we fall into heresy when we refuse to change our view, even when the shortcoming is made clear.

Tritheism

Tritheism views God as being composed of three equally powerful entities, which while they share a similar (but not identical) nature, are essentially three independent divine beings. It leaves the impression that we believe in a 'species' called God, and that the Father, Son and Spirit are the three members of the species, having a great deal in common, but in the end essentially being three gods, rather than one God eternally existing in three persons.

Not only was my youth group leader a modalist (albeit an extraordinary nice modalist), but he also lapsed into tritheism, when he explained that the Trinity was rather like an egg, made up of shell, albumen and yolk. The egg is one, even though made up of three parts. The trouble is that each of the substances that make up the egg is definitely distinct. The yoke is completely separate in nature from the shell. Even worse, most people don't say that they have not eaten an egg because it is presented to them minus the shell – which could lead to a belief that one member of the Trinity is disposable. So it is best not to pursue this analogy.

Subordinationalism

This is really a subset of tritheism, but worth a special mention. If you are a subordinationalist, you are also a tritheist by definition, though the reverse is not necessarily true. While the subordinationalist acknowledges one God in three persons, they suggest that the essence of each person exists in a hierarchy. While they wouldn't necessarily put it this crassly, most subordinationalists believe that God the Father is the most important and powerful member of the Trinity. Coming in a relatively close second is God the Son, while the distant third place is held by the Holy Spirit. By contrast, orthodox Trinitarianism confesses an essential equality among all the members of the Godhead. None are greater in essence than the other. That doesn't mean that the Father's role is the same as that of the Son, or that the Spirit does what the Father does. But they are equal in essence.

A raft of others . . .

Historically, many other errors were identified. Some dealt with the divinity of a particular member of the Trinity.

Arianism taught that while the pre-existent Christ was the first and greatest of God's creatures, he was not fully divine. The rationale was that, to use the words of Arius (c. 250–336), 'There was a time when he was not' – a period before God created the Son. Of course, if there was a time when Jesus did not exist, then there was period when the Father was not a father. Implications from that flow thick and fast. The Arian controversy was of major importance in the development of Christology during the fourth century. The First Ecumenical Council which met in Nicea in 325, declared that Jesus was 'God from God, Light from Light, very God from very God, begotten not made (not created), and one in essence with the Father.'

Docetism taught that Jesus Christ is a purely divine being who only had the 'appearance' of being human. When it came to Christ's suffering, some versions taught that Jesus' divinity abandoned or left him when he was on the cross (because it was felt that God could not suffer) while others claimed that he only appeared to suffer (in much the same way as he only appeared to be human).

At the opposite end of the spectrum was *Ebionitism* which taught that while Jesus was endowed with special gifts which distinguished him from other humans, he was nevertheless a purely human figure. Thus while docetism denies the full humanity of Jesus, ebionitism denies his full divinity.

A variation was *adoptionism* which suggested that Jesus was born totally human, but was later adopted by God in a special way. Again, it is the full divinity of Jesus that is called into question.

Predictably, there were also those who relegated the status of the Holy Spirit, the best known being *Macedonianism* which taught that the Holy Spirit was created by the Son, and is therefore lesser.

Partialism taught that Father, Son and Holy Spirit are separate components of the one God. The implication is that each of the persons of the Trinity is only part God, only becoming fully God when they come together.

This is not an exhaustive list of heresies that have been sparked in the quest for an adequate Trinitarian theology, but it identifies the key kinds of errors being made. When push comes to shove, most can be classified as either a form of modalism or tritheism, with subordinationist errors often resulting from an underlying tritheism. Lest we tut-tut over the errors from the past, and smugly conclude that we are unlikely to fall prey to them, we should again acknowledge that because Trinity names who God is, we should approach the topic with awe and reverence. We will never fully understand it – though that does not excuse us from the effort of trying.

A word on Rahner's rule

One more qualification is appropriate before we explore the impli-cations of Trinitarian theology. It concerns what has sometimes been called 'Rahner's rule', and answers the question whether the God revealed in history (often known as the economic Trinity) is in any way different to what God is eternally like (often known as the immanent Trinity). Given that we can never fully know what God is like, and that our revelation of God is partial, can we be sure we have not jumped to faulty conclusions about God on the basis of insufficient evidence? There are other more subtle but related questions. Is God in any way changed or altered by God's revelation in history, or are the relations between Father, Son and Spirit impacted by the incarnation so that in some way God's ontological being is impacted?

The debate quickly reaches a level of complexity far beyond the intended reach of this text, but citing Rahner's rule is helpful. The rule states that the economic Trinity is the immanent Trinity and the immanent Trinity is the economic Trinity.[1] Put differently, God is not other than the God who has been revealed to us, or as the other great Karl of the twentieth century, Karl Barth, puts it, 'The reality of God which meets us in revelation is His reality in all the depths of eternity.'[2] In short, the God revealed in three persons as Father, Son and Spirit is the God we can speak of with confidence without thinking that there is some profoundly different Other who has escaped our attention.

Now it is true that Rahner's rule has its critics, but the critique is usually at the level of nuance and shades of difference, rather than of fundamental disagreement.

Why does this matter? At its simplest, we need to be confident that the God revealed in history is the God of eternity. If this is not the case, we are doomed to perpetual uncertainty. Whilst it is not inappropriate to speak with a certain hesitancy and humility when we speak about God (for we are speaking about that which is well beyond us), we need to be sure that our journey leads in essentially the right direction. It might not be accurate in every detail, but it is not fundamentally misguided. Rahner's rule assures us that the God revealed through Christ's incarnation is the God of eternity. We will not discover a God who is fundamentally different to the baby in the manger, the boy Jesus in the temple, the miracle worker from Galilee, the Saviour on the cross, or the Christ of the empty tomb. Of course the Father is not the Son, nor is the Son the Spirit, but we have every reason to trust Jesus' words in John 14:9: 'Anyone who has seen me has seen the Father.'

So what? A study of some Trinitarian implications for the church[3]

This book started with a lament that the church today often comes across a little like the naked emperor who was fooled into thinking he was wearing the finest of clothes, whilst the reality was that he was stark naked. Our claims often soar well beyond the experienced reality, and we need to burrow back into what we believe if we are to set about clothing the emperor. How would a robust Trinitarian theology help in this quest?

Let's imagine what the church would look like if it were shaped by the relationships that exist in the divine life of the Trinity. If the God in whose image we are made comes to us as Father, Son and Spirit, what does it mean to be image-bearers of such a God, and what should the faith communities we form look like, given that such communities would presumably be profoundly impacted by the nature and being of this God?

Whilst what has been written thus far in this chapter might sound a little theoretical, I hope it has laid the foundation for a simple thesis which we can now unpack. It is this: The best apologetic for the truth and reality of the gospel is when the church is the church. The thesis has a second part: We are most truly church when we participate in the rich Trinitarian life of God.

We need an adequate image of God to guide and direct our ecclesiological quest, and this quest will only have an appropriate apologetic outcome if it is rooted in what has been revealed of the triune life of God. God has acted in the world, being shown as Father, Son and Spirit. As we reflect on some key characteristics of the three who are one, and explore what they reveal about God's own self, we are in a position to shape our ecclesiology accordingly. I would like to suggest that if our churches were modelled on the Trinitarian life of God they would be communities of surprise (Father), embrace (Son) and witness (Spirit), communities of gentle persuasion, communities that are inviting and winsome, indeed communities that quickly break down the wall between church and world, for the revealed God is assuredly not trapped within the four walls of any particular version of the church, past, present or future.

A quick example will serve to highlight what I am writing about, and thereafter I'd like to develop the implications for the church of serving a God of surprise, embrace and witness – a God who is triune.

An example: Beyond individualism

I think it is worth reminding ourselves of an example given in the opening chapter.

The revealed God is triune. The mathematical complexity of demonstrating that one plus one plus one equals one has proved a theological red herring. The only God we can know is the God who is revealed and we can safely assume that God is as God is revealed – one essence in three persons. So we must work with what we know. The revealed God is never an isolated, lonely God, but comes to us in the rich relational life of Father, Son and Spirit. To image such a God would therefore presumably require a comparable rich communal life in the entity that we call church. At the very least, the triune God is a rebuke to any excessive stress on individuality that comes at the expense of the life of the community. That a strong stress on the individual, often at the expense of the communal, has been a characteristic of many churches should be of concern to us.[4]

In Ephesians 3 Paul reminds us of two conditions that help the church to partially comprehend the width, length, height and depth of Christ's love for us. The first is that 'Christ may dwell in your hearts through faith' so that we would be 'rooted and established in love' which naturally leads to the second, which is of us being 'together with all the saints' in the communal quest to discover the love that 'surpasses knowledge'.[5] All this is a world away from the drift towards what Alan Jamieson calls 'churchless faith'.[6] The problem with churchless faith is that 'together with all the saints' simply disappears. The lonely self-embarked on the 'me, myself and I' quest to discover God is quickly pulled up when the realization that this God is triune, dawns. The self cannot enter into a one-on-one relationship with God, for the one it attempts to relate to is three. The self is immediately thrust into community.

This is not to suggest that the self disappears in community. Again, the triune nature of God helps us avoid this potential trap. The Father is not the Son, the Son is not the Spirit, the Spirit is not the Father. Colin Gunton titled his 1992 Bampton Lectures 'The One, the Three and the Many' which is richly suggestive of the paradox that we enter into.[7] Rather than the disappearance of the self, the self is most truly self in relationship, in community. Outside of community, the self cannot image the God whose likeness it is invited to reflect.

Let's now explore some key ways in which the revelation of God should shape our expectation of the likely life of the church. I suggest that our communal experience of each of the three persons of the triune God should lead us to expect a church of surprise, embrace and witness. I'll work through each in turn.

A community of surprise

The church of the living God will always be a community that surprises. The God who is Father and Creator is never dull.

Our very existence starts with surprise. At its most basic level it is the surprise that we are here – that we live and that in a world of substance not nothingness. We intuitively reason that nothingness would be more logical. It would make sense if an implied but non-existent creed proclaimed to the nothingness, 'In the beginning was nothing, its absence unknown and unlamented, a nothingness with neither form nor force to shape it, world without beginning, and therefore without end.' Instead we are born into a clearly existent order filled with others with whom we are invited to interact and participate – participate in the mystery of existence that we can only ascribe to the surprise of a God who is there. Our amazement that we exist is logically linked to an awareness of the wonder of a God who simply must be.[8]

By contrast, picture your average church service. Your thoughts probably go straight to Sunday. Then there are the rows of people. The heads are probably all oriented in the same direction. The short range view is of the rear hairstyles of those immediately ahead, the longer range view can be of anything from a pipe organ to a drum kit and keyboard. For a while the people stand and sit at the behest of a group of musicians who may or may not be talented. These musicians may or may not persuade the people in the straight lines to join them in their singing. At some point someone will inform the people in the rows what the church will be doing in the coming weeks and will then take up an offering to support its work. Some will give generously, others will pop in a fiver, yet others will ignore the quest for funds. Soon after, a talking head will pontificate on some aspect of Christian faith, reflecting views which might be considered orthodox or other. Depending on the skill of the speaker, after what seems like a brief or interminably long period, the community will sing again and then be dismissed. If the church is of a more liturgical bent, some responsive readings would have been part of the mix, and the Eucharist might have been celebrated. After dismissal, some probably remain behind for a cuppa. Better communities of faith might serve a quality brew, but that assuredly cannot be taken for granted.

The obvious question to ask is what this portrait of church has to do with the portrait of the God of surprises who has been revealed to us. It is all so tamely predictable. The talking head of the preacher at the front may assure us that the God of the Bible is, like Lewis's Aslan, not a tame lion, but the version we actually experience seems pretty domesticated. Undoubtedly the church has made many errors in its 2,000-year existence, but its attempt to trivialize God has been one of the more outrageous.

By contrast, the revealed God is unpredictable and exciting. Adrio König rightly points out that the self-revealed name of God, I am who I am, is in essence a promise that God will continue to be who God has always been.[9] The promise should not be understood in terms of some immovable inner essence, or in terms of ontological being, but rather as faithful continuity to the revealed mission of God. God will continue to do what God has always done. Rather than a *Deus Absconditus* we are to expect a perpetually involved God, a God's whose activity in our midst ensures that we never doubt the divine existence.

This is the God of 1 Samuel 5. The local wisdom was that when nations went into battle, those fighting were simply vehicles in the hands of their gods, and that victory came not to the people who were stronger but to the god or gods who were stronger. 1 Samuel 5 tells us that this was the Philistines' day, Yahweh supposedly defeated by Dagon. The Ark of the Covenant is captured by the Philistines and placed in submission to their god Dagon in his temple in Ashdod. Dagon is left to gloat over this presumably lesser and clearly defeated deity. Instead Dagon falls off his stand, desperately scampering for the exit to the temple, losing his head and hands in the process. Clearly Dagon is under no illusion as to who the more powerful deity is. Shortly after, tumours break out amongst the people of Ashdod, and in the end they beg to have the Ark of the Covenant returned. The surprising discovery is that even when God's people seem to be defeated, Yahweh still reigns. Victory comes with or without the aid of the people of God. This God is no tame lion. This God surprises. The question is, what is the relationship of this God to the God experienced Sunday by Sunday?

There have been many times in the history of the church when the God of surprises has empowered the church to be a community of surprise. The early church was often, though not always, such a community. Luke's summary of their early life together found in Acts 2:44–47 and 4:32–37 gives a feel for the new way of life adopted by this fledgling community. Those who observed it found it compelling. There were many converts.

The God who is not a tame lion can clearly not be forced to dance to any tune that the church cares to announce. The church cannot set the agenda for God. It can only work the other way around. But the church can pray. Indeed, we can pray the opening petition of the Lord's Prayer a little more urgently: 'Our Father, who art in heaven, hallowed be Thy name.' That little request, 'may your name be considered holy', or 'may your name be held high', or 'may your name be venerated' should be prayed with passion and urgency. It should also be prayed with expectancy. The revealed God is more than capable of ensuring the hallowing of the divine name. While willing to participate in bringing this petition to fruition, the churches primary responsibility is to observe the signs of its fulfilment. As we spot the *missio Dei* within and beyond the four walls we label church, we should find a new sprightliness within our step, and the courage to embrace the surprising, delightful, new works of God.

A community of embrace

In Jesus we meet the God who is Immanuel – the God who is with us, the God of embrace. Indeed, if the actions of the Father surprise, the embrace of the Son is just as remarkable. In selecting Bethlehem rather than Rome as birthplace, in appearing to be more at ease with tax collectors, prostitutes and sinners than with religious leaders, and in choosing not to throw the first stone at the unaccompanied, adulterous woman, the Son embraces fallen humanity with an empathy that sits uneasily with the average religious institution. Indeed, on the basis of his track record, one could easily conclude that Jesus is an unlikely patron for the organization founded to further his mission – the Christian church. But we would make that mistake because, to use Stanley Hauerwas's memorable insight, we forget that we shouldn't be looking 'only for the church that does exist but for the church that should exist'.[10]

Often our communal life falls short of what it should be. Some years back Michael Griffiths wrote a book about the church which he called *Cinderella with Amnesia*.[11] Too often it is true. A consequence of forgetting who we are is a willingness to embrace that which is lesser – and to the extent that sin is at least in part a falling short of the mark – embracing a smaller vision of what God intends for the church is part of the sinfulness from which she must repent.

There are times when the church is a pale version of the community of surprise and embrace she is called to be – certainly if she is called to reflect the Trinitarian life of the God who calls her into being. It often bears many similarities to the water polo club my family were part of when we lived in Auckland, New Zealand. We were a respectable little group committed to ensuring our children had a great experience with water polo. At times we could be quite generous. We were welcoming to new families, especially those whose children showed some natural aptitude for the game. If they were willing to provide transport to away games, umpire, or better still, help to raise funds, they were doubly welcome. We'd chat pleasantly about the game as we sat in the stands together, and we'd try to remember to make favourable comments about the performance of the child of the parents we were talking to. When that was impossible, we'd retreat to a diplomatic silence. Other than that the conversation reverted to water polo more frequently than in other contexts, the chitchat we engaged in was much the same as in the school parking lot, the workplace and the local church. Nothing wrong with that, but it left me wondering in what way the local church was really any different to the water polo club. While my family had no major crisis during those years, I don't doubt that if we had, someone from the club would have phoned to find out how we were and to offer their assistance. Certainly when we were stuck for transport, others quickly came to our aid, as we did to theirs in comparable situations. So in what ways is the church different to the water polo club we were part of? True, we didn't sing at the water polo club (mercifully we had no karaoke evenings!), and it was a lot less expensive, but in so many ways there wasn't much difference.

Surely one of the great differences between the water polo club and the church should be the latter's willingness to unconditionally reach out, welcome and embrace, to affirm that people belong, before they have met a multitude of preconditions? To get into the water polo club there were a fair number of water polo-related hurdles that we had to cross. While not insurmountable, this was not a club that anyone could get into. Not so the church. Christ's incarnation was not delayed until such time as the planet engaged in impeccable behaviour. This openness to the other is part of what it means to participate in Christ's movement into the world.

While in the past atheists were usually content to justify their lack of belief in God's existence on the basis of intellectual objections, it is now increasingly common for that justification to be based on moral objections.[12] To quote from the title of Christopher Hitchens's bestselling book, it is alleged that God is not great and that religion poisons everything.[13] Some would have us believe that religious faith is an evil akin to greed, poverty and disease and that it is a significant social problem to be obliterated if we are to attain a more utopian existence. While the famous G.K. Chesterton paradox claims, 'The Christian ideal has not been tried and found wanting. It has been found difficult and left untried',[14] a growing tide impatiently dismisses the sentiment as escapist and is unwilling to endure what they claim is the poisonous harvest of religious faith.

That harvest is described in different ways, but ten common components (in no particular order) include:

- religious warfare
- colonial exploitation
- racial bigotry
- the oppression of women
- homophobia
- the exploitation of the environment
- retarding the progress of science, especially medical science
- academic censorship with a resultant intellectual dishonesty
- intolerance of anything new
- hypocrisy

Clearly there is nothing attractive about this list, and if it is seen to be the normative result of religious faith, evangelists should expect audiences who are increasingly hostile to their message – presupposing they can find any audience at all.

David Kinnaman's study of the attitude of 16 to 29-year-old Americans towards Christians saw six recurring images.[15] They considered Christians to be:

- hypocritical
- interested in 'saving' people rather than in relating to them
- anti-homosexual
- sheltered
- too political
- judgemental

Again, the list is far from winsome, and represents significant barriers to the likely receptivity to messages about the love and mercy of God. It is also very far removed from the way in which Jesus' ministry was experienced by his peers – sheltered, too political, judgemental – well, that's hardly the way anyone from his time would have described him.

We could argue that these negative images are the fruit of the Christendom era, when membership of the Christian faith was assumed for almost all who lived in the Western World. Christendom was often more about sanctioning the status quo than following Jesus, and we could be hopeful that its demise might free the church to find more authentic expressions of faith in this 'after Christendom' era.[16] If the harvest of Christendom was our poisonous list of ten (and I acknowledge that it is excessively one-sided to suggest that the list is fair),[17] is it possible that in the post-Christian era a Christianity that more closely represents and reflects the life of Jesus might emerge?

In popular expressions of Christian faith it has become common to ask the WWJD question – 'What would Jesus do?' Perhaps in becoming a community of embrace we need to supplement this with two additional questions – 'What would Jesus think?' and 'What would Jesus feel?' – put differently, we need to focus on the trio of orthodoxy, orthopraxy and orthopathy.

There is another reason to develop a holistic understanding of Jesus and his mission. Theologians routinely note that humans are made in the image of God. It is less common for them to explore the implications of Jesus as the *imago Dei*.[18] We cannot discover what it means to be human unless our quest is rooted in an understanding of the humanity of Jesus. In pondering his humanity, we discover our own.

To be sure, our thinking is likely to be filtered through our preconceived portraits of Jesus, and inevitably these will reflect more than a touch of contemporary culture. Up to a point, we should simply shrug our shoulders and say, 'So be it; we can only live in the world in which we find ourselves.' But this is a little too defeatist. We can immerse ourselves in the biblical narratives. We can also trust that the Spirit-inspired Scriptures are also the Spirit-illuminated Scriptures. And we can guard against excessively individualistic interpretations of the text by studying it together in community, confident, 'that the Spirit guides the church, and that the community of faith will therefore by pneumatologically guided as it communally attempts to discern truth in a changed context'.[19]

This brings us to the third person of the Trinity, the Spirit.

A community of witness

If God the Father ensures a community of surprise, and God the Son a community of embrace, God the Spirit ensures a community of witness, presence and power. The apologetic impact of this trio is likely to be profound.

Is aspiring to be a community of witness, presence and power a hankering back to Christendom, a quest to reclaim the influence and importance the church had in the Christendom era?

It depends on how we say it. If the tone is strident and rousing – 'We're a community of witness, presence and power' (aren't we great) – then our past has taught us little. If it is a quietly confident, 'The triune God's love for the world always keep flowing outwards, therefore we are called to move out as a community of witness, presence and power', we are on surer ground.

The revealed God constantly moves out to the world through the Spirit. Rather than creating arrogant, self-sufficient church communities, the Spirit calls us to be communities that readily chant Zechariah 4:6: '"Not by might nor by power, but by my Spirit," says the LORD'. Unless the Spirit equips us, we will be communities with high, but unrealized, ideals.

Theologians often comment that while the early church paid attention to the work of the Spirit, thereafter pneumatology acted as little more than an afterthought until the second half of the twentieth century. Perhaps in Christendom the church thought the work of the Spirit was superfluous. That risk is long past. In the West the societal move from a soft to a hard secularism is becoming increasingly obvious. 'Not by might nor by power, but by my Spirit' is our only hope.

For a brief moment forget every image that promptly springs into mind when you hear the word 'church'. Imagine instead the rich Trinitarian life of the God revealed as Father, Son and Spirit. Ponder the way the Father is revealed though the pages of Scripture. Remember the embrace of the Son to a multitude of unlikely candidates. Recall the transformation of the disciples at Pentecost. If God will be who God has been, and if God will do what God has done, could it be that we can expect new versions of church to spring into being? Perhaps in the future we might participate in communities of surprise, embrace and witness. The nature of our triune God should prompt us to settle for nothing less. And if we were shaped by a God of surprise, embrace and witness, the emperor would no longer parade naked.

An interview with Stephen Holmes

Dr Stephen Holmes is senior lecturer in theology at the University of St Andrews, Scotland and is the author of several books, including the widely acclaimed *The Holy Trinity: Understanding God's Life*.[20]

1. The Big Picture *is written for thoughtful readers, rather than professional theologians. Some might be tempted to put the doctrine of the Trinity into the too hard basket. What would you say to them?*
   What we call 'the doctrine of the Trinity' is the church's best attempt (in my humble opinion . . .) to articulate who God must be if our habitual ways of speaking about God – both biblical language, which we read, and our own prayers – are good ways of speaking. So if we want to pray well, or speak well about God, we need to think a bit in this area.

2. *Your book on the Trinity makes it clear that you are doubtful about some of the so-called advances in Trinitarian theology made in the last half century. Why?*
   The book is about the history of doctrine, and argues a historical point: that much of what went on in the last half century was just

very different from visions of Trinitarian doctrine in the previous nineteen centuries of the church's life. I probably don't hide my desire to be on the side of the historical majority here, but I don't really argue that point in the book . . .

That said, the historical point I argue is something like this: in the last few decades there have been a lot of people finding a vision of perfect society in the Trinity – three persons in relationship. This vision has been used to suggest that Trinitarian doctrine is useful in telling us how to order church and society more widely; there has also been a strong historical claim that this vision was the original doctrine of the Trinity; I think that historical claim is wrong.

3. *In your book you argue that Basil of Caesarea and Gregory of Nyssa, in defending the Nicene understanding of the Trinity, were more concerned with finding a 'grammar' than a 'logic' for the Trinity. What do you mean by this and why does it matter?*
The doctrine of the Trinity is fundamentally about how to speak adequately about God; we do not pretend to know what it is like to be God, or how God's life works; we claim to be able to say things about God that are true and meaningful. That's all I mean by 'grammar' not 'logic'.

4. *People often find talk of the three persons of the Trinity to be confusing. What do we mean when we link the word 'person' to God, and equally, what don't we mean?*
Our modern notion of person is very heavily conditioned by the sensibility of the nineteenth-century Romantic Movement; there, the essence of who we are lies in our interior selves, that place deep within that no one else can truly reach, and that is independent of any external influence. The task of the artist, and of every human being, is to be true to this interior self.

Now, if we think of God as three 'persons' like that we're going to go very badly wrong; the people who started using the word 'person' (or rather the Latin word *persona*) for God had never read a poem by Wordsworth, heard a symphony by Beethoven, or seen a painting by Turner – their loss, of course, in each case, but we really should not read them as if they had.

By 'person' they meant something like 'particular existence of a thing'. So the Trinitarian claim was that the one God exists three times over, as Father, Son, and Holy Spirit. If 'interior self' means anything (and I'm not sure it does), then Father, Son, and Spirit share the same 'interior self'.

5. *And the question I ask everyone: What do we really, really need to know about God?*

That God created the world; that for us and our salvation God the Son came down from heaven and became incarnate, that he suffered for us, died, and rose again; that he will come in glory to judge the living and the dead and bring in a kingdom without end; that God the Spirit, the Lord and giver of life, has spoken in the Scriptures and is poured out on the church – the old creeds sum up the essentials of the faith rather well, I believe.

To ponder and discuss

- What is your first response when you hear the name 'Trinity', and why?
- The chapter claims: 'The self cannot enter into a one-on-one relationship with God, for the one it attempts to relate to is three. The self is immediately thrust into community.' Do you agree, and what implications does this have?
- Does your church ever overlook the work of any member of the Trinity? If so, what might it mean if this were to change?
- The chapter describes the triune God as a God of surprise, embrace and witness. To what extent does your local church community reflect a God who is like this?

8.

All Creatures Great and Small: Building a World with a Better Name

Imagining a better world into being

The apartheid era in South Africa was drawing to a grizzly close. Violence had become so widespread that rather than report on individual cases of politically motivated murder, the major newspapers simply showed a map of the country and inserted numbers in each region. A '10' over Kwazulu-Natal meant that there had been ten political deaths in that region in the last twenty-four hours; a '12' in the Eastern Cape indicated that the violence there has been even worse. There were simply too many bad news stories to tell each one. Keeping up with the statistics was the best that could be hoped for.

In the midst of this early 1990s chaos, South African Breweries produced an improbable series of adverts to promote their main product, Castle Lager Beer. It told a story of a young black soccer player who had been given a chance to follow his dream and trial for a prestigious European soccer club . . . but funds were needed to get him there, and he didn't have any. In a show of great solidarity, his team mates, many of them white, put themselves out to raise the necessary funds, and in due course the money was raised, the achievement celebrated together over a cold Castle Lager.

It was so unlike the South Africa that was; where were these soccer teams where people of all races worked harmoniously to help any player in need? The apartheid world wasn't like that at all, but as those adverts played over and over again, people started to wonder, 'Could we ever have a world like this?'

It would be an enormous exaggeration to say that the Castle Lager beer adverts were the reason for the end of the apartheid era, but they did play their part. They helped people to conceive of a world that until then had been inconceivable, and so they helped to hasten its birth. Post-apartheid, South African Breweries continued its strategy of visioning a world that could be, and as Bafana Bafana (the name of the South African national soccer team) entered its first soccer World Cup in 1998, Castle launched its memorable advertising jingle 'One Nation, One Soul; One Beer, One Goal'.[1] It was more than clever. It was inspiring, a genuine force for good. And it sold lots of beer.

If a little hopeful imagining could prove so helpful in that situation of quiet desperation, what difference could Christ followers make if we were to delve deeply into the story which shapes and challenges us? What if we imagined the world not as it currently is, but as it both could and should be? What if we invited people to live in the light of that story? Reflect on the creation mandate.

Genesis 1:26 announces that as image-bearers, humanity is to rule over creation. This is given a little more content in the expanded creation account which starts at Genesis 2:4. Verses 19 to 20 recount that God brought the birds and beasts to Adam to see what he would name them. The second half of verse 19 spells out the result – 'and whatever the man called each living creature, that was its name.' Names are so important, a truth repeatedly recognized in the Bible. They are often aspirational, giving an ideal to strive after. They get to the heart of who we are, and if our name fails to do this, we might need a new one.

The Bible has many accounts of people whose names were changed by God. Abram becomes Abraham, Sarai is changed to Sarah, Jacob is named Israel, and Simon is invited to become Peter. The message is clear. Names matter. A new name usually means that God has spotted a potential or possibility that isn't presently being realized, or that a promise of a better future is being gifted.

When Adam is instructed to name creation, his mandate is to create a world where each has a suitable name. By naming creation, Adam is calling it to fulfil its potential – to become the name it is invited to carry. As Adam named creation, God watched to 'see what he would name them'.[2] It is a beautiful image. God, the Creator of all, watching while the creature made in God's image takes creation to a new realm of possibility by naming other created beings. God doesn't interfere in the process, but simply looks on. What God begins, humanity extends – and this with God's approval. This creative responsibility is assuredly a key part of what it means to be an image-bearer.

In this chapter we will explore the role that those made in the image of God should play in building a world with a better name. This world should not be viewed anthropocentrically – as though only people matter. The creation mandate requires all to have a name. Building a better world means better for all creatures great and small. This task helps delineate one of the major contours of a genuinely Christian world view, but it is one that is often overlooked, largely because we have allowed some unnecessary blocks to get in the way.

Blocks to a better name

Sadly, while it would seem reasonable to imagine that Christians would champion a thoughtful and creative response to issues which prevent the world finding a better name, the evidence does not fully support this.

Take the issue of climate change. After analyzing the results of the Australian National Church Life Survey of 2006, a study by Pepper, Leonard and Powell concludes that while overall church attendees in Australia have a fairly high level of concern about climate change, anxiety being expressed by 66 per cent of the 3,400 respondents, the figure is essentially the same as that of non-church goers.[3] There were some differences on the basis of denomination. Those who attended Anglican churches were the most likely to believe that the matter was urgent, while those at Pentecostal churches were the least likely to affirm this, with those belonging to Uniting, Catholic and Evangelical Protestant churches being somewhere in the middle.[4] The study concluded that: 'There is nothing here to suggest that Australian churchgoers are different from the Australian population in the urgency attributed to climate change.'[5]

An American study which focused on the attitudes of American evangelicals to global warming concluded that when compared to the rest of the population, they were less likely to believe that climate change was happening, or that human activity was its cause, or that it should be a reason for worry or concern.[6] This should not be interpreted as suggesting that overall American evangelicals had no concern about global warming – just that it was at a lower level than the rest of the population.

Given that Christians should take their mandate as stewards of creation seriously, we must ask why this vision apparently has no positive practical impact with an issue such as climate change. Put differently, why is the emperor naked when it comes to the realm of creation care?

Not that we should only read the negatives. The field of ecotheology is generating significant interest, and as Clive Ayre notes, 'ecotheologians generally take it as a "given" that Christianity has a role to play in environmental care, and that ecotheology calls for a response'.[7] Furthermore, some Christian groups are sparkling examples of concern and engagement. Operation Noah, a British group, describes itself as an ecumenical Christian charity providing leadership, focus and inspiration in response to the growing threat of catastrophic climate change, and claims to be 'Faith-motivated. Science-informed. Hope-inspired'.[8] Blessed Earth, with its slogan of 'Serving God, Saving the Planet' is another notable example.[9]

While there are these pleasing exceptions, it is important to unpack why they are not automatically the norm. As is often the case, the reasons often flow from a poor comprehension of the major contours of the Christian faith. Let's unpack four common blocks . . .

Stewardship as exploitation

Whilst the creation mandate to steward the earth confers a clear duty of care for creation, it has sometimes been misinterpreted to justify an anthropocentric view of the world, where nature exists simply for the use and benefit of humans. When we forget that the call is to name creation, and thereby invite it to realize all its potential and glory, we run the risk of viewing stewardship as an excuse for exploitation.

The confusion is sometimes caused by interpreting the instruction in Genesis 1:26, let them 'have dominion over' all the earth (to cite the well-known words from the King James Version) as an invitation to dominate. The later call to 'subdue' the earth (Gen. 1:28) was often given more air time than the earlier call in the same verse to 'Be fruitful, and multiply, and replenish the earth' (KJV).

In 1967, medieval historian Lynn White Jr published a still widely cited article, 'The Historical Roots of our Ecological Crisis'.[10] In it, White argues that a Western Christian world view (which he differentiates from an Eastern Christian world view) encouraged humanity to aggressively dominate nature. Complaining that 'Especially in its Western form, Christianity is the most anthropocentric religion the world has ever seen', White writes: 'Christianity, in absolute contrast to ancient paganism and Asia's religions (except, perhaps, Zoroastrianism), not only established a dualism of man and nature but also insisted that it is God's will for man to exploit nature for his proper ends.' He argues that in ancient paganism every tree and stream was seen to have its guardian spirit. One could therefore not destroy a tree without first placating the spirit in charge. 'By destroying pagan animism, Christianity made it possible to exploit nature in a mood of indifference to the feeling of the natural objects.'[11] White acknowledges that there have been exceptions to this model, and towards the end of the article points to the example of St Francis of Assisi, and wonders if a renewed Franciscanism could help foster a closer sense of inter-relationship between humanity and all of creation.

White's argument alerts us to the possibility of a partial reading of the creation mandate that fosters a context in which an anthropocentric exploitation of the surroundings is more probable. It is important to note all the qualifiers in any biblical passage. To read the creation account and focus only on the call to have dominion over the earth or to subdue the earth, without heeding the instruction to be fruitful and to replenish the earth, and to name every creature on earth, is to be guilty of an incomplete reading of Scripture. As image-bearers, humanity is called to represent God to the planet. God's verdict on creation was that all that was made was good. We cannot look at the degradation of rainforests or the extinction of animal and plant species and claim to have upheld God's standards. This is not the world as God made it, let alone a world with a better name.

Rather than the Christian faith objectifying creatures others than humans, and thus allowing an unhelpful dualism to creep in, the act of naming creation intentionally invites us to enter into a tender relationship with all of creation.

During the thirteenth century, Thomas of Celano recorded many stories of St Francis and his interaction with birds, fish and animals. Whilst we cannot be sure of the veracity of each story, they point to the profound respect and delight Francis took in each creature. His sermons were not simply directed to humans, but to birds and animals as well. He would bless and make the sign of the cross over fish, rabbits and ducklings. Most famously, it is alleged that he tamed the ferocious wolf terrorizing the people of Gubbio with the sign of the cross, and went on to broker a peace deal between the people of Gubbio and the wolf. In return for food from the townsfolk, the wolf would stop terrorizing the people. A relationship of genuine friendship developed between the people in the town and the wolf.

St Francis recognized the close inter-relationship between God, humans and animals. In an oft-cited quote he notes, 'If you have men who will exclude any of God's creatures from the shelter of compassion and pity, you will have men who will deal likewise with their fellow men.' In a greatly loved hymn he wrote in 1225, he urges all creatures to lift their voices in praise to God. By all creatures he meant all creatures, and in different stanzas personifies sun, moon, stars, wind, cloud, rivers, fire, flowers and fruit. Whilst some might chide him for failing to draw appropriate boundaries between people who have been made in the image of God, and the rest of creation which is not, he grasped that the creation mandate was not about exploitation, but harmonious inter-relationship.

Why then has St Francis's example of a caring and responsible relationship with creation not been the automatic default drive for the Christian church?

Perhaps the underlying muddle is reflected in a comparable way when Abraham is elected by God to be the father of a nation through whom the whole earth will be blessed.[12] While Abraham's call was an enormous privilege, the reason he was called was to bless the entire world. Genesis 12:3b makes this clear – 'and all peoples on earth will be blessed through you.' The reason behind

Abram's election and call was that multitudes would be blessed. In reality, Abraham's offspring quickly started to interpret their election in terms of privilege rather than responsibility. Instead of having a heart for the Gentiles, they quickly viewed them as aliens and as 'other'. They focused on the benefits of the relationship for their nation, rather than on their need to be careful stewards. Their neglect saw them face the judgement of God.

Likewise, the Bible clearly teaches that humanity stands in a privileged position in creation. Only humans are made in the image of God. But this privilege does not confer the right to exploit and abuse. It confers the responsibility to bless. It is a responsibility which must be taken with the utmost seriousness, for all stewards are called to account for their stewardship. We must answer for the name we give the earth during our watch.

Excusing ourselves, for we're too fallen to make a difference

Another block to being constructive change agents in the world is to assume that the impact of the Fall is so great that fallen humanity will never achieve anything of lasting value. A lot depends on how the judgement issued after the Fall of Adam and Eve is interpreted. Genesis 3:14–19 outlines the losses. There will be pain in childbirth. Male-female relationships will be distorted by male domination. The earth will not be spontaneously fruitful, and painful toil rather than joyful work will be Adam's lot. Even more seriously, death now takes hold, and humanity is doomed to return to the dust of the earth from which it originally came.

Adam and Eve leave their garden paradise clothed in the skin of animals that had been slaughtered so that their fur would protect the fallen couple from the winter cold and rain. Death is not just a reality for humans. With the Fall, it is the destination of animals as well.

Clearly this is a bleak picture, and one that is intended to impact with a sense of loss and gloom. Lest there be any danger of missing the point, the follow-up stories are of immense sadness. Adam and Eve give birth to two sons. We are not told how much pain Eve actually had in childbirth, but her later pain would have been unspeakably intense, for the one son, Cain, murders the other, Abel. Paradise would have seemed a very long time ago.

Should this proclamation of judgement forever impact our assessment of the worth of human endeavour? Should we passively accept that children will bring pain, that male-female relationships will be fraught with tension, that work will be a curse, and that death will perpetually be the victor?

It is this last claim that is decisively overturned at the resurrection of Jesus. His defeat of death, says Paul in 1 Corinthians 15:20, is 'the firstfruits of those who have fallen asleep'. Verse 22 gives the triumphant follow-through: 'For as in Adam all die, so in Christ all will be made alive.' This is more than a little heartening. It is the decisive proclamation of the reversal of a terrible evil. The curse of the Fall will be reversed. No longer do we move from life to death, but from life to life – albeit that this transition is still mediated by our death and departure from the present order of things.

Where does the proclamation of judgement at the Fall leave us in our quest to build a world with a better name? Are we forever doomed to hobble in a shadow world of failed dreams – a world with endless reminders of what could have been, but isn't?

The biblical vision is far more hopeful. While the ultimate restoration of all things awaits a future fulfilment, we should not ignore the radical change that has been brought about as a result of Jesus' life, death and resurrection. Nor should we ignore the impact of the birth of the church on the day of Pentecost. When we place together the incarnation, crucifixion and resurrection of Jesus, and add to it the empowering of the church at Pentecost, we have news of a radically changed order – a new reality that has already started to be birthed. While a long way from being God's last word with humanity, it is a definite sign of the birth of an alternate kingdom – the kingdom of God. This kingdom operates with a different mandate. It is to shape itself not in the light of either past or present reality, but in the light of future reality. Jesus instructed us to ask that God's will would be done on earth as it is in heaven – a solid reason to get us to ask, 'How is it done in heaven?' before committing to any course of action. In other words, if we are to clothe the emperor, we need to look to the future, not the Fall.

When we passively accept that distorted male-female relationships will forever be our lot, or that work will be joyless, or that the grave cannot be defeated, we have allowed our gaze to settle on the wrong point in the story. Judgement has indeed been issued. We see evidence of that everywhere. However, of far greater importance is the promise of a new order. Christ followers are called to build a visible community of faith and hopefulness. In doing so they are a sign of the coming kingdom.

To excuse ourselves from building a world with a better name because we consider ourselves doomed by the Fall is to deny the impact of forgiveness and the power of the resurrection. We are called to live in the light of our new name, not our old name.

Having said that we should not use the Fall as an excuse for actively working to bring needed change to the world, we must be careful of not making the opposite error, namely of trivializing the Fall, and thinking that its impact no longer affects us. We live in an 'already' and 'not yet' world. Jesus defeated the powers of death and darkness on the cross, but the full benefit of that will only be realized after his return. The church is called to be a sign of the coming new reality. She is a sign of hope, a countercultural presence alerting to a new and better future. But that future has not yet fully dawned. We are indeed a candle in the dark, but sunrise might be a while off.

At times we will still be hopelessly muddled. The history of the church is one of lofty highs, but also of tragic lows. This also works its way out at an individual level. In Romans 7:19, Paul describes a universal human dilemma when he agonizes, 'For what I do is not the good I want to do; no, the evil I do not want to do – this I keep on doing.' If we are naïve and deny the constant pull towards Adam's sin, we are made the more vulnerable.

What does this mean in practice? Should we strive to build a world with a better name? Of course we should. This is God's good world and we are called to be responsible stewards of that which has been entrusted to us. Indeed, we will be called to account for our stewardship. But if we ever think that we will build Utopia, we have lapsed back into the original sin of thinking that we can replace God, and sort out the difference between good and evil unaided. Rather, we should recognize that our call is to spot the work that God is already doing in the world. As we identify the *missio Dei*, we align ourselves with the future that God is building for this planet.

Secularizing the mission

Lofty though it is to talk of building a world with a better name, it is possible to become entranced by an entirely secular version of paradise . . . a world without sickness, hunger, injustice; a world where every plant and animal is named and cherished. Such a world is indeed desirable, but if it is not in relationship with the Creator of all, it will still hobble along as a deeply flawed fragment of what was meant to be. We can become so enamoured with the challenges facing the human race that we attempt to tackle them outside of a deeply committed relationship with God.

Jonathan Wilson, in his outstanding book, *God's Good World*, talks of teleological amnesia.[13] Whilst the term might sound daunting, the concept is not too hard to understand. Teleological is about the ultimate goal or purpose of something, and amnesia – well, I've forgotten what that means.

Wilson cites as an example of teleological amnesia our changing vocabulary. Where our ancestors would have spoken of the need to care for the creation, we speak of the need to care for the environment. So what is wrong with caring for the environment? Nothing, except that caring for the environment without an awareness of why it exists is to forget that there is an ultimate purpose behind our immediate surroundings. You don't make that mistake when you speak about creation. After all, talk about creation implies a Creator. If there is a creation, there is a Creator, and there is a strong likelihood that the Creator created for a purpose. Teleology springs to life, as we ask the relevant question, 'So what is the meaning and purpose of life?'

Secular societies talk of the environment. They make no reference to the possibility of there being something behind our surroundings. Naturally enough they soon have to rally the troops to care for the environment – after all, there is no inherent reason why we should care for an accidental universe. If there is no purposeful reason behind this planet, all behaviours become disturbingly optional. To tell someone they 'should' or they 'ought' to do something makes no sense if our ultimate conviction is that this planet is essentially purposeless, apart from any purpose we impose on it.

A secular agenda to build a world with a better name will always fall far short of its ultimate *telos*, for the ultimate goal of the universe is found in Jesus the Christ. In Colossians 1:17 Paul makes the bold but illuminating claim that in Jesus 'all things hold together'. He elaborates in verses 19,20: 'For God was pleased to have all his fulness dwell in him, and through him to reconcile to himself all things, whether things on earth or things in heaven, by making peace through his blood, shed on the cross.' The reconciliation of 'all things' strongly alerts against adopting too small an agenda. An entirely secular version of reality excludes the deeper and more comprehensive range of reconciliation envisioned in a Christian world view.

Whilst an entirely secular agenda to build a world with a better name will fall well short of the mark, we should be wary of excusing ourselves from this endeavour because so many secular organizations adopt this as their ultimate goal. A dualistic world, where some things are seen as spiritual (and therefore worthy) and others as unspiritual (and therefore unworthy) must be rejected as unbiblical. In Christ, all things hold together. Nothing is unworthy of our attention, and no aspect of life is too trivial to matter. As God is the ultimate creator or all, like God we should be concerned at the sparrows fall, and marvel at the way the lilies of the field are clothed.[14] Simply because many secular organizations operate from an abbreviated agenda, one unwilling to allow belief in God to shape the nature of the programme, does not justify Christ followers having no interest in their endeavours, or worse still, caricaturing them as a waste of time.

To constantly remind ourselves that we are committed to creation care is a helpful corrective. Talk of creation sets the right tone. We are dealing with wonder and mystery. We are also dealing with a plot, plan and purpose. We should not subvert it by our neglect to care for the world God created.

Embracing the status quo

A fourth block is a residue from the Christendom era, when the agenda of the Christian church was seen as synonymous with the interests of Western society. 'For God and country' has often been a catchphrase justifying an uncritical attitude towards colonization, war and a range of social programmes. Biblical passages such as Romans 13:1–7 (which encourages respect for the ruling authorities) have sometimes been used to encourage a passive indifference to the activity of the state. At times this has led to a naïve embrace of the status quo, perhaps the worst example being the complicit compliance of the majority of Christians in Germany during the rise of Hitler and the Third Reich.

However, it is not only during the more dramatic moments in history that we might default towards the existing state of affairs. Christians often have an ambivalent attitude to change. Henry Lyte's hymn, 'Abide with Me' illustrates the point. Written in 1847 by a seriously ill Lyte (1793–1847), its second verse speaks of change and decay being all around. Given the frail condition of the author, it is understandable that the hymn associates change with decay, but its enormous popularity makes one wonder if the link between change and decay isn't often drawn a little too quickly, and whether it sometimes becomes an assumed Christian attitude towards all change.

We should take this question seriously. After all, change and decay bear no necessary relationship to each other. Change often brings renewal and fresh hope. Change is usually a prerequisite to something new being birthed. An instinctive opposition to the new would see us opposed to the new heaven and new earth that the Scriptures encourage us to expect. The promise of Revelation 21:5 is that we will hear the one on the throne say, 'Behold, I make all things new' (KJV).

Our attitude to change seriously impacts our openness to building a world with a better name. We face many fresh challenges. Medical advances have unearthed a raft of new questions. Likewise, technology has dramatically opened up new possibilities for creating community. Globalization is the new normal . . . the list could go on. Each has the potential for great good. An instinctive caution away from the new is unlikely to prove helpful. Whilst we should not veer in the opposite direction (it must be good if it is new), we need to think carefully about the principles available to guide us in our decision-making. We should be willing to repeatedly ask both 'Why?' and 'Why not?' and we should not assume that answers valid in a previous era will automatically apply in a changed context. Technological advances never anticipated by the biblical authors necessitate a deep understanding of why they approved certain visions of life, and why they opposed others.

Humility and hopefulness should walk hand in hand. We are not God, and our early ancestors did not gain their wish when they ate the forbidden fruit in the hope that it would enable them to distinguish good from evil. Differentiating between the two often remains elusive, and if we decide too quickly or are too certain that we have got it right, we should proceed with great caution. Church history teaches us many things, but one lesson that cannot be missed is that the people of God do make mistakes. This should not paralyze us into inactivity, but it should leave us committed to lives of prayerfulness and humility. God is constantly at work in the world, but spotting the *missio Dei* is not always easy.

Stewards of creation

What then should we conclude? It is perhaps as simple (and complex) as this. As image-bearers, humans carry great responsibility. We are called to be stewards of creation. We are the voice of the voiceless. God still watches to see what we will name the birds and animals. And while God will ultimately birth a new heaven and a new earth, we should align ourselves with the mission of God by taking seriously our brief to build a world with a better name.

An interview with Jonathan Wilson

Dr Jonathan Wilson is the Pioneer McDonald Professor of Theology at Carey Theological College, Vancouver, and the author of many books, including *God's Good World: Reclaiming the Doctrine of Creation*.

1. *In a nutshell, why do you think it is important for Christians to reclaim the doctrine of creation?*
   If we take seriously Paul's declaration in Colossians 1:16 that all things in heaven and on earth are through Christ and for Christ, then reclaiming a doctrine of creation is also a matter of expanding our recognition of the greatness of Christ and the work that God accomplishes in him. If we do not bring creation

into our account of salvation, then we have an understanding of reconciliation that is less than fully biblical.

2. *This chapter explores some reasons Christians are often slow to embrace their mandate to steward and replenish the earth. Can you think of some others?*

The list here is a good one, full of insight and illumination. In some parts of the church around the world we have disembodied human life and the gospel. That is, we have de-emphasized the physical and overemphasized something that we call 'spiritual'. And at the same time we disconnect physical and the spiritual. So all we are left with is 'the spiritual'. Then we take the next step: if our essence and our future is purely spiritual, then 'creation' is meaningless. Against this mistake, I ask my students and others to imagine something 'spiritual' that they can do without their bodies. Or is there some way of loving God that does not require creation? So to steward creation and replenish the earth is to love God, our neighbour and ourselves.

3. *Are there some signs of encouragement that Christians are reclaiming the doctrine of creation?*

There are encouraging signs. One is the way everyday practices of creation care are growing among Christians. Another is the growth of ministries (like A Rocha International) that practise and encourage care for creation as acts of Christian discipleship. A third is the growing focus on and cry for justice. This passion for justice is a cry for creation to be redeemed. This cry needs to be carefully brought under the reality and guidance of the gospel. It must not be left to secular ideologies. And Christians must not succumb to simply choosing one of these secular ideologies as our version of justice. To develop a mature, gospel-grounded account of God's justice, we need to reclaim the doctrine of creation.

4. *In your book* God's Good World *you encourage us to remember the 'eighth day of creation'. What do you mean by that and why is it important?*

'The eighth day of creation' is a teaching that I learned from Eastern Orthodoxy. It is a reference to the resurrection of Jesus

Christ which 'completes' the Genesis account of the seven days of creation. This teaching and the celebration of the 'eighth day of creation' reminds us that the ongoing life of the world and the promise of the redemption of creation depend upon the power of the resurrection of Jesus Christ.

5. *And the question I ask everyone: What do we really, really need to know about God?*
We need to know that God the Father, Son and Spirit are, simply, LIFE and LOVE as they give themselves to one another as Father, Son and Spirit: that they give themselves as LIFE and LOVE to creation, most fully in Jesus Christ; and that our lives and the life of all creation is sustained by giving and receiving in the grace and mercies of God.

To ponder and discuss

- If a beer advertisement could help build a better world, how might we tell the Christian story so that it opens hopeful possibilities for people?
- How can the example of St Francis help us to be better stewards of creation?
- The chapter explores four blocks that often prevent Christians from being responsible stewards. Are you tripping over any, or have you seen any of these blocks hinder the mission and witness of the church?
- Did anything from this chapter strike you as being especially relevant, and if so, what and why?

9.

Ever Hopeful: Living in the Light of Eternity

About apocalyptic terrorism

Granted my youth group days were back in the 1970s, but I still remember what was standard fare at many evenings. I probably watched the film *A Thief in the Night* at least a dozen times.[1] For those unfamiliar with the show, it is a Christian scare movie that follows the fortunes of Patty Myers, who wakes one day to find that her Christian husband, along with millions of others, has mysteriously disappeared in the rapture. As a non-believer she has been left behind, and the movie goes on to depict the horrors of living on a post-rapture earth. Most famously the productions credit line is not content to finish with 'The End' but adds with a final flourish ' . . . is near'.

Often viewed by children, the film has sparked many discussions on the ethics of terrifying people into faith. There are those who defend the practice, noting that the Bible does speak about the reality of judgement and that while views on what will take place after the return of Christ differ, most agree that only those who have come to a saving faith in Christ can be confident of eternal life with Christ. If this is the case, they argue, movies which depict the dangers of not being a Christian are, in principle, no different from advertisements which graphically display the dangers of smoking or the accidents which sometimes result from driving under the influence of alcohol.

Others protest that Christian conversion is a response to God's loving invitation and grace, and that scare tactics seriously distort people's understanding of the Christian faith. They often argue that whilst fear might see some raise their hands to an appeal to put their trust in Jesus, it rarely results in a long-term commitment to the journey and at best leads to following Christ from shallow and muddled motives.

I have been a pastor for long enough to know that when the term 'eschatology' is mentioned, those whose eyes show a flicker of recognition usually assume that the ensuing discussion will be about the 'end times' and also imagine that some apocalyptic speculation will soon follow. They will be curious to see if the preacher of the day adopts a pre, post or a-millennium line, and might be interested as to what path an exploration of the beast in Daniel 7 will follow.

Whilst understanding the natural curiosity associated with such discussions, in this chapter I will argue that a Christian world view is better served when we avoid apocalyptic terrorism and refuse to link eschatology to escapism and idle speculation. Rather, we should build a world view emboldened by the resurrection of Jesus, and the confidence that gives of our long-term security. You can't believe in Easter and live timidly. It gives the courage to do that which is right, for as a result of the resurrection death has become a toothless tyrant. Initially it might still seem a little scary, but when we probe more deeply we discover its power is now illusionary. Consequently, hopefulness is a settled disposition in our lives.

This chapter explores what it means to live in the light of eternity, and the implications of such an orientation for the present moment. It asks whether our belief in an afterlife reduces or alters our commitment to our present life, and explores the implications of a belief in a new heaven and a new earth for the present earth. It takes the model prayer of Jesus seriously, and asks what it means to pray, 'your kingdom come, your will be done on earth as it is in heaven.'

But first we should ask the even more fundamental question – what is it that Christians believe about the future?

Some things we believe about the future

All religions do not teach essentially the same thing, and this becomes obvious when you study the teaching of what happens after death found in the world's major religions. Tom Wright insightfully comments:

> There is a world of difference between the Muslim who believes that a Palestinian boy killed by an Israeli soldier goes straight to heaven, and the Hindu for whom the rigorous outworking of karma means that one must return in a different body to pursue the next stage of one's destiny. There is a world of difference between the Orthodox Jew who believes that all the righteous will be raised to new individual bodily life in the resurrection, and the Buddhist who hopes after death to disappear like a drop in the ocean, losing one's own identity in the great nameless and formless Beyond.[2]

If religions differ as to what happens after death, what are the agreed contours of a Christian vision of life beyond the grave?

That there is life after death is a fundamental Christian teaching. At the very least, the resurrection of Jesus confirms that rigor mortis is not our permanent destiny. It is impossible to interpret 1 Corinthians 15 in any other light.

Although we speak loosely of Jesus coming back from the dead, it is more biblical to speak of Jesus showing us what is on the other side of death. His resurrection body was not the same as it had been prior to the crucifixion, and it was able to appear and disappear in a manner previously unknown. By contrast, Lazarus came back from the dead.[3] However, he was not, like Jesus, the 'firstfruits of those who have fallen asleep'.[4] Lazarus, after all, died again at a later stage. His temporary return from death provided no decisive clue as to our future destiny.

When the apostle Paul writes of the resurrection of Jesus in 1 Corinthians 15 he spells out the implications for Christian believers. He argues that at the resurrection of the dead, a resurrection made certain by the resurrection of Christ, we will see the contrast between our current body and our resurrection body. Listen to his words in verses 42–44a: 'So will it be with the resurrection of the dead. The body that is sown is perishable, it is raised imperishable; it is sown in dishonour, it is raised in glory; it is sown in weakness, it is raised in power; it is sown a natural body, it is raised a spiritual body.'

So much, then, is clear. Those who have placed their trust in Jesus can expect, at the resurrection of the dead, to receive a resurrection body that is imperishable. This is guaranteed by the resurrection of Jesus, whose resurrection is a sign of the future harvest to come for all those who have received his grace and forgiveness. 'Are the dead raised to life?' asks Paul. His logic is clear, and found in 1 Corinthians 15:16–20:

> For if the dead are not raised, then Christ has not been raised either. And if Christ has not been raised, your faith is futile; you are still in your sins. Then those also who have fallen asleep in Christ are lost. If only for this life we have hope in Christ, we are of all people most to be pitied.
> But Christ has indeed been raised from the dead, the firstfruits of those who have fallen asleep. (NIV 2011)

In short, in Paul's thinking everything stands or falls on the resurrection of Jesus. If it has not taken place, we have no eternal hope. Indeed, if the dead are not raised, we might as well adopt an existentialist philosophy, for as Paul writes in 1 Corinthians 15:32, 'If the dead are not raised, "Let us eat and drink, for tomorrow we die."'

1 Corinthians 15:22–26 gives a sense of the chronological order of things:

> For as in Adam all die, so in Christ all will be made alive. But each in his own turn: Christ, the firstfruits; then, when he comes, those who belong to him. Then the end will come, when he hands over the kingdom to God the Father after he has destroyed all dominion, authority and power. For he must reign until he has put all his enemies under his feet. The last enemy to be destroyed is death.

We are, therefore, urged to hope for the death of death and a radically new order where God's reign is unchallenged.

What does this mean for the future of this planet? Whilst we can be assured of our personal future, will this be in a heavenly realm where memories of this earth rapidly fade and become increasingly irrelevant? If so, does it really matter how we live on this planet? Surely 7 billion years in eternity will make the seventy we spent here appear to be of very little significance.

A closer reading of Scripture does not support this understanding. There is a gentle insistence that Christian hope is rooted in God's new creation, and that this lies in a new heaven and a new earth. Quoting from Isaiah 65:17, John in Revelation 21:1 announces a vision of 'a new heaven and a new earth.' 2 Peter 3:13 announces a similar expectation, confirming that 'we are looking forward to a new heaven and a new earth, where righteousness dwells' (NIV 2011). Clearly if those resurrected from the dead are to be whisked away to heaven, we must ask what role the new earth plays and why a new earth is required. Indeed, why is a new heaven also needed?

Whilst it is important to acknowledge that Revelation 21 and 22, like most apocalyptic literature is difficult to understand (and it is therefore best to be a little provisional in making claims as to its meaning), it does suggest some fairly clear lines. The current heavens and earth will either be replaced or renewed with a new heaven and a new earth. The new earth will be the residence and permanent dwelling of all believers. When we misleadingly speak of going to heaven, we should qualify the sentiment by noting that 'heaven' is located on the new earth, and it is here that the New Jerusalem will be positioned. It is a physical place where we will dwell in our glorified resurrected bodies. It will be free from sickness, suffering and death, and sin will have disappeared.

The announcement in Revelation 21:3 that 'God's dwelling-place is now among the people, and he will dwell with them' (NIV 2011), perhaps suggests that the old divide between heaven and earth will be removed. Certainly access to God is no longer an issue. As John puts it in Revelation 21:22,23: 'I did not see a temple in the city, because the Lord God Almighty and the Lamb are its temple. The city does not need the sun or the moon to shine on it, for the glory of God gives it light, and the Lamb is its lamp.'

If we are to wait for a new earth, does the fate of the old one matter?

First, it is as well to acknowledge that some believe that in talking of a new earth, the Bible is primarily talking about the renewal of the earth, or the restoration of this planet. As I would rather focus on the large lines of agreement between Christians, I will not dive into this, but would rather note the obvious. When we talk of a new earth, we immediately imply that there is both continuity with the past (else how would we know that it is the earth?), as well as some discontinuity (else why consider it new?).

Put differently, if after the death of a pet dog I am informed that I will receive a new dog, I know that some things will be the same, and some different. My new dog will not be a cat. It might not be the same breed as the old one, and might have a fairly different personality, but it will bark like a dog, and not roar like a lion. Continuity and discontinuity. This seems to be the thrust of talk of a new heaven and earth. Are things going to continue exactly as they were before? No! Are things going to be so different that the earth no longer bears the name earth – no again. While this is the new earth, it is still earth.

Is this relevant and does it make any difference to the way we currently live on this planet? It should make every difference, because the portrait of the new earth gives us an idea of what lasts and what does not. A new earth is God's radical and permanent 'yes' to the concept of earth. God does not look at the old earth and say, 'Dreadful idea. Don't know what I was thinking.' To the contrary, whilst some things must disappear when the new earth is birthed, the basic idea behind the earth is affirmed for all eternity. Even more significantly, those things that disappear on the new earth are the things that resulted from the Fall. John's Revelation notes the disappearance of sorrow, death, mourning and pain. This will be a world without tears.[5] Put differently, sin is defeated on the new earth. God's original plan for creation now flourishes.

This has a very practical outworking in the present – when we steward the world well, or when we say no to sin, or when we work to alleviate pain and suffering, we announce our 'amen' to the future of God. When we do the opposite, we proclaim an attachment to a doomed way of living. As we have been given a sufficiently clear portrait of that which will be upheld forever, we should live in accordance with future reality. It makes absolutely no sense to proclaim that we are 'longing for heaven' if we hold tightly to those things which disappear on the new earth.

As it is in heaven: An orienting prayer

Let's develop some of the closing thoughts from the last section a little more fully. What does it mean for us to announce our 'amen' to the future of God?

In the model prayer which Jesus taught his disciples, we are instructed to pray, 'your kingdom come, your will be done, on earth as it is in heaven'.[6] It seems only reasonable to ask what it would look like if this prayer were answered in the affirmative. Note that the underlying request is that God's *will* be done on earth, just as God's *will* is done in heaven. In the first instance the prayer is about obedience to God's will, rather than a petition that the activities of heaven be slavishly duplicated on the earth.

When we ask what life on earth would look like if it were in accord with God's will, we should expect an answer that is paradoxically both clear and vague.

On the one hand, we have the clarity of God's law revealed in the Bible. The Ten Commandments, for example, are not that difficult to understand. If wondering if we are entitled to help ourselves to an interesting trinket from the local store, and contemplate doing so without paying for the item, the 'You shall not steal' command in Exodus 20:15 leaves us in no doubt that we should expect divine displeasure – regardless of if the shopkeeper notices our pilfering or not. Likewise, Exodus 20:3 informs us to have no other gods but Yahweh, which leaves us without excuse if we hedge our bets and petition fifteen different deities for the new job we are applying for. Such things are clear, and it is unwise to make them seem complicated.

However, the original sin of our ancestors should alert us to the risk of assuming that the ethical quest is easily conquered. When Eve and Adam ate from the tree of the knowledge of good and evil, they did so in the hope that like God they would be able to definitively differentiate between good and evil.[7] Equipped with such knowledge, they would be able to stake their ethical independence from God. The act is seen as one of deep rebellion not simply because they had been told not to do it, but because the underlying motivation was to stake autonomy from God. Rather than a life of close relationship with God, humanity hoped to make ethically sound decisions in a secularized garden. But God's will can never be done outside of relationship with God precisely because God wills to be in relationship with the creatures made *imago Dei*. If we are not in relationship with God, life is not as God wills it to be. In short, the ethical quest and our spiritual formation should not be separated. Mechanically living in accordance with virtue is not the same as living from virtue, and the latter is only possible when our lives are lived in a close, trusting and warm-hearted relationship with our Creator.[8]

If we are to live in the light of eternity, and attempt to do so by committing to the prayer that God's will be done on the earth, a sound starting point it to take seriously those aspects of God's will clearly revealed in the Bible. Perhaps Jesus' summary of the law and the prophets in Mark 12:28–33 is a solid starting point. It has been suggested that these verses constitute Jesus' own creed, and if good enough for Jesus, should be good enough for us.[9]

As I have said earlier, love which engages our heart, soul, mind and strength brings us face to face with every other human being, and requires us to explore and enact whatever genuine love for them will mean. In ascertaining if our attitudes and actions are in accord with the will of God, we can litmus test them against love for God and love for the neighbour.

As God's will is destined to reign through eternity, by taking seriously the prayer to make God's will a reality on this planet we align ourselves with that which lasts forever. A commitment to God's will also provide contours for an active agenda. There is so much on this earth that is clearly not in accord with God's will. As we resist every such temptation, we allow the future reality of God to shape the present moment.

Not that we should make the mistake of thinking that our obedience to God's will ushers in the kingdom of God. While some aspects of life on this planet can more closely resemble God's original intent for creation, others are in need of radical transformation, and will only be achieved when God's kingdom arrives. For example, whilst medical advances and a better distribution of the world's resources have seen human life expectancy increase, death itself is not progressively defeated. We all face death, even if on average it arrives a decade or two later than 100 years ago. We can delay death, but cannot defeat it. The final destruction of death awaits the vertical irruption from beyond. It will be an eschatological reality, something achieved through the triumphant return of Christ, not something we can slowly chip away at achieving in the present moment. As such, whilst we pray that God's will be done on the earth, we realize that the full answer to that prayer will be an eschatological rather than a present reality. However, this should be viewed as an invitation to humility, rather than as an excuse to ignore the prayer.

Living in the light of eternity

Eschatology can easily become escapist, and it is not unreasonable to ask, 'If everything is going to be made new, why bother about what happens in the present moment?'

There are many examples of belief in an afterlife dulling the call to change in the present. At times circumstances on this planet have been so appalling that only the hope of an alternate reality has made survival possible. Think for example of the song, 'Swing Low, Sweet Chariot'. Sung by slaves, it was totally understandable that their hopes were nested in a better afterlife. They did indeed long for the sweet chariot to come and sweep them away to a place which could more validly bear the name 'home'. If at times it made the present more bearable, perhaps even being what Marx suggested was an 'opiate for the masses', it never stopped the quest for a better today, but made it possible to get up in the morning when such a day was clearly only on a far distant horizon. We who live in far more comfortable circumstances should avoid being critical of eschatological escapism by those who lived during untenable times. However, given that our circumstances are radically different, we should be cautious if our eschatology has too similar a flavour.

The thirteenth chapter of Paul's first letter to the Corinthians is justifiably famous. Often read at weddings, its insights on love are both profound and moving. The chapter ends with the memorable lines, 'And now these three remain: faith, hope and love. But the greatest of these is love.'[10] In chapter 2 I suggested that this verse should serve as an orienting passage for us as we examine the meaning of Scripture. The reason is not hard to fathom. We are assured that three things will remain for all eternity: faith, hope and love. When we engage in pursuits that flow from faith, hope or love, we deal with the stuff of eternity. To live in the light of eternity is to be willing to ask of every activity, 'In what way has this been birthed by faith? In what way has this been birthed by hope? In what way has this been birthed by love?' If an awkward silence follows each question, we are probably tinkering in trivia, and should explore an alternate agenda.

Not that it will always be easy to reply to these questions. Nor should we too quickly buy into the answer. Reading a novel to relax might seem escapist and non-productive, but it could help us regain inner peace and quiet, such that love rather than irritation motivates our later actions. The importance of this should not be overlooked. The ideal is not that we become driven people, frenetically trying to justify our existence by our busy (albeit noble) agenda. The creation account describes a world where each day begins with the night – there was evening and morning, the first day.[11] Night is the time when work cannot be done, and where we simply trust ourselves to the loving care of God. From the refreshing renewal of sleep, we then embark upon the day, when activity can begin. Our value to God is not linked to our usefulness to God, but to our being in a tender and loving relationship with the maker of all. Alternatively, we could note that we are called to live from the grace of God, and should be wary if grace retreats into legalism. The question, 'Has this been birthed by faith? Or hope? Or love?' is not intended as a legalistic trap, but as an invitation to check the overall orientation and direction of our life.

But let us probe a little deeper. What does it mean to embark on activities birthed by faith? In the first instance it means that we put our faith and confidence in the revealed agenda of God. It means trusting, even without obvious evidence to back our trust. It means being willing to do what we believe God calls us to.

To operate from hope means to look to the future and to live in the light of what we see. The resurrection points us to an empty tomb. It helps us to see the death-defeating Jesus welcoming us in the future. That welcome relativizes all fear in the present. An example that might seem a little trivial could nevertheless help.

I enjoy watching rugby on television, but have noticed that I can get a little too intense when watching live matches. This is especially so when the team from my childhood town of Durban are playing. One year it was especially bad. Almost without exception they were ahead until the closing ten minutes of the match, and then inexplicably they would crumble, and lose the game. Watching was heartbreaking – and really bad for my blood pressure! So I decided to record all matches, and find out the score before I committed to watching. If my team won, I would watch the game. If not, I would mutter and grumble but not subject myself to viewing their humiliation.

It makes an enormous difference when you watch a rugby game knowing that your team has already won. The referee can make a poor call, and instead of hurling abuse and suggesting the name of an appropriate optician, I philosophically note that even good referees make some mistakes. The other team can score a try, and instead of being gripped by a cold panic that this spells the end, I calmly comment that it is rather nice that the other team gets the occasional point – after all, there is no need to humiliate them simply because they are on the other side. Or my team can be awarded an extremely easy penalty kick in front of the posts, and miss. If I don't know the score, I am likely to explode, 'My granny can kick better than that . . . and she's dead!' Knowing that we win, however, I serenely suggest that even the best players miss occasionally.

The entire experience is transformed by knowing the final outcome.

Living in the light of the resurrection is a little like that. Having seen the future, we live backwards from the knowledge gained. Christ's kingdom will come and it will last forever. Current opposition is simply a temporary setback that should not unsettle us unduly. Not that this makes it unreal at the time, but it reminds us that the last word has yet to be spoken – and the last word vindicates our hope. A sign has already been given that this is the case – that sign being the resurrection of Jesus. Hope lasts forever, because our hope in Jesus does not disappoint us.

What then does it mean to live from love? It means that we know that we are loved by God. We have perhaps heard that so often that the news does not impact us as much as it should. When love is the context of our life, we are liberated to love others, and to love God's good world. Love releases us from the need to be self-protecting and self-absorbed. Love lasts forever because it frees us to be without fear, shame or hiding. Love lasts, because God lasts forever, and God is love.[12]

Eschatology is not about speculative timelines, or an avoidance of the present. It is the quietly insistent affirmation that God's love triumphs, and that this love lasts forever. It is the invitation to live in the light of the future, a future which while perhaps distant, has been rendered certain by the resurrection of Jesus. This hope does not disappoint us.

An interview with John McClean

Dr John McClean is the vice-principal of Christ College, Sydney, where he teaches theology. He is the author of *From the Future: Coming to Grips with Pannenberg's Thought*.[13]

1. *Why do you think that eschatology is often understood in escapist terms?*
   Tom Wright has pointed out how many Christian hymns finish with believers 'in heaven' rather than in a renewed creation. The old saying is that 'the law of prayer is the law of faith' – the way we think about our faith follows the way we worship. If that is right, then escapist eschatology is the Christian default.
   I doubt there is just one reason for this. Partly, we in the West have a folk memory of 'heaven' as 'somewhere else' where we are freed from the prison of the body. That memory comes from the Greek tradition which is built on a longing for an end to change and decay. (Of course, the same themes are even stronger in Eastern thought.)
   I suspect we also have trouble believing that God's promises about the future are real. And it is easier to keep believing in a hope that doesn't touch this world than to talk about Jesus returning to 'here' and transforming the things that surround us – and us. Changing this world sounds like the way religious 'crazies' talk!
   Most seriously, escapist eschatology lets us off the hook. We can tell ourselves that what we do with our bodies and our possessions doesn't matter to God (much like the Corinthian church seems to have thought). We can ignore our neighbours, our society and the environment because God will get rid of all that in the end.

2. *How should we live with the tension between the now and the not yet?*

It has to be a tension. We'll always find we notice one side and then have to remember the other. One day it is exciting to see a Christian friend growing and changing; the next day I am depressed by my own sinfulness. Remarkable church growth is followed by ugly division. So in one sense we can't help but live with the tension.

It is important to see the shape of God's work now. We have to learn to look for the signs of the intrusion of the kingdom in our own lives, in our churches and in the world. They should encourage us, and we should celebrate them. At the same time it is foolish to build expectations which will inevitably be crushed. Christians still get sick, they sin and they fight. Church can be discouraging. Jesus followers are still people who mourn, even though we rejoice. So living in the tension is not about 'optimism' or 'pessimism', but well-grounded hope in real struggle.

2 Corinthians 4:16 is a key verse to remind us that the reality of new life is usually experienced as inner renewal, even while we are outwardly wasting away. In Christ we have spiritual life now, but not yet physical resurrection.

3. *Anticipation plays a key role in Pannenberg's thought. How can this work out in the lives of ordinary Christians?*

Pannenberg's idea of 'anticipation' is fairly unusual. He suggests that all things are what they are now because of what they will be in God's future: reality flows from the future to the present and the present 'anticipates' the future. Fascinating as that is, I think the Bible puts more stress on how things are now, but understands them in the light of the future. In that sense Christians have to live in anticipation (or another word would be 'hope'). Knowing God's future gives us direction and confidence. We don't know enough about God's plans for the new creation that we can make it for ourselves now (1 John 3:2). We do know that God will renew bodies and societies and the whole creation, and we can anticipate that in how we act now. I can also live with myself, weak and struggling, because God promises what I am now in Christ will one day be obvious (Col. 3:3,4).

4. *What is your understanding of the new heaven and the new earth?*
When Jesus returns, God will do with the whole created order what he has already done with Jesus' own body. He won't destroy it, purify it in judgement and glorify it in wonderful fulfilment of all it is now. We shouldn't imagine a 'patch-up job'. The whole of creation will be filled with God's glory: he will fill our existence with unutterable wonder, his life will fill and empower us, his light will enlighten and bedazzle us, his holiness will purify us, his joy will enrapture us and God will be all in all. It will not be a 'spiritual' creation which is no longer physical, but truly physical and fully penetrated by God's Spirit.

5. *And the question I ask everyone: What do we really, really need to know about God?*
'The one who calls you is faithful, and he will do it' (1 Thess. 5:24). He has established the future already by giving himself for us in Christ and to us in the Spirit. 'Salvation' is not a mechanical transaction and the gospel is not simply a set of true propositions. If, like me, you've been a Christian for a while, it is easy to take things for granted and to treat them this way. What I need to keep on seeing is that God is personally, intimately, graciously involved in his world and on that basis he calls us to get involved with him and live for his kingdom. Since he has given himself for us, we can take him at his word and trust him. So in fellowship with God we can now live for his future on the basis of his work in the past.

To ponder and discuss

- The chapter claims that 'You can't believe in Easter and live timidly'. Why? Think through the implications.
- What do you think it means to 'live in the light of eternity'?
- The chapter states, 'When we engage in pursuits that flow from faith, hope or love, we deal with the stuff of eternity.' Put some flesh on this. What does it mean in practice?
- How do you respond to the idea that the new earth will contain elements of continuity and discontinuity with the old earth?

What do you think will be different? And what do you think will be the same?

Section C:

The Big Picture
at Church and Work

An Ethical Mandate: Hospitality and Openness to the Other

The 'belong, believe, behave' thing . . .

It was a throwaway comment made by Craig Vernall at the Mission to New Zealand Conference, June, 2003.[1] Talking about the changes that had seen his congregation grow from a weekly attendance of around one hundred and fifty to 700, he said that a key ethos change had been from 'behave, believe, belong' to 'belong, believe, behave'. In other words, in the past you would only feel welcome in the church if your behaviour was consistent with certain subcultural expectations of what was acceptable for churchgoers. Having met the implied ethical requirements of church attendance, you would imbibe the setting and doctrine so that you came to a place of belief which in turn would lead to formally belonging to the church community. But now, Vernall suggested, his church community had found a way to welcome and embrace the community in such a way that they belonged before they either believed or behaved in a manner that reflected traditional Christian norms.

I thought it a comment worth pondering. It was reinforced when reading Webber's *The Younger Evangelicals*.[2] Again it was an incidental comment. Webber attributes it to an email he received from Dawn Haglund where, speaking of paradigm shifts, she suggests that the old paradigm was 'behave, believe, belong' but the new is 'belong, believe, behave'. Since then I have often heard it described as the journey to 'belong, believe, become' – behave now sounding a little passé. I'll use both in the pages that follow.

As I reflect back on some of my pastoral experiences, I realize that there have been many times when 'behave' was the opening impression given of what really mattered about the Christian faith. Whatever I might have preached about grace, the things that actually troubled and bothered the church communities I was part of were violations of a largely unwritten but powerful code of behavioural expectations. They have shifted over the years, so I will give some of the more dated examples as they help underline how subcultural some of the expectations were.

I remember the outcry when one of the young students on our welcoming team arrived to fulfil her duty barefooted and wearing Bermuda shorts. She had come straight from the beach. Several members of the congregation approached me and asked if I would give her a talk on the importance of appropriate dress. 'After all,' as some of them said, 'if you were going to visit the Queen you'd wear your smartest clothes. And worship is entry into the presence of one greater than royalty.'

I also recollect the delightfully eccentric academic who came to faith through the ministry of the church. Post-conversion he was as eccentric as before. For some this was offensive. I remember one regular at the church prayer meeting routinely praying that he would really be converted. I always wondered what that prayer meant . . . Did he want the professor to become as boringly predictable as others in the congregation?

Another memory (and this goes even further back) was of the longhaired young man who had formerly struggled with drug addiction. In an era when church expectations were for short hair, he left his locks intact. A few days after giving the moving story of his journey to faith he received a letter thanking him for what he had said. Enclosed was some money to enable him to get a haircut, the donor being anxious that he should now 'look like a Christian'.

Fortunately my pastoral experience has usually been loftier than these examples might suggest, but each serve as a reminder that acceptance into the Christian community is often via conformity to a set of unscripted but powerful behavioural norms. In other words, behave dominates the trio of 'behave, believe, belong'.

In chapter 2 I suggested that two key reasons an increasing number of people view the Christian faith as 'naked' are that the Christian faith is considered to be intellectually vacuous and morally suspect. In earlier chapters of the book I have tried to argue against the accusation of being intellectually vacuous by helping to unpack and outline some of the big building blocks of the Christian faith, suggesting they provide broad contours for *a* (rather than *the*) Christian world view. In the remaining two chapters I would like to explore ways to explode the 'morally suspect' myth. One way is by genuine openness to others and by a willing participation in the journey to discover what it means to be human – a quest those who believe they have been made *imago Dei* should embark upon with delight.

I'll suggest that if the emperor is to be clothed, and accusations of moral dubiousness dropped, we need to find ways to make the hospitable journey away from 'behave, believe, belong' to 'belong, believe, become'.

Two questions immediately spring to mind. Is such a paradigm shift desirable? If so, is it possible?[3] Should we desire a church characterized by actual openness (as opposed to superficial openness) and a genuine welcome (as opposed to a conditional, 'on our terms' welcome)?

Embracing the paradigm

Initially the desirability question seems self-evident. Surely the church is nothing if not a community of welcome and embrace. Christ's incarnation was not delayed until such time as the planet engaged in impeccable behaviour. Both Bethlehem's cradle and Calvary's cross speak of the divine 'yes' to humanity in spite of its indifference, cruelty and fallenness. Tax collector Zacchaeus, the five-times married and now co-habiting woman at the well and the Christ-denying Peter all had life narratives where the journey of faith was possible because of the divine welcome rather than a promising behavioural record. Add to this that the first divine 'no' was to human aloneness ('It is not good for the man to be alone', Gen. 2:18) and the case seems pretty compelling.

In addition, the postmodern context sees community (and thus belonging) as an ideal. So taken was he with the concept that North American theologian Stanley Grenz chose 'community' as the integrating theme for his theology.[4] Grenz says he adopted the theme of community after reading *Habits of the Heart*, a seminal sociological work which explores the tension between individualism and the need for community in the USA.[5,6] One of the issues highlighted in *Habits of the Heart* is the link between religion and individualism. The privatization of faith, be it the plea from evangelicals to come into a personal (individual) relationship with God, or the more liberal invitation to worship God in whatever shape or form the individual chooses to conceive the divine, tends to see the emphasis fall back to individual response rather than to community mediation. While individualism might lead to ownership of decisions taken, it can also lead to a sense of isolation and alienation. Against a pendulum that had swung too far in its emphasis on the individual, Grenz suggested community as a correcting and integrating motif. You cannot be part of a community unless it has an open door – people who are willing to welcome you in and treat you as friends, not strangers.

One could also explore the biblical theme of hospitality. From the record of Abraham's welcome to the three visitors in Genesis 18 to the affirmation in Hebrews 13:2 that in welcoming the stranger one might entertain angels without being aware of it, or the great multitude in Revelation 19, delighted to be invited to the wedding feast of the Lamb, the Bible extols the virtue of hospitality. By contrast, the shameful and sordid events at Sodom, recorded in Genesis 19 include, amongst other significant wrongs, a failure of hospitality.

Noting the emphasis on hospitality in the ancient Near Eastern world, Ewing writes, 'In the desert, every tent, however poor its owner, offers welcome to the traveller . . . It is the master's pride to be known as a generous man; any lack of civility or of kindness to a guest meets severe reprobation. In the guest's presence he calls neither his tent, nor anything it contains, his own. During his sojourn, the visitor is owner.'[7]

It could be argued that the welcome of hospitality is a different matter to the conferring of the status of one who belongs, but that misses the point that the first stage in the trio under investigation is of an ethos that notices, reaches out, includes and incorporates the other. If we are not to be dismissed as naked emperors, self-righteously evaluating others while our own house is in disarray, it is an ethos which should be seriously considered.

It could be that the motivation behind belong-believe-behave is not essentially theological but pragmatic. Simply put, the welcome of belonging creates an openness to explore new systems of belief and new models of being.

Similarly, one could argue that creating an atmosphere of acceptance and belonging is psychologically sound. Psychologist Carl Rogers is well known for his insight that unconditional positive regard is key to individuals being freed to embrace constructive and life-serving change. A little counterintuitively Rogers suggests that a person who feels fully and unconditionally accepted is far more likely to be open to change and grow than one who does not feel accepted. The very act of accepting the other helps give them the courage to look more deeply within. Although one might fear that acceptance would lead to complacency, Rogers argues that the opposite results.[8]

Theologically this could mean that instead of starting with an emphasis on sin and the Fall, our opening announcement might be of grace and hope.[9] The discussion is not purely theoretical. I have friends who serve as street chaplains. Their ministry begins with their being on the streets at inhospitable hours. They listen to those who have sold their bodies, or imbibed excessively, or who simply want to feel a little less alone. Often the stories they hear make no sense. Many meander meaninglessly. But one thing is always understood. As Christ's representative, their willingness to listen and be present is a tentative sign of the willing incarnation of Jesus 2,000 years ago. Their ministry is about being there with open hearts and hands. If they started with the wagging finger and expressions of moral outrage, they would have no ministry at all.

Questioning the paradigm

Significant though these arguments are, the paradigm shift to belonging before believing or behaving should not be accepted without question. Five issues spring quickly to mind:

- Is the journey to faith really linear? Linked to this, isn't the model too static? When, for example, does one get the tick of approval affirming that one is now behaving as a Christian?

- Is it possible to 'belong' to something that one does not yet believe in or whose ethics do not guide one's behaviour?
- In both paradigms, 'believe' is placed in the middle. Is the role of belief really secondary?
- Does the model imply that we are all really 'anonymous Christians' and that the invitation to belong is therefore appropriate regardless of personal belief or behaviour?[10]
- By placing behaviour at the end of the trio, do we run the risk of endorsing what Bonhoeffer classifies as 'cheap grace'?[11]

These are not trivial questions, so let's work through them systematically.

Is the journey to faith really linear?

In older evangelical understandings of Christian conversion, the journey to faith was seen to go through clear and predictable stages. It was taught that all were sinful from birth and in need of a saviour from sin.[12] Those who recognized this need and accepted Christ's substitutionary death on the cross on their behalf would then ask for forgiveness of sin, and accept Jesus into their life. Having done this, they were 'saved' or 'justified'. Justification occurred at the moment of conversion and ensured an eternal future as a child of God. An oft-cited example was the thief on the cross who, because he asked for Jesus' help, was assured that on that very day he would be together with Jesus in paradise.[13] Justification was instant and sufficient to guarantee that thief a place in heaven, even though his imminent death prevented any significant progress on the route of sanctification. The most important step was therefore that of justification, as this guaranteed eternity in the presence of Christ.

Post-justification, the journey of sanctification began and was usually understood as becoming more Christ-like. On Christ's return or after death (whichever came first) there was the expectation of glorification when all believers would live with God forever.[14]

While this understanding of Christian conversion remains amongst evangelicals, the neat division into tidy stages is increasingly questioned, as is the precise nature of conversion. The validity of simply making a decision for Jesus is challenged. Robert Webber writes: '. . . the postmodern world is fertile ground for the Christian message, but it must be the full message and not a reductionism to a decision without an in-depth follow up to Christian thought and practice. If we are to evangelise effectively, we must set about building community and providing healing to the hurts of life.'[15]

Linked is the growing claim that the felt need in communities is no longer for a release from guilt and sin, but revolves rather around finding meaning and purpose. Richard Harries writes:

> During the late medieval and Reformation period people were gnawed by a sense of guilt, and in our time it is predominantly a feeling of meaningless which oppresses us . . . whereas in the late medieval and Reformation period the Christian faith could be powerfully preached as deliverance from sin and a sense of guilt, it is much more difficult to do that today when there has been a widespread loss of a sense of sin . . .[16]

A more holistic understanding of conversion is thus being called for. A problem with the shift from 'behave, believe, belong' to 'belong, believe, behave' is that it retains a sense of stages to be passed and ticked off the list. The more likely trajectory is one of simultaneously feeling a sense of identification with and acceptance by a Christian community while increasingly understanding and accepting traditional Christian teaching and, where required, making gradual ethical course corrections. Dictating the precise order serves no useful function, nor is it likely to be accurate. The biblical image of growing towards maturity, with the fruit of the Spirit slowly but steadily impacting our life, is probably both more accurate and more helpful.

Is it possible to 'belong' to something that one does not yet believe in or whose ethics do not guide one's behaviour?

At another level of query we should ask if it is possible to 'belong' to something not yet believed in or whose ethics have not been adopted. Underneath is the question of what it means to 'belong'.

Certainly if 'belong' implies 'having been formally accepted into membership of', the 'belong, believe, become' model has little likelihood of success in a postmodern era. A common concern expressed by many church leaders is that while they can get people to attend and participate in the ministry of the local church, they find it hard to get them to officially join the church. The experience of the Baptist Churches of Western Australia is probably representative, where in 2003 the combined average Sunday service attendance for all churches in the Union was 10,904 compared to a membership of 5,419.[17] The number attending each Sunday was roughly double the number of those who were actual church members.

However, to think of 'belong' in the narrow terms of church membership is probably not what was intended by Vernall's or Haglund's comments.[18] More probable is that they envision a community where one feels one has found a 'place' in the sense used by Paul Tournier in his classic *A Place for You*. The book opens with this account:

> The words were those of a young student with whom I had formed a deep friendship. He was sitting by my fireside, telling me of his difficulties, of the anxiety that never left him, and which at times turned to panic and to flight. He was trying to look objectively at what was going on inside himself and to understand it. Then, as if summing up his thoughts, he looked up at me and said: 'Basically, I'm always looking for a place – for somewhere to be.'[19]

Though the incident was recounted back in the 1960s, it has a strikingly contemporary ring. Perhaps the longing for 'a place – for somewhere to be' is universal. It could be argued that the psalmist expresses a similar sentiment in Psalm 84:10 'Better is one day in your courts than a thousand elsewhere'.[20] It sees other images of church spring to mind such as church as community, or church as family.

Church as family brings us back to the heart of the question being looked at. When told that his mother and brothers were waiting for him, Jesus turned to his disciples and declared that 'whoever does the will of my Father in heaven is my brother and sister and mother'.[21] The behavioural component of doing 'the will of my Father in heaven' was a necessary companion to the declaration of being part of Christ's family. To return to the question, is it possible to 'belong' to something that one does not yet believe in or whose ethics do not guide one's behaviour? Or can the sequence really be 'belong, believe, become'?

Is the role of belief really secondary?

A third issue is over the place of belief. In both the new and old paradigm the suggestion is that belief comes in the middle. While a welcome invitation to humility for those who insist on theological precision, the validity of the claim must be questioned.

One could argue that the sentiment is correct. Jesus urged his listeners to have the faith of little children. It was their intuitive and spontaneous faith that seemed to impress him, not their doctrinal orthodoxy.[22] In more critical vein, James 2:19 notes that even demons hold some accurate beliefs. However, to dismiss the importance of sound doctrine on such a basis would be trite. Much of the New Testament explores the struggle for accurate and sound teaching.

Perhaps what is called for is a chastened view of doctrinal formulations. Certainly the multitude of books published on 'apologetics for a postmodern era' stress that if apologetics is to have a future, it will need to be more relational and more willing to listen.[23]

In addition, the call for a post-foundational basis for theology is becoming widespread. Images for doctrinal orthodoxy now revolve around webs of coherence rather than undisputed foundations, and for truth to be seen as a centred rather than a boundaried set.[24] While some worry about the demise of traditional understandings of truth,[25] others argue that a contextual, relational view of truth is both more accurate and appropriate for a postmodern context.

The implication that belief now flows from belonging rather than from behaving should probably be modified to acknowledge that belief is usually related to multiple factors. In reality, belief cannot often be divorced from one's community of reference. Openness to a community of faith often leads to greater openness to its belief system. It is debatable if the two can be separated. Uneasiness with the beliefs of a community would make identification with (belonging to) the community improbable. In the sense that one might identify with a community (belong), accept its beliefs but only aspire to its behaviour ('behave' being a goal rather than a reality) the progression might well be 'belong, believe, behave'. If belief is not seen as a stand-alone category, it is probably best placed at the centre of the trio. Certainly the emphasis that beliefs are communal rather than individual is consistent with post-modern thinking. Thus belief would not head the trio, as there can be no understanding of what the Christian faith is apart from the community of faith who uphold it.

Does the model imply that we are all really 'anonymous Christians'?

The fourth question around a shift to 'belong, believe, behave' asks if the affirmation of belonging before any requirement to believe or behave might imply that a person is already an 'anonymous Christian' waiting to be included into the family they are part of – albeit without their knowledge. In this view, the acknowledgement of belonging without other prerequisites is an affirmation of a person's true, though previously unknown, status.

The stance is not without merit. Those who stumble into the faith community, no matter how tentatively, have arrived at their true home. Made to reflect the image of the Creator God, we discover our humanity the moment we respond to the voice calling in Eden's garden, 'Where are you?' Hearing that voice is the start of finding our true identity and the place where we belong. Discovering where we most truly belong will be accompanied by a realization that all other allegiances are, at best, a pale shadow of this new allegiance. We are set free to discover who we have been made to be. So we 'belong' the moment we enter our true home. Of course, if we never enter it . . . well, that raises too many questions to explore here.

By placing behaviour at the end of the trio, do we run the risk of endorsing what Bonhoeffer classifies as 'cheap grace'?

A fifth objection is that a stress on belonging without prerequisites of belief or behaviour could imply that cheap rather than costly grace is operative. While the danger exists, it is worth noting that it was a risk Jesus was prepared to take. Jesus accompanied Zacchaeus to his home before the tree-climbing tax collector offered to relinquish his ill-gotten gains. Jesus appears to have affirmed the importance of acceptance prior to moral change.[26] Add to this Jesus' reputation of associating with drunkards and people with questionable morals, and the earlier paradigm of 'behave, believe, belong' is shown to be inconsistent with Jesus' model of ministry. If Jesus was confident that a genuine experience of grace would lead to transformation, perhaps we should follow his example.

From quibbling to ethos

While the detailed scrutiny of 'belong, believe, behave' leaves some significant questions, rather than treat the statement as one of absolute truth it is probably more fruitful to view it as indicative of a needed ethos change. It affirms that Christians should be warmly open-hearted and inclusive. At this level, the model is hard to fault. One of the major missiological barriers faced by the church is that it is perceived to be self-righteous, judgemental and hypocritical. To make matters worse, it is usually believed that it does not live up to its own standards of morality – and is thus judging others by standards it fails to meet itself. It is this perception that raises another, perhaps more compelling, missiological question. Indeed, it could be another paradigm shift that we need . . .

Another paradigm shift

Thus far we have been working from the assumption that if the church were to be a community of welcome and embrace, it would find a steady stream of people grateful for the ethos change and waiting to swell its ranks. This assumption is almost certainly flawed. Suspicion of and even hostility towards the church has increased. While not facing religious persecution, churches in the West are in serious danger of being marginalized. On the basis of current trends, Peter Brierley predicts that whereas in 1970, 80 per cent of those living in the 'first world' claimed some kind of allegiance to the Christian faith (however nominal), by 2050 the percentage is likely to have declined to 57 per cent.[27]

The irony is thus that while we debate if we are willing to accept people whose belief or behaviour might not conform to our standards, the line of those waiting to belong has dwindled. Perhaps it has completely disappeared or more probably, perhaps it never existed.

It could be that the paradigm shift from 'behave, believe, belong' to 'belong, believe, behave' is too late.

Has this therefore been an exercise in futility, comparable to debating the number of angels that can fit on a pinhead?

The model can be salvaged if an additional paradigm shift takes place. It depends on how one interprets 'belong' and on how one answers the question, 'Who belongs to who?' In traditional models, conversion marked the leaving of one's former lifestyle and adopting the lifestyle of the new community. While certain aspects of this model are valid, perhaps discontinuity with the past was overstressed. In short, perhaps the queue to belong to the church does not exist because the church is perceived to criticize and critique the world it seeks to win.

In other words, the believing community requires others to 'belong' to it, but the community it seeks to win is not sure that those who make the call have ever belonged to their world in a constructive way. Put differently, incarnation must precede any invitation to belong to a new community.

We can better understand the dilemma by placing ourselves in the shoes of the average 17-year-old.[28] She probably hasn't been to church before, and if she has, is likely to have felt out of place. But she would have been fed information about the church. The media have portrayed it as an uncomfortable relic from the past. That could be acceptable, if it weren't a relic with an opinion. But it is enormously opinionated! Apparently it believes that sex and fun are distasteful. Its leaders are invariably hypocrites and paedophiles. It condemns homosexuals to hell while its clergy can't keep their hands off young boys. And though not exactly the flat earth society, it insists that the world is around six thousand years old.

True, most of what she would believe about the church would be stereotypical and unfair. But she is part of a generation for whom image is reality. Even though the majority of young people believe in God, most rate Christianity as irrelevant to a genuine spiritual quest.[29] No matter how welcoming the church might attempt to be, the likelihood of her ever coming within its embrace is slight. Even if she did, she is unlikely to want to 'belong' to a group associated with such images.

In chapter 3 we explored the paradoxical dilemma that in many areas this generation's values are probably closer to Christian values than any previous generation. In contrasting modern to postmodern values, Jones suggests that there has been a shift from the

- rational to the experiential
- scientific to the spiritual
- unanimous (or the homogenous) to the pluralistic
- exclusive to the relative
- egocentric to the altruistic
- individualistic to the communal
- functional to the creative
- industrial to the environmental
- local to the global
- compartmentalized/dichotomised to the holistic
- relevant to the authentic

Jones also notes that both modern and postmodern audiences value relational approaches.[30]

Most striking is the positive nature of most of these shifts. While many Christians are anxious about the shift to a postmodern ethos, Jones's analysis suggests that the emerging values are closer to core Christian values that those held during the modern era.[31] To a desire for greater community, altruism, creativity and indeed most of the contemporary values Jones outlines, the gospel gives loud agreement.

This, then, is the dilemma. Historically the church has felt that it holds the moral high ground, whilst those outside the church no longer consider the ethical superiority of the church to be self-evident. The current values of the Western world often reflect a kinder and more charitable face than 'the average face' shown by the church in its 2,000 year history.[32]

Missiologically we have created significant hurdles for ourselves, and they are not the stumbling-blocks posed by the cross of Christ. While clearly needing an ethos shift from 'behave, believe, belong' to 'belong, believe, become', on its own, this will accomplish little. Repentance for past and present wrongs, as well as a willingness to affirm and embrace the positive change that has taken place in society, is also needed. If the emperor will humbly agree to be clothed and supported by the big building blocks of the Christian faith, perhaps a new start can be made.

For 'bottom line' thinkers

In summary, then, while applauding an ethos change from 'behave, believe, belong' to 'belong, believe, become' a more dramatic paradigm shift is required. In the book of Jonah, the prophet turns out to be harder to reach than the Ninevites. It could be that the scenario has not changed significantly. Missiological obstacles in the West are not limited to a failure to welcome and embrace, but a failure to convince that the Christian message leads to a life-affirming transformation of both individuals and communities. Seeing such transformation incarnated in communities of care and embrace could prove a powerful apologetic for the Christian faith in the 21st century. If we open our hearts to God's world, perhaps its heart will open in response.

An interview with Carolyn Tan

Dr Carolyn Tan worked for many years as a paediatric surgeon in Singapore, and has more recently embarked on a career as a theologian. She teaches Greek at Vose Seminary, and also serves in the lay leadership of Perth Baptist Church, which is noted for its open-hearted ministry to students from around the world.

1. *So which do you think it is? 'Behave, believe, belong' or 'belong, believe behave'?*
   Many years ago, I would have flowed with 'behave, believe, belong'. Today I'm not so sure.

Jesus extends his hand of fellowship to people who are at the margins, even outcasts, of the community of God's people. He invites himself into Zacchaeus's home before Zacchaeus does his public turnaround (Luke 19:5). He calls Levi even as Levi sat collecting the hated taxes (Luke 5:27). It is the sinner that Jesus has come for. He accepts them because he already knows what he will do on the cross. I am now convinced that 'belonging' must be grounded in Jesus and what he has done, and not on an adherence to a code of conduct. But should we not at least believe before belonging? From an earthly perspective, yes. However, ours is a God who looks at us from the future. Our own vision is often limited by our unidirectional experience of time. Instead, following Christ, I think we should regard newcomers as 'pre-believers', beginning on their own journey of faith. I believe that we come to believe by the grace of God, a grace extended to us because for God, we have always belonged to him – we've just been lost. So I now say – 'belong, believe, behave'.

2. *It's one thing to say that the church should not be so judgemental, but aren't we called to be prophetic? Is it possible to be prophetic and sensitive at the same time?*
   Judges stand over against the people. True prophets stand with the people. Moses was prepared to be blotted out together with the Israelites if God chose not to forgive them (Exod. 32:32); Isaiah saw himself as one of a people with unclean lips, a sinner like the rest (Isa. 6:5); Jeremiah was shamefully treated by the people he was sent to warn, and yet, when his prophecies mate-rialized, and although he was given the chance to escape, he stayed with the people even when they continued to disobey God and stubbornly headed into disaster (Jer. 40:2–6; 43:4–7); Jesus could have run away from the Garden of Gethsemane, but he stayed, waiting for the soldiers (Mark 14:32–42). True prophets feel God's wrath, and also his deep sorrow, and they weep with the people. True prophets are incarnational. It is not a question of being diplomatic or sugar-coating an unpalatable truth. There is no feeling of superiority or the gleeful triumph of 'I told you so'. There is only pain and sorrow in a proph-et's heart, and a very great godly love for God's humanity. As

God's children, when we think we are being prophetic, are we speaking for God or for ourselves?

3. *You have lived in different cultures, and serve in a multi-cultural church. Does being hospitable and open to others mean different things in different contexts?*
I live in two cultures, and see life through two cultural lenses. To be genuinely open to others and hospitable in such a way that the other person feels included and welcome must begin first, I believe, with a perspective of shared humanity and shared fallenness. It calls for humility. The minute our hand of welcome is extended on the basis of superiority ('Aren't *we* being so kind to *them*?'), God's grace has been thwarted. Openness and hospitality is linked to acceptance and inclusion. Second, our way of doing things is not the only 'right' way. Often there is no 'right' or 'wrong', just differences. And differences in cultural signals should be respected. For example, patting a child on the head, a gesture of warmth in Anglo-Saxon communities, is rude in Thai-Cambodian societies. Third, misunderstandings and conflicts should be identified and lovingly addressed rather than avoided – bearing in mind that many cultures find such confrontation difficult and uncomfortable. Fourth, we must be willing, ourselves, to embrace change. Our triune God is at the centre of who we are and what we do; everything else around us can change without threat to the core of our being.

4. *As a medical specialist you would often have been with families at times of extreme stress and grief. What does incarnation mean at such times?*
The area I loved most was neonatal surgery, meaning that I often looked after tiny, premature babies. Sometimes they become so ill that nothing we do, medically or surgically, helps. There comes that moment when the ventilator has to be switched off. When the parents feel ready, my colleagues and I remove their child from the machine and place him or her in their arms, and we grieve.
Having journeyed with the parents thus far, I believe that if able, I should be with them at this time. I often say to them

that their baby is now in a much better place, and will wait for them there, and most parents seem to draw comfort from this, whatever their own beliefs. God created this child, and physical death does not uncreate him or her; they are just home with him. But I am sorry that the parents will not have the privilege of getting to know their child this side of eternity.

5. *And the question I ask everyone: What do we really, really need to know about God?*
Karl Barth boiled it down to 'Jesus loves me, this I know'. The more I think I learn about God, the more a mystery he is. Yet God must want us to know him, because he has revealed himself in many ways, and most of all, through Jesus. Although I am in the business of reflecting on who God is and what he does, and I believe he has invited me to do this, I recognize that my intellect is not his equal, and it is his love for me that I will be holding onto when I cross the threshold to meet him.

To ponder and discuss

- If you are part of a local church, what has it done to win the right to speak to its community? Do you think that is a fair question to ask? Why or why not?
- If you were to ask your community what it thinks of your local church, what do you think it would say?
- Do you feel a part of a local church? Why or why not?
- What might incarnation and hospitality look like in your context?

11.

The Big Picture at Work

Faith in the marketplace

If we are to clothe the emperor, the broad contours that make up a Christian world view will need to find practical expression. Whilst some of this will be through church communities, often the implications will be worked out in the marketplace. It is here, after all, that we spend so many of our waking hours. If faith is vibrant and alive only on Sunday, something is seriously wrong. We need to think about what Paul Stevens calls *The Other Six Days*.[1]

If we are indeed the image-bearers of a God who makes everything from nothing, imagine the creativity we can expect from those who follow Jesus the Christ. If we are a community shaped by grace, how will this flow through into the workplace, with its many complex relationships, competitiveness and compulsive need for ever-better results? If we are committed to responsible stewardship, and to consequently strive to build a world with a better name, how will this impact our career decisions, and will it mean that there are some vocational prospects we will always say no to? Questions keep bubbling to the surface.

Perhaps we can begin with some general observations. The incarnation of Jesus around two thousand years ago forever commits us to an agenda that is rooted in the reality of daily life. Jesus was located in a specific community at a particular time in history. He tasted the dust of the Palestinian soil, encountering real people at a complex and discouraging time in their historical story. While mindful that people cannot live by bread alone, he recognized that they also cannot live without it. There was a practical earthiness about his ministry (such as washing his disciples' feet, or spitting to make mud to place on a blind man's eyes), even as he pointed to lofty alternatives – indeed, he calmly instructed that we should be perfect, even as our Father in heaven is perfect.[2] It is impossible for us to claim to be serious followers of Jesus the Christ and to simultaneously cloister ourselves away in a ghetto of detached irrelevance. Jesus does not walk down that street. We therefore cannot follow him there.

Let's think about what it might mean to live a little more creatively, and thereby image a little more closely the creativity of God.

In discussing the arts, Leland Ryken has observed, 'What we habitually take into our minds and imaginations becomes a permanent part of us. If we consistently immerse ourselves in mediocre literature or painting or music, we become, in that sphere of our lives, mediocre people . . . Christians are obligated to excellence because of who God is.'[3]

Perhaps we should soften Ryken's comments a little, lest we embrace a new legalism, where impeccable taste in art and literature becomes a key performance indicator of effective Christ following. We are not seeking to create an elitist club. But Ryken's point is valid. As bearers of God's image, why would we settle for the tedious and boring? We are made for more and should strive to achieve it. We should have an infectious openness to the creative possibilities inherent in God's good world.

While as image-bearers we will be excited by the ingenious, the Fall means we are also pulled in the opposite direction. David Rushton notes the consequence of this in our approach to music, and observes, 'A basic problem with many of us is that we are in a musical rut. We say, "We know what we like," but in reality it would be more accurate to say, "We like what we know."'[4] Those who believe in a Creator God are freed to be a little more adventurous. Christianity, rather than placing people in insufferable straightjackets, liberates them to explore the full range of God's creation. The only thing forbidden is to try to explore the world outside of a relationship with God – for relationship with God is the key that unlocks everything.

Naturally, we are called to be responsible stewards of what we have – not of what we don't have. If we are created with the potential to be crafters of words, symbols and sounds, we should do so with our entire God-given ability. However, if that ability is stretched when confronted by a word of more than two syllables, we should be released to aspire to a different standard. For the Christian, excellence is not about being better than everyone else, but about being the best that we can be. Yet even that is a little too private and individualistic. Usually we are better together, and so within communities of affirmation and grace we soar to places we might otherwise have found impossible. I have a responsibility to help you to become a little more than you otherwise might have been, just as you have a similar responsibility to me.

In the workplace, this means that we approach our employment as an invitation to be God's incarnated representatives in a specific setting. We need to imaginatively look for answers to the 'What would Jesus do?' question in our particular location. Let's try to earth this by exploring a few vocational options.

Teaching, and Christ following

Teaching is often cited as a fruitful vocation for those seeking to follow Jesus. It is not hard to understand why. A Year Three teacher usually spends more time with the children in their class than their parents do. Children of that age aspire to be like their teachers, so the impact of educators is great. But what might it mean to approach education from a Christian perspective?

I was enormously impressed at the 2012 Christian Schools Australia conference in Western Australia. The keynote speaker, David Smith, had been given the impossible topic, 'Teaching from a Christian world view'.[5]

So how do you teach mathematics from a Christian world view? Well, simple, isn't it? How many books in the Old Testament? Thirty-nine. How many books in the new? Twenty-seven. So children, how many books in the Bible? Sixty-six. Behold, mathematics from a Christian perspective. Bah, humbug – or no, no and no again. Nor is it teaching English from a Christian perspective if we simply replace a Shakespearean sonnet with a psalm. But what does it then mean to teach or approach something from a Christian world view – or is the concept meaningless? How does the Christian story we believe in shape every story that we tell?

Smith gave a helpful example. He had been a teacher of German, teaching in a Christian school, and was told to approach his discipline from a Christian perspective. Would that mean translating Bible verses into German? While not closed to that possibility, he hoped it could mean more. He noted that the standard school German text gave the predictable language examples. It was a kind of 'how to survive in Germany' text, and suggested phrases to ask for directions and the like – all very useful if you are visiting a country. In fact, the book started with arriving at the airport and built outwards from there. It advised you how to ask for price of things, 'How much does the beer cost?' Or where to access transport, 'Where can I get a taxi?' Now, there is nothing wrong with any of these, but they are all about tourists being able to get by and consume happily in countries they happen to be visiting. And that is not at all what Christian faith is about. Our faith is somewhat nobler than simply scrabbling around to find what I can get from this place and how I can make sure I get the best deals whilst here.

So Smith devised a new syllabus. It started with an evocative photograph, taken during the Nazi era, of some members of the White Rose, a non-violent, intellectual resistance group from the University of Munich. The black and white photo showed brother and sister Hans and Sophie Scholl, with some Nazi soldiers hovering in the background. The sense of anxiety is palpable. Smith starts by asking the question, 'So what do you see in this photo?' The class begins to answer. Smith introduces the occasional German word as they unpack the picture, 'or as the Germans say', and gets the class to repeat it. This is a portrait with a story. Because the young people in it were part of the White Rose, they were arrested shortly after the photograph was taken. Sophie and Hans Scholl were to be beheaded on 22 February 1943 at the age of 21 and 24 respectively. They were convicted of high treason because they had dared to question a despotic dictatorship. Hans's final words were 'Long Live Freedom'. You can almost hear the class bellow it back as Smith gives them the German words to use.

The story of the White Rose is one of great pathos and sadness. As Smith tells it to his pupils, more and more German words get introduced. It moves on to a picture of their graves and a shrine where their heroism is remembered. The whole learning experience is about entering into different slithers of time in Germany and trying to understand what it felt like to be a German then – with vocabulary and grammar seamlessly introduced.

What is the difference between the original travellers' textbook and this approach, and why is the one Christian and the other not? Well, the one is all about me and what I can get from being in Germany; where I can find cheap beer or how I can be sure the taxi driver is not exploiting my ignorance. The other approach is about incarnation. Trying to be there, trying to feel what it was like for those there, trying to understand, and trying to be helpful. This is a Christian approach not only because incarnation is a key Christian value but also because another key biblical theme is that of hospitality, by which we mean openness to the other. The Christian starting point is not about how I get my needs met, but about the larger story that God is shaping – a story I am invited to participate in. The Bible itself starts as a story of hospitality as it tells of the God who created a world that was in every way perfect for us.

The point is hopefully clear. Teaching from a Christian perspective is not about trotting out Bible verses to a captive audience. It is about what we choose to talk about, what we highlight, the stories we tell. If those stories encourage a myopic view of the world, they do an injustice to the God whose love for the world led to an active agenda which entailed incarnation and participation in the woes and struggles of this planet.

Not that a Christian world view is captured by content alone. The teacher who is a distant and remote authority figure has not yet caught a glimpse of Jesus at the wedding in Cana. The teacher who writes off the disobedient child has not yet pondered the story of Zacchaeus, or of the woman caught in adultery. Teachers who are not willing to take a little extra time discussing the more complex aspects of their subject with interested students have not really considered the dynamic at play as Jesus and Nicodemus talk together at night. The physical education teacher who only has time for the most gifted athletes has not internalized the psalmist's joy that we are all fearfully and wonderfully made. The social studies teacher who is content to limit historic and geographic studies to a syllabus that is little more than a 'ra ra' in support of the local status quo, has not yet captured the heartbeat of a global God. This is the God to whom every story is known, and to whom every story matters.

Teachers who operate from a Christian view of the world know that they will be remembered long after the content they taught has been forgotten. They remember that they need to win the right to speak to their pupils about the love of God, and that God's love needs to flow through their own life into the lives of their students. Paul describes his converts as living letters, able to be read by all.[6] What will be read and remembered over the longer haul are acts of kindness and sincerity. Or to quote another Pauline insight, the three things that remain are faith, hope and love.[7] Teachers guided by these sure lights leave behind a legacy to be cherished.

Economics, and Christ following

While relatively few people are formally employed as economists, economics impacts the life of all. Economists study those activities that involve money and its exchange between people. Economists explore our attempt to distribute scarce resources, and what methods of distribution produce optimal returns. They are concerned with what will be produced in society and with how it will be produced. They investigate who will consume what is produced. They are interested in employment and unemployment, with inflation and its impact, and with ways to increase the productive capacity of an economy.

While this summary statement cannot capture even a fraction of the nuances in the field, perhaps it gives a feel for the importance of the economists' task. After all, few things impact our life as much as our access to wholesome food, clean water, hygienic and comfortable housing, competent healthcare, sound education and the opportunity to find stretching and enjoyable work. The economic structure of each country greatly influences how such resources are distributed amongst its citizens, and how many resources it has to allocate.

Although it is never a comfortable question, economists have to ask how to assess the value of a human life. Here are two economic dilemmas that are often discussed in introductory courses on economics and justice.

In 2001 the Czech Republic contemplated raising the excise tax on cigarettes to offset the increased healthcare costs of those who smoke.

The Czech division of the Philip Morris Group (a tobacco company) conducted a cost-benefit analysis of smoking on the Czech economy and concluded that when you take the short-term expense of additional health costs incurred by smokers, and offset it against the benefits of the additional tax revenue generated by the smoking excise tax, as well as the healthcare savings that resulted from the early death of smokers (elderly people being the most costly to the health care system), plus the savings of not having to provide pensions or pensioner housing for smokers (as smokers on average die younger), the net gain to the economy of smokers in the Czech republic in 1999 was $147 million or $1,227 per smoker. The unspoken conclusion was that if anyone should pay extra tax, it should be non-smokers for their lack of consideration in living so long.

While the report created an uproar and was widely ridiculed and condemned (the Philip Morris group subsequently apologizing for and disavowing the report), it did raise a key question. What value should we attach to a human life, and how should we calculate it? Indeed, can it be calculated?

This brings us to the second case study.

In the 1970s the Ford Pinto was a popular small car. Unfortunately it had one significant drawback – its petrol tank at the rear of the car made it far more vulnerable in accidents. It was calculated that the cost of providing a shield for the fuel tank to protect it in the event of a rear-end collision was, in 1970 dollars, $11 per car. Ford had been diligent in doing the calculations. For 12.5 million cars the cost of the safety shield would have been $137 million. The benefit of this expenditure would have been to save 180 lives, a further 180 injuries, and repairs to 2,100 cars. Ford then attached dollar values to each of these benefits and worked out the maths. The benefit of saving a life was valued at $200,000/life, preventing an injury was valued at $67,000/injury, and repairs to cars at $700/vehicle. When totalled, it was concluded that the economic benefit of adding the protective shield was $49.5 million, considerably less than the $137 million to provide the shield, which consequently was not added.

The families of the victims took a different view to Ford and sued the company in 1978. Ford lost the case, and was fined $128 million, ensuring that subsequently they pondered the value of a human life a lot more carefully.

Fascinating though these studies are, the underlying economic dilemma came home to me forcefully in a recent visit to Jakarta in Indonesia. Those who have been there will be aware that the traffic on the roads is more than a little challenging. One portrait remains with me.

When travelling on major roads, it is almost impossible to turn right across the ceaseless stream of oncoming traffic to access the side road you may need to use. You therefore overshoot your destination, and wait for a break in the traffic island that will allow you to make a U-turn and then drive back to your side road. You now need to glide off to the left, which is not a problem. Although there are designated points to make the U-turn, it can be a hazardous process. The point at which my hosts needed to make the turn was staffed by a young boy, who proudly and courageously darted out into the traffic, getting it to either slow down or stop to allow the turning vehicles to enter. In return for his services, some motorists (but certainly not all), provided a modest tip. Presumably this helped the boy's family to make ends meet.

I still remember his face – youthful and enthusiastic. I am not sure how old he was – 10 seems a reasonable estimate. He seemed to love his job, but I was struck by how dangerous it was. The statistician in me pondered the odds of it leading to a serious accident. They struck me as being unacceptably high – probably around 1 in 2. If in an accident, will he be killed, or maimed, or left a cripple for life? And even if not injured, what future does he face if uneducated (it was a school day when he guided our car). At 10 he might be loving his job, but the future it leads to is desperately bleak. This is a question of economic justice played out in a billion different ways, every day of the year.

For Christian economists, there are no easy answers. But there are some principles to guide us.

- Every life matters, because it matters to God.
- We are blessed to bless. Making money can never be end in itself. It is how it is used for the greater good that counts.
- Justice matters. We should strive to achieve a fair distribution both of opportunity and of reward for effort.
- God has a heart for the poor. While all people matter, God is acutely aware of the vulnerability of the poor. The Bible repeat-

edly refers to the needs of widows and orphans, as well as of the stranger in the land. All policies should be evaluated in the light of their impact upon the most vulnerable members of society.
- I am my brother's keeper, and am part of a global family.
- Future generations matter. Present greed cannot be allowed to jeopardize the future.
- The earth is the Lord's and must be respected and replenished.

Work as curse, work as calling

While we have sampled some implications of a Christian world view in two vocations, it is as well to explore some broader Christian attitudes to work. Two views dominate.

The first sees work as a drudge or as an unpleasant necessity. A man asked why he was digging a hole replied: 'I'm digging a hole to earn the money to buy the bread to give me the strength to dig the hole.' From a biblical perspective, this negativity is a result of the Fall. Genesis 3:17–19 relays the consequences, a part of it reading: 'Cursed is the ground because of you; through painful toil you will eat of it . . . By the sweat of your brow you will eat your food until you return to the ground, since from it you were taken . . .'

Every day that we trudge to work resentfully, we are entitled to explode, 'Thanks very much, Adam. What a marvellous great-great granddad you turned out to be. This is your legacy to us.'

Sadly, some Christians are foolish enough to leave it there. Work is a consequence of the Fall, so that is that. This is however a completely sub-Christian view because it leaves no place for the redemption we find in Christ. With the coming of Jesus, a different view of work surfaces. You see it in passages such as John 9:4,5, where Jesus says, 'As long as it is day, we must do the work of him who sent me. Night is coming when no-one can work. While I am in the world, I am the light of the world' (italics mine). Note that we must do the work of him who sent Jesus. This becomes even more fascinating when we link it to a second statement of Jesus, found in Matthew 5:14: '*You* are the light of the world. A city on a hill cannot be hidden.' Jesus is the light of the world, yet proclaims that we are the light of the world. And we are called to do the work of the one who sent Jesus into the world.

This second view is far more hopeful and opens a window to the redeemed community, which is invited to view work as participation in the *missio Dei* – the mission of God in the world. This is why Christians through the ages have usually seen work as a vocation or calling from God. Rather than a drudge, it is lofty, because whatever the shape of our particular vocation, it is engaging together with God in God's work in the world.

Finding our particular vocation can take time. Frederick Buechner has memorably noted that 'The place God calls you to is the place where your deep gladness and the world's deep hunger meet.'[8] God does call us to a particular place. We might service air-conditioners, work at a fast-food outlet, or fix plumbing. Wherever located, we are invited to follow the Pauline injunction found in Colossians 3:17: 'And whatever you do, whether in word or deed, do it all in the name of the Lord Jesus, giving thanks to God the Father through him.' Those who are the recipients of our services will notice the Jesus difference in our approach to work. They are likely to find it refreshing. Perhaps it will lead to yet deeper questions being asked

When it is not that obvious

As I have noted a few times in this book, I grew up in apartheid South Africa. It was an extraordinary difficult period of history, and each day posed new ethical challenges. Armchair critics can look back at those tragic years and pontificate about which courses of action were morally responsible, and which were not. They might give the impression that those trapped in the system should have found it easy to decide upon a course of action, and that the only issue was whether one had the will to do what was obviously right.

I can only say that I found the reality to be very different. Morally noble decisions sometimes have devastating unintended consequences, and we are never exempt from trying to predict what those consequences might be.

I remember being wakened by a persistent knocking at the door at 4:30 one morning. Sleepily staggering my way to open it, on the doorstep was a 30-something black South African man. He pleaded with me to give him work in my garden for the day, explaining that he had been employed at the General Motors factory in Port Elizabeth, and that as a result of the economic sanctions imposed upon South Africa, and the decision of General Motors to withdraw from the country, he was one of several thousand who had been left unemployed. He had six children, and with no work he had absolutely no prospect of being able to feed them. He was sorry to have woken me so early, but he knew that if he didn't start very early, he would lose out on any small possibility of finding work for the day. The man's sheer sense of desperation haunts me to this day. I could give him work for one day; I have no idea what happened to him and his family after that.

I also remember standing with a black South African grandmother as she wailed and wailed at the news that her first grandchild had died of malnutrition. The family breadwinner had also lost his employment as a result of the economic sanctions imposed on the country. Her tiny grandson Abedi (the name means 'worshipper') was the victim.

I tell these stories not because they are edifying, but because they are sobering. Any objective analysis of the reasons for the end of the apartheid era will invariably (and validly) cite the imposition of economic sanctions as a significant factor. Actually, sanctions achieved a great good; they also caused immense and immeasurable suffering. Should a Christian have supported the imposition of sanctions? Probably yes. Should they have slept peacefully at night after doing so? Probably not.

Knowing the right thing to do is not always easy. When Adam and Eve ate the forbidden fruit in the hope of being able to discern good from evil, they embarked upon an impossible quest. They also severed links with the God who could have guided them in their search. Indeed, knowing good from evil outside of relationship with God can prove nigh impossible.

Perhaps, then, the most distinctive quality found in those living in accordance with a Christian world view is humility. Although we are image-bearers of the God who made us, we are not God. And the difference between us is immense. We tentatively embark upon the journey we are called to, but we know that without God as our guide and companion, we have little hope of living or acting wisely. For all that, we have the courage to believe that with the empowerment of the triune God, we might live a life of significance. Regardless of whether our aspirations and dreams are realized or not, we are quietly confident that we are loved by God. With God's grace enfolding us, the love of Jesus inspiring us, and the presence of the Holy Spirit empowering us, we dare to hope and dream of eternity, even as in the present we set about building a world with a better name. Deep within, we have the Spirit's reassurance that our hope will not disappoint us, for like faith and love, it abides forever.

An interview with Kara Martin

Kara Martin is the associate dean of the Marketplace Institute at Ridley Melbourne, a mission and ministry college in Australia, where she also coordinates its online certificate programme. A former director of the Australian College of Theology, and human resources policy adviser, she is particularly interested in issues of faith and work.

1. *So what do you think? Should we view work as curse or calling?*
   I think it is simplistic to put those things as either/or. In fact, I think that the 'work is a curse' statement is within a larger gospel framework of creation–Fall–redemption–glory. So work was created as something good. We are told that God worked in creation, and the first conversation with humankind is an invitation to join in his work. Rather than work being cursed, a close reading of Genesis 3 reveals that the process of working was cursed. Working is hard and frustrating and annoying and drains our energy. However, that is not the end of the story. Work still has elements that are good, that we enjoy, that motivate and energize us. What is more, Jesus demonstrated that his redeeming work was not simply for our spiritual lives, but impacts on every part of our lives. Hence, we can use our imagination to create work relationships and workplaces that better represent what God intended, and there is a great sense of purpose and achievement in working with God in that task. This area of redemption is linked to our sense of calling, which is primarily a call back to

relationship with God, but is also a call to use all our gifts and abilities and intellect in the work where he has placed us. We can also be encouraged that there are aspects of our working that will survive when Jesus returns, ushering in the new earth. The relationships we form, the new ways of working we pioneer, the way we love, our modelling of Jesus, and our proclamation of the gospel in word and deed, all has eternal consequences. I really loved your example of the teacher of German who is not just thinking through a more faith-full way of teaching, but pioneering an approach that is a better way, whether you are a Christian or not.

2. *Many Christians struggle to relate the faith they experience on Sunday to the workplace on Monday. Why do you think this is so?*
The Sunday/Monday divide is unfortunately something that has developed over a very long period of time. It comes from the Platonic view of the body as separate and inferior to the spirit. Therefore the physical work we do is inferior to the spiritual work we do. This has been reinforced by some misreading of biblical texts that appear to elevate the work of the church. It has also been cemented in as work has left the domestic situation, as the industrial revolution created something called 'a job', and as we have come under increasing pressure to separate our public world of work from our private world of faith. Someone told me that he is a Christian until he gets on the bus to go to work on Monday morning. And he becomes a Christian again when he gets in the car to drive to church on a Sunday. This, of course, is ridiculous, but it is perpetuated through the pulpit, whenever we celebrate the work of missionaries and ignore the world where 98 per cent of those in the pew spend 95 per cent of their lives.

3. *Are there any occupations where you long to see Christians more actively engaged?*
I think we desperately need Christians to be more visible in politics and media, because these are places that are helping to set the cultural agenda. I know of a guy who works for a firm involved in gambling, and while his friends are appalled, he points out that he is the only Christian who works there, and

how else will they hear or see a gospel difference? The reality is Christians need to permeate every occupation, as conscience allows.

4. *You often provide guidance to Christian groups about their employment practices. Is there sometimes a risk that we can abuse a person's sense of call, and if so, how can we safeguard against this?*
Unfortunately, some Christian organizations act as if a sense of 'call' to 'ministry' puts them above the law of the land. It allows them to pay people less than they should or deny them other benefits. Or they feel they don't have to pay the government certain fees or taxes. I believe that God wants us to be ethically pure, and have faith that God will provide for the work that needs to be done. Unfortunately, I have also seen this view of 'ministry' as higher mean that administrative staff are bullied and neglected, and leaders of those organizations act as if the organization, its resources and its people belonged to them, rather than belonging to God.

5. *And the question I ask everyone: What do we really, really need to know about God?*
We really, really need to know God. Knowing about him is useful, and the Bible has lots of resources. Knowing God, though, is something different, and that is what he wants: intimate, creative, dynamic, generous, loving relationship with us. Knowing God helps us to be consistent with our faith at work, helps us to see the good, helps us to recognize and avoid sin, helps us work in tune with God's redeeming purposes, and ensures that in the end he gets the glory.

To ponder and discuss

- What ways have you found to honour God in the marketplace?
- Reflect on John 9:4,5. What will it mean for you to 'do the work of him who sent me'?
- How do you cope with ambiguity and uncertainty, and not always knowing what is the right thing to do?
- Do you agree that a key distinctive of those following a Chris-

tian world view should be humility? What might this mean in practice?

References

Ayre, Clive W. 'Climate Change and a Climate of Change in the Church' in *Climate Change, Cultural Change: Religious Responses and Responsibilities* (ed. Anne Elvery and David Gormley-O'Brien; Preston: Mosaic, 2013).

Barrett, Matthew, and Ardel B. Caneday, eds. *Four Views on the Historical Adam* (ed. Stanley N. Gundry, Counterpoints; Grand Rapids, MI: Zondervan, 2013).

Barth, Karl. *Church Dogmatics* (trans. G.W. Bromiley. Vol. 1/1. 2nd ed. Edinburgh: T.&T. Clark, 1975).

Bass, Diana Butler. *The Practicing Congregation: Imagining a New Old Church* (Herndon, VA: Alban Institute, 2004).

Bebbington, David. *Evangelicalism in Modern Britain: A History from the 1730s to the 1980s* (Grand Rapids, MI: Baker, 1989).

Bellah, Robert N., Richard Madsen, William M. Sullivan, Ann Swidler, and Steven M. Tipton. *Habits of the Heart: Individualism and Commitment in American Life* (Berkeley, CA: University of California Press, 1985).

Berkhouwer, G.C. *Studies in Dogmatics: Sin* (trans. Philip C. Holtrop; Grand Rapids, MI: Eerdmans, 1971).

Bonhoeffer, Dietrich. *The Cost of Discipleship* (trans. R.H. Fuller; revised by Irmgard Booth (London: SCM, 1959).

_____. *Ethics.* (trans. Neville Horton Smith; New York: Macmillan, 1965).

Browning, Don S. *Reviving Christian Humanism: The New Conversation on Spirituality, Theology and Psychology* (Minneapolis, MN: Fortress, 2010.

Carson, D.A. *The Gagging of God: Christianity Confronts Pluralism* (Grand Rapids, MI: Zondervan, 1996).

Cohen, David. *Why O Lord? Praying Our Sorrows* (Milton Keynes: Paternoster, 2013).

Collins, Francis S., ed. *Belief: Readings on the Reason for Faith* (New York: HarperCollins, 2010).

Enns, Peter. *The Evolution of Adam: What the Bible Does and Doesn't Say About Human Origins* (Grand Rapids, MI: Brazos, 2012).

Erickson, Millard J. *Christian Theology* (Grand Rapids, MI: Baker, 1985).

_____. *Postmodernizing the Faith: Evangelical Responses to the Challenge of Postmodernism* (Grand Rapids, MI: Baker, 1998).

Ford, Lance. 'Foreword' in *Servantship: Sixteen Servants on the Four Movements of Radical Servantship* (ed. Graham Hill; Eugene: Wipf and Stock, 2013).

Franklin, R.W., and Joseph M. Shaw. *The Case for Christian Humanism* (Grand Rapids, MI: Eerdmans, 1991).

Grenz, Stanley J. *Theology for the Community of God* (Nashville, TN: Broadman and Holman, 1994).

_____. 'Jesus as the Imago Dei: Image-of-God Christology and the Non-Linear Linearity of Theology'. *Journal of the Evangelical Theological Society* 47, no. 4 (2004), pp. 617–628.

Grenz, Stanley J., and John Franke. *Beyond Foundationalism: Shaping Theology in a Postmodern Context* (Louisville, KY: WJKP, 2001).

Griffiths, Michael. *Cinderella with Amnesia: A Restatement in Contemporary Terms of the Biblical Doctrine of the Church* (Downers Grove, IL: Inter-Varsity Press, 1975).

Gunton, Colin E. *The One, the Three and the Many: God, Creation and the Culture of Modernity.* The Bampton Lectures 1992 (Cambridge: Cambridge University Press, 1993).

Harries, Richard. *God Outside the Box: Why Spiritual People Object to Christianity* (London: SPCK, 2002).

Harris, Brian. 'The Need for a Double Conversion: A Response to "Doing Ministry in the Helix of Post Modernism"' in *Mission New Zealand Consultation* (Auckland, NZ: 2003).

_____. 'From "Behave, Believe Belong" to "Belong, Believe, Behave" - a Missional Journey for the 21st Century' in *Text and Task: Scripture and Mission* (ed. Michael Parsons; Carlisle: Paternoster, 2005), pp. 204–217.

_____. *The Theological Method of Stanley J. Grenz: Constructing Evangelical Theology from Scripture, Tradition and Culture* (Lewiston, NY: Edwin Mellen Press, 2011).

_____. 'Trinitarian Apologetics: Participating in Communities of Surprise, Embrace and Witness' in *Beyond Four Walls* (Vose Seminary, Perth, 2011).

_____. 'Faithful Thinking: The Role of the Seminary in Promoting a Thoughtful Christian Faith', *The Pacific Journal of Baptist Research* 8, no. 1 (2013): 27–35.

_____. *The Tortoise Usually Wins: Biblical Reflections on Quiet Leadership for Reluctant Leaders* (Milton Keynes: Paternoster, 2013).

Hill, Graham, ed. *Servantship: Sixteen Servants on the Four Movements of Radical Servantship* (Eugene: Wipf and Stock, 2013).

Hitchens, Christopher. *God is Not Great: How Religion Poisons Everything* (New York: Twelve, 2007).

Hoggard Creegan, Nicola. *Animal Suffering and the Problem of Evil* (New York: Oxford University Press, 2013).

Holmes, Stephen R. *The Holy Trinity: Understanding God's Life Christian Doctrine in Historical Perspective* (Milton Keynes: Paternoster, 2011).

The Holy Bible: New International Version. International Bible Society, 1984.

Jamieson, Alan. *A Churchless Faith: Faith Journeys Beyond Evangelical, Pentecostal and Charismatic Churches* (Wellington, NZ: Philip Garside Publishing, 2000).

Jones, S.L., and R.E. Butman. *Modern Psychotherapies: A Comprehensive Christian Appraisal* (Downers Grove, IL: Inter-Varsity Press, 1991).

Jones, Tony. *Postmodern Youth Ministry* (Grand Rapids, MI: Zondervan, 2002).

Kant, Immanuel. *Religion within the Limits of Reason Alone* (trans. Theodore M. Greene and Hoyt H. Hudson; New York: Harper & Row, 1960).

Kinnaman, David, and Gabe Lyons. *Unchristian: What a New Generation Really Thinks About Christianity . . . And Why it Matters* (Grand Rapids, MI: Baker, 2007).

König, Adrio. *Here I Am! A Believer's Reflection on God* (Pretoria: University of South Africa, 1978).

Konyndyk DeYoung, Rebecca. *Glittering Vices: A New Look at the Seven Deadly Sins and Their Remedies* (Grand Rapids, MI: Brazos, 2009).

Lebacqz, Karen. 'Alien Dignity: The Legacy of Helmut Thielicke for Bioethics' in *On Moral Medicine: Theological Persepectives in Medical Ethics* (ed. Stephen E. Lammers and Allen Verhey; Grand Rapids, MI: Eerdmans, 1998), pp. 184–192.

Lennox, John. *God's Undertaker: Has Science Buried God?* (Oxford: Lion, 2009).

_____. *Gunning for God: Why the New Atheists Are Missing the Target* (Oxford: Lion, 2011).

Mager, Anne. '"One Beer, One Goal, One Nation, One Soul": South African Breweries, Heritage, Masculinity and Nationalism 1960–1999', *Past and Present* 188 (2005), pp. 163–194.

McClean, John. *From the Future: Coming to Grips with Pannenberg's Thought* (Milton Keynes: Paternoster, 2013).

McCool, Gerald, ed. *A Rahner Reader* (London: Darton, Longman & Todd, 1975).

McGrath, Alister E. *Evangelicalism and the Future of Christianity* (London: Hodder & Stoughton, 1993).

McKnight, Scot. *The Jesus Creed: Loving God, Loving Others* (Brewster, MA: Paraclete Press, 2004).

Migliore, Daniel L. *Faith Seeking Understanding: An Introduction to Christian Theology* (Grand Rapids, MI: Eerdmans, 1991).

Miller, Calvin. *The Singer: A Classic Retelling of Cosmic Conflict* (Downers Grove, IL: Inter-Varsity Press, 2001).

Murray, Stuart. *Church after Christendom* (Carlisle: Paternoster, 2004).

_____. *Post-Christendom* (Carlisle: Paternoster, 2004).

Newbigin, Lesslie. *Truth to Tell: The Gospel as Public Truth* (London: SPCK, 1991).

Niebuhr, H. Richard. *Christ and Culture* (New York: Harper & Row, 1951).

O'Neil, Michael D. *Church as Moral Community: Karl Barth's Vision of Christian Life, 1915–1922* Paternoster Theological Monographs (Milton Keynes: Paternoster, 2013).

Pepper, Miriam, Rosemary Leonard, and Ruth Powell. 'Denominational Identification, Church Participation, and Concern About Climate Change in Australia' in *Climate Change, Cultural Change: Religious Responses and Responsibilities* (ed. Anne Elvery and David Gormley-O'Brien; Preston: Mosaic, 2013), pp. 25–47.

Peterson, Eugene. *Practice Resurrection: A Conversation on Growing up in Christ* (Grand Rapids, IL: Eerdmans, 2010).

Placher, William C., ed. *Callings: Twenty Centuries of Christian Wisdom on Vocation* (Grand Rapids, IL: Eerdmans, 2005).

Rahner, Karl. *The Trinity* (trans. Joseph Donceel; New York: Crossroad, 1997).

Rogers, Carl. *On Becoming a Person: A Therapist's View of Psychotherapy* (London: Constable, 1961).

Ross, Hugh. *Why the Universe is the Way it Is* (Grand Rapids, IL: Baker, 2008).

Rushton, David W. 'A Christian Perspective on Music' in *Christian Worldview and the Academic Disciplines: Crossing the Academy* (ed. Deane E.D. Downey and Stanley E. Porter, pp. 324–335 (Eugene, OR: Pickwick, 2009).

Ryken, Leland, ed. *The Christian Imagination: Essays on Literature and the Arts* (Grand Rapids, IL: Baker, 1981).

Schmidt, Alvin J. *Under the Influence: How Christianity Transformed Culture* (Grand Rapids, IL: Zondervan, 2001).

Shelley, Bruce L. *Church History in Plain Language*, 2nd edn (Dallas, TX: Word, 1995).

Sire, James W. *The Universe Next Door*, 5th edn (Downers Grove, IL: Inter-Varsity Press, 2009).

Smith, David I. *Learning from the Stranger: Christian Faith and Cultural Diversity* (Grand Rapids, IL: Eerdmans, 2009).

Smith, David I., and James K.A. Smith, eds. *Teaching and Christian Practices: Reshaping Faith and Learning* (Grand Rapids, IL: Eerdmans, 2011).

Smith, N., and A Leiserowitz. 'American Evangelicals and Global Warming'. *Global Environmental Change* 30 (2013).

Stackhouse, Ian. *Primitive Piety: A Journey from Suburban Mediocrity to Passionate Christianity* (Milton Keynes: Paternoster, 2012).

Stevens, R. Paul. *The Other Six Days: Vocation, Work, and Ministry in Biblical Perspective* (Grand Rapids, IL: Eerdmans, 1999).

Stott, John. *The Cross of Christ* (Leicester: Inter-Varsity Press, 1986).

Strom, Mark. *Breaking the Silence: The Abusiveness of Evangelicalism* (Sydney: Robert Menzies College, 1993), 1:11.

Thielicke, Helmut. *The Ethics of Sex* (trans. John W. Doberstein; Grand Rapids, IL: Baker, 1964).

Thompson, Donald W. *A Thief in the Night* (Carlisle: Mark IV Pictures, 1972).

Tournier, Paul. *A Place for You* (trans. Edwin Hudson; Crowborough: Highland, 1968).

Walton, John H. *The Lost World of Genesis One: Ancient Cosmology and the Origins Debate* (Downers Grove, IL: Inter-Varsity Press, 2009).

Webber, R.T. *Ancient Future Faith: Rethinking Evangelicalism for a Postmodern World* (Grand Rapids, IL: Baker, 1999).

Wells, David F. *No Place for Truth or Whatever Happened to Evangelical Theology?* (Grand Rapids, IL: Eerdmans, 1993).

_____. *God in the Wasteland: The Reality of Truth in a World of Fading Dreams* (Grand Rapids, IL: Eerdmans, 1994).

White Jr, Lynn. 'The Historical Roots of Our Ecological Crisis', *Science* 155, no. 3767 (1967): 1203–1207.

Wilson, Jonathan R. *God's Good World: Reclaiming the Doctrine of Creation* (Grand Rapids, IL: Baker, 2013).

Witherington III, Ben. *Matthew Smyth and Helwys Bible Commentary* (Macon, GA: Smyth and Helwys, 2006).

Wolterstorff, Nicholas. *Reason within the Bounds of Religion* (Grand Rapids, IL: Eerdmans, 1976).

Wright, Tom. *Surprised by Hope* (London: SPCK, 2007).

Yancey, Philip. *What's So Amazing About Grace?* (Grand Rapids, IL: Zondervan, 1997).

_____. *Rumours of Another World: What on Earth Are We Missing?* (Grand Rapids, IL: Zondervan, 2004).

Endnotes

Foreword

[1] Francis S. Collins, ed. *Belief: Readings on the Reason for Faith* (New York: HarperCollins, 2010), pp. xi-xii.

[2] Cited in William C. Placher, ed. *Callings: Twenty Centuries of Christian Wisdom on Vocation* (Grand Rapids, MI: Eerdmans, 2005), p. 3.

Chapter 1

[1] Alister E. McGrath, *Evangelicalism and the Future of Christianity* (London: Hodder & Stoughton, 1993), p. 10.

[2] John 10:10 TLB.

[3] Galatians 5:25.

[4] Zechariah 4:6.

[5] Psalm 8:5 (NIV 2011).

[6] Helmut Thielicke, *The Ethics of Sex* (trans. John W. Doberstein; Grand Rapids, MI: Baker, 1964), p. 26.

[7] This is essentially the position adopted by Bonhoeffer in the opening chapter of *Ethics*. Dietrich Bonhoeffer, *Ethics* (trans. Neville Horton Smith; New York: Macmillan, 1965).

[8] Matthew 5:43–48.

[9] Mark 15:39.

[10] Luke 23:34.

[11] See, for example, Robert Bellah's *Habits of the Heart*. One of the issues highlighted in *Habits of the Heart* is the link between religion and individualism. The privatization of faith, be it the plea from evangelicals to come into a personal (individual) relationship with God,

or the more liberal invitation to worship God in whatever shape or form the individual chooses to conceive the divine, tends to see the emphasis fall back to individual response rather than to community mediation. While individualism might lead to ownership of decisions taken, it can also lead to a sense of isolation and alienation. Robert N. Bellah and others, *Habits of the Heart: Individualism and Commitment in American Life* (Berkeley, CA: University of California Press, 1985).

[12] Conversionism is one of the four distinctives cited by Bebbington as forming a quadrilateral of priorities for evangelicalism. The others are activism, biblicism and crucicentrism. David Bebbington, *Evangelicalism in Modern Britain: A History from the 1730s to the 1980s* (Grand Rapids, MI: Baker, 1989), pp. 2,3.

[13] Matthew 6:9 (NIV 2011).

[14] Ephesians 3:17–19.

[15] Alan Jamieson, *A Churchless Faith: Faith Journeys Beyond Evangelical, Pentecostal and Charismatic Churches* (Wellington, NZ: Philip Garside Publishing, 2000).

[16] Stanley J. Grenz and John Franke, *Beyond Foundationalism: Shaping Theology in a Postmodern Context* (Louisville, KY: WJKP, 2001).

[17] James W. Sire, *The Universe Next Door*, 5th edn (Downers Grove, IL: Inter-Varsity Press, 2009), p. 20.

[18] Sire, *The Universe Next Door*, pp. 22,23.

[19] Ian Stackhouse, *Primitive Piety: A Journey from Suburban Mediocrity to Passionate Christianity* (Milton Keynes: Paternoster, 2012).

Chapter Two

[1] An example is Christopher Hitchens, *God is Not Great: How Religion Poisons Everything* (New York: Twelve, 2007).

[2] See Nicholas Wolterstorff, *Reason within the Bounds of Religion* (Grand Rapids, MI: Eerdmans, 1976). The title of Wolterstorff's work is intentionally opposite to Kant's. Immanuel Kant, *Religion within the Limits of Reason Alone* (trans. Theodore M. Greene and Hoyt H. Hudson; New York: Harper and Row, 1960).

[3] Wolterstorff, *Reason within the Bounds of Religion*, p. 63.

[4] Wolterstorff, *Reason within the Bounds of Religion*, p. 64.

[5] Wolterstorff, *Reason within the Bounds of Religion*, p. 82.

⁶ I have written at greater length on this passage in chapter 3 of Brian Harris, *The Tortoise Usually Wins: Biblical Reflections on Quiet Leadership for Reluctant Leaders* (Milton Keynes: Paternoster, 2013).

⁷ Scot McKnight, *The Jesus Creed: Loving God, Loving Others* (Brewster, MA: Paraclete Press, 2004).

Chapter Three

¹ H. Richard Niebuhr, *Christ and Culture* (New York: Harper and Row, 1951).

² Lesslie Newbigin, *Truth to Tell: The Gospel as Public Truth* (London: SPCK, 1991), p. 7.

³ Mark Strom, *Breaking the Silence: The Abusiveness of Evangelicalism* (Sydney: Robert Menzies College, 1993), 1:11, p. 5.

⁴ Matthew 10:30 and Luke 12:7.

⁵ Bruce L. Shelley, *Church History in Plain Language*, 2nd edn (Dallas, TX: Word, 1995), p. 98.

⁶ 2 Samuel 12:1–14.

⁷ 'All Things Bright and Beautiful', Cecil Frances Alexander (1818–95), first published in *Hymns for Little Children* (1848). Public domain.

⁸ I have also told this story in my book on 'quiet leadership', *The Tortoise Usually Wins: Biblical Reflections on Quiet Leadership for Reluctant Leaders* (Milton Keynes: Paternoster, 2013), pp. 82,83.

⁹ Jonathan R. Wilson, *God's Good World: Reclaiming the Doctrine of Creation* (Grand Rapids, MI: Baker, 2013), p. 207.

¹⁰ Matthew 6:24.

¹¹ An excellent exploration of this topic is found in William C. Placher, ed. *Callings: Twenty Centuries of Christian Wisdom on Vocation* (Grand Rapids, MI: Eerdmans, 2005).

¹² Matthew 22:30 (NIV 2011).

¹³ Whilst the most common reading of this passage, there are those who disagree. See for example, Ben Witherington III, *Matthew, Smyth and Helwys Bible Commentary* (Macon, GA: Smyth and Helwys, 2006), pp. 414–417.

¹⁴ This is not intended to be a serious examination of this topic, but simply to counterculturally ask, 'Is sex really that important?' or 'Why do we think sex is so important?'

¹⁵ Graham Hill, ed. *Servantship: Sixteen Servants on the Four Movements of Radical Servantship* (Eugene, OR: Wipf and Stock, 2013), pp. 4–9.

[16] Lance Ford, 'Foreword', in Graham Hill, ed. *Servantship: Sixteen Servants on the Four Movements of Radical Servantship* (Eugene, OR: Wipf and Stock, 2013), p. xv.

[17] I have written much more fully on the need for 'quiet leadership' in my book *The Tortoise Usually Wins*.

[18] Much of this section is an updating of a conference paper I presented. Brian Harris, 'The Need for a Double Conversion: A Response to "Doing Ministry in the Helix of Post Modernism",'in *Mission New Zealand Consultation* (Auckland, NZ: 2003).

[19] See for example D.A. Carson, *The Gagging of God: Christianity Confronts Pluralism* (Grand Rapids, MI: Zondervan, 1996); Millard J. Erickson, *Postmodernizing the Faith: Evangelical Responses to the Challenge of Postmodernism* (Grand Rapids, MI: Baker, 1998); David F. Wells, *No Place for Truth or Whatever Happened to Evangelical Theology?* (Grand Rapids, MI: Eerdmans, 1993); David F. Wells, *God in the Wasteland: The Reality of Truth in a World of Fading Dreams* (Grand Rapids, MI: Eerdmans, 1994).

[20] Tony Jones, *Postmodern Youth Ministry* (Grand Rapids, MI: Zondervan, 2002).

Chapter Four

[1] To some extent this depends on the level of detail one expects. Some argue that the broad lines provided by the Genesis account are not inconsistent with contemporary scientific explanations for the origin of the universe. A vast literature exists on this topic, and it ranges from the seriously suspect to the reputable. An interesting and accessible beginning point is Hugh Ross, *Why the Universe is the Way it Is* (Grand Rapids, MI: Baker, 2008). There are those who believe that any such attempts to harmonize are essentially misguided. See, for example, John H. Walton, *The Lost World of Genesis One: Ancient Cosmology and the Origins Debate* (Downers Grove, IL: Inter-Varsity Press, 2009).

[2] But if you can't resist these questions, John Walton's *The Lost World of Genesis One* (op cit) provides excellent food for thought on the topic. An interesting overview of the range of questions sparked, with differing responses, is Barrett, Matthew, and Ardel B. Caneday, eds. *Four Views on the Historical Adam* (ed. Stanley N. Gundry, Counterpoints; Grand Rapids, MI: Zondervan, 2013).

[3] Genesis 1:31.

[4] Genesis 4:9.

[5] Genesis 4:2.

[6] Bonhoeffer explores this idea in the opening chapter of his book on ethics (op cit).

[7] Genesis 6:5.

[8] Berkhouwer writes, 'We are of the opinion that an explanation for sin is truly impossible. Furthermore, when we say this we are not implying a hiatus in our knowledge that may soon be overcome. For the riddle of sin is of an entirely different kind. It is completely sui generis.' G.C. Berkhouwer, *Studies in Dogmatics: Sin* (trans. Philip C. Holtrop; Grand Rapids, MI: Eerdmans, 1971), p. 26.

[9] Nicola Hoggard Creegan, *Animal Suffering and the Problem of Evil* (New York: Oxford University Press, 2013).

Chapter Five

[1] This is a true story, told with permission, though I have changed names and setting to preserve confidentiality.

[2] Romans 7:15.

[3] Psalm 8:5 (NIV 2011).

[4] Romans 3:23.

[5] Psalm 139:14; Romans 3:10.

[6] Compare Genesis 1:4,10,12,18,21 and 25 with Genesis 1:31.

[7] Karen Lebacqz, 'Alien Dignity: The Legacy of Helmut Thielicke for Bioethics' in *On Moral Medicine: Theological Persepectives in Medical Ethics* (ed. Stephen E. Lammers and Allen Verhey; Grand Rapids, MI: Eerdmans, 1998), p. 186.

[8] Genesis 2:18.

[9] Genesis 1:26–30.

[10] Peter Enns, *The Evolution of Adam: What the Bible Does and Doesn't Say About Human Origins* (Grand Rapids, MI: Brazos, 2012), p. xv.

[11] For a brief but helpful overview of some of these views see Stanley J. Grenz, *Theology for the Community of God* (Nashville, TN: Broadman and Holman, 1994), pp. 218–233.

[12] Name changed to preserve confidentiality.

[13] Daniel L. Migliore, *Faith Seeking Understanding: An Introduction to Christian Theology* (Grand Rapids, MI: Eerdmans, 1991), p. 128.

[14] See for example Don S. Browning, *Reviving Christian Humanism: The New Conversation on Spirituality, Theology and Psychology* (Minneapolis, MN: Fortress, 2010); R.W. Franklin and Joseph M. Shaw, *The Case for Christian Humanism* (Grand Rapids, MI: Eerdmans, 1991).

[15] Philip Yancey, *Rumours of Another World: What on Earth Are We Missing?* (Grand Rapids, MI: Zondervan, 2004).

[16] David Cohen, *Why O Lord? Praying Our Sorrows* (Milton Keynes: Paternoster, 2013).

Chapter Six

[1] Cited in Philip Yancey, *What's So Amazing About Grace?* (Grand Rapids, MI: Zondervan, 1997).

[2] Name changed to preserve confidentiality.

[3] Calvin Miller, *The Singer: A Classic Retelling of Cosmic Conflict* (Downers Grove, IL: Inter-Varsity Press, 2001).

[4] Discussed in Adrio König, *Here I Am! A Believer's Reflection on God* (Pretoria: University of South Africa, 1978), pp. 44,45.

[5] Stott's discussion on forgiveness and sin is outstanding. See John Stott, *The Cross of Christ* (Leicester: Inter-Varsity Press, 1986).

[6] Romans 6:23.

[7] Isaiah 53:5.

[8] Dietrich Bonhoeffer, *The Cost of Discipleship* (trans. R.H. Fuller; revised by Irmgard Booth (London: SCM, 1959), p. 35.

[9] Romans 6:1,2.

[10] Michael D. O'Neil, *Church as Moral Community: Karl Barth's Vision of Christian Life, 1915–1922*, Paternoster Theological Monographs (Milton Keynes: Paternoster, 2013).

[11] Eugene Peterson, *Practice Resurrection: A Conversation on Growing up in Christ* (Grand Rapids, MI: Eerdmans, 2010), pp. 94,95.

Chapter Seven

[1] Karl Rahner, *The Trinity* (trans. Joseph Donceel; New York: Crossroad, 1997), p. 22.

[2] Karl Barth, *Church Dogmatics* 2nd ed., vol. 1/1 (trans. G.W. Bromiley; Edinburgh: T&T Clark, 1975), p. 548.

³ This section is a vigorously modified version of a paper I presented in 2011. Brian Harris, 'Trinitarian Apologetics: Participating in Communities of Surprise, Embrace and Witness', in *Beyond Four Walls* (Vose Seminary, Perth: 2011).

⁴ See, for example, Robert Bellah's *Habits of the Heart* (op cit) which highlights the link between religion and individualism.

⁵ Ephesians 3:17–19.

⁶ Jamieson, *A Churchless Faith*.

⁷ Colin E. Gunton, *The One, the Three and the Many: God, Creation and the Culture of Modernity*. The Bampton Lectures 1992 (Cambridge: Cambridge University Press, 1993).

⁸ Aquinas's first mover argument is well known. For a contemporary elaboration of the argument by a currently popular apologist, see John Lennox, *God's Undertaker: Has Science Buried God?* (Oxford: Lion, 2009); John Lennox, *Gunning for God: Why the New Atheists are Missing the Target* (Oxford: Lion, 2011).

⁹ König, *Here I Am!*, pp. 78,79.

¹⁰ Stanley Hauerwas, *A Community of Character: Toward a Constructive Christian Social Ethic* (Notre Dame, Ind.: University of Notre Dame Press, 1986), p. 6.

¹¹ Michael Griffiths, *Cinderella with Amnesia: A Restatement in Contemporary Terms of the Biblical Doctrine of the Church* (Downers Grove, IL: InterVarsity Press, 1975).

¹² The remainder of this section is a modified form of part of my paper Brian Harris, 'Faithful Thinking: The Role of the Seminary in Promoting a Thoughtful Christian Faith', *The Pacific Journal of Baptist Research* 8, no. 1 (2013).

¹³ Hitchens, *God is Not Great*.

¹⁴ G.K. Chesterton, *What's Wrong with the World*, Kindle edition, ch. 5.

¹⁵ David Kinnaman and Gabe Lyons, *Unchristian: What a New Generation Really Thinks About Christianity . . . And Why it Matters* (Grand Rapids, MI: Baker, 2007).

¹⁶ For a discussion of and rationale for the conclusion that we live in a 'post-Christendom' era, see Stuart Murray, *Church after Christendom* (Carlisle: Paternoster, 2004); Stuart Murray, *Post-Christendom* (Carlisle: Paternoster, 2004).

¹⁷ For a very different (and far more positive) interpretation of the church's contribution to society, see Alvin J. Schmidt, *Under the*

Influence: How Christianity Transformed Culture (Grand Rapids, MI: Zondervan, 2001).

[18] See Grenz's discussion of this in Stanley J. Grenz, 'Jesus as the Imago Dei: Image-of-God Christology and the Non-Linear Linearity of Theology', *Journal of the Evangelical Theological Society* 47, no. 4 (2004).

[19] Brian Harris, *The Theological Method of Stanley J. Grenz: Constructing Evangelical Theology from Scripture, Tradition and Culture* (Lewiston, NY: Edwin Mellen Press, 2011), p. iii.

[20] Stephen R. Holmes, *The Holy Trinity: Understanding God's Life, Christian Doctrine in Historical Perspective* (Milton Keynes: Paternoster, 2011).

Chapter Eight

[1] Anne Mager, '"One Beer, One Goal, One Nation, One Soul": South African Breweries, Heritage, Masculinity and Nationalism 1960–1999', *Past and Present* 188 (2005), pp. 163–194.

[2] Genesis 2:19.

[3] Miriam Pepper, Rosemary Leonard and Ruth Powell, 'Denominational Identification, Church Participation, and Concern About Climate Change in Australia', in *Climate Change, Cultural Change: Religious Responses and Responsibilities* (ed. Anne Elvery and David Gormley-O'Brien; Preston: Mosaic, 2013), pp. 40,41.

[4] Pepper, Leonard and Powell, 'Denominational Identification, Church Participation, and Concern About Climate Change in Australia', p. 42.

[5] Pepper, Leonard and Powell, 'Denominational Identification, Church Participation, and Concern About Climate Change in Australia', p. 44.

[6] N. Smith and A. Leiserowitz, 'American Evangelicals and Global Warming', *Global Environmental Change* 30 (2013).

[7] Clive W. Ayre, 'Climate Change and a Climate of Change in the Church', in *Climate Change, Cultural Change: Religious Responses and Responsibilities* (ed. Anne Elvery and David Gormley-O'Brien; Preston: Mosaic, 2013), p. 56.

[8] See their website, http://www.operationnoah.org/

[9] See their website, http://www.blessedearth.org/

[10] Lynn White Jr, 'The Historical Roots of Our Ecological Crisis', *Science* 155, no. 3767 (1967).

[11] White Jr, 'The Historical Roots of Our Ecological Crisis', p. 1205.

[12] Genesis 12:1–3.

¹³ Wilson, *God's Good World*, pp. 33,34.
¹⁴ Matthew 10:29; Matthew 6:28.

Chapter Nine

¹ Donald W. Thompson, *A Thief in the Night* (Carlisle: Mark IV Pictures, 1972).
² Tom Wright, *Surprised by Hope* (London: SPCK, 2007), p. 7.
³ John 11:1–44.
⁴ 1 Corinthians 15:20b.
⁵ Revelation 21:4.
⁶ Matthew 6:10.
⁷ Genesis 3:1–7.
⁸ For an outstanding exploration of this theme, see Rebecca Konyndyk DeYoung, *Glittering Vices: A New Look at the Seven Deadly Sins and Their Remedies* (Grand Rapids, MI: Brazos, 2009).
⁹ McKnight, *The Jesus Creed*.
¹⁰ 1 Corinthians 13:13.
¹¹ Genesis 1:5.
¹² 1 John 4:8.
¹³ John McClean, *From the Future: Coming to Grips with Pannenberg's Thought* (Milton Keynes: Paternoster, 2013).

Chapter Ten

¹ This is an edited and updated version of a paper originally published as Brian Harris, 'From "Behave, Believe Belong" to "Belong, Believe, Behave" – a Missional Journey for the 21st Century', in *Text and Task: Scripture and Mission* (ed. Michael Parsons; Carlisle: Paternoster, 2005), pp. 204–217.
² Robert Webber, *The Younger Evangelicals: Facing the Challenges of the New World* (Grand Rapids, MI: Baker, 2002), p. 48.
³ The question might not be 'Is it possible?' but 'Has it already happened?' In *The Practicing Congregation*, Bass makes the perceptive comment that 'This book does not argue that mainline churches should change. Rather, it argues that mainline churches are changing and have already changed.' Diana Butler Bass, *The*

Practicing Congregation: Imagining a New Old Church (Herndon, VA: Alban Institute, 2004), p. 3.

[4] See, e.g. Stanley Grenz, *Theology for the Community of God* (Nashville, TN: Broadman and Holman, 1994) or Stanley Grenz and John Franke, *Beyond Foundationalism.*

[5] See e.g. Grenz' use of Bellah in Stanley Grenz, *Revisioning Evangelical Theology: A Fresh Agenda for the 21st Century* (Downers Grove, IL: Inter-Varsity Press, 1993), pp. 148,149.

[6] Robert N. Bellah, William M. Sullivan, et al, eds, *Habits of the Heart: Individualism and Commitment in American Life* (New York: Harper & Row, 1985).

[7] W. Ewing, 'Hospitality' in *Dictionary of the Bible*, 2nd edn (eds F.C. Grant and H.H. Rowley; Edinburgh: T&T Clark, 1963), p. 400.

[8] See, for example, Carl Rogers, *On Becoming a Person: A Therapist's View of Psychotherapy* (London: Constable, 1961), p. 63.

[9] Evangelicals usually critique Rogers for his optimistic view of human nature and the absence of a category for human sinfulness. See e.g. S.L. Jones and R.E. Butman, *Modern Psychotherapies: A Comprehensive Christian Appraisal* (Downers Grove, IL: Inter-Varsity Press, 1991), pp. 255–277.

[10] The term 'anonymous Christian' is associated with Karl Rahner. It should be noted that Rahner did not suggest that all are automatically Christians, but rather than those who do not consciously reject God are believers. He writes: 'It is true that it would be wrong to go so far as to declare every man, whether he accepts the grace or not, an "anonymous Christian". Anyone who in his basic decision were to really deny and reject his being ordered to God, who were to place himself decisively in opposition to his own concrete being, should not be designated a "theist", even an anonymous "theist"; only someone who gives – even if it be ever so confusedly – the glory to *God* should be thus designated. Therefore no matter what a man states in his conceptual, theoretical and religious reflection, anyone who does not say in his *heart*, "there is no God" (like the "fool" in the psalm) but testifies to him by the radical acceptance of his being, is a believer.' In *A Rahner Reader* (ed. Gerald McCool; London: Darton, Longman & Todd, 1975), pp. 213,214.

[11] Bonhoeffer's words at the start of *The Cost of Discipleship* remain as startling and relevant today as they were in the 1930s: 'Cheap grace is the deadly enemy of our Church. We are fighting today for costly grace.' In Dietrich Bonhoeffer, *The Cost of Discipleship*, p. 35.

[12] Augustine's doctrine of original sin was usually accepted. Original sin was understood to mean the dimension of sin with which we begin life, or the effect which the sin of Adam has upon us as a precondition of our lives. See e.g. Millard J. Erickson, *Christian Theology* (Grand Rapids, MI: Baker, 1985), pp. 627–639.

[13] Luke 23:43.

[14] The exact sequence and process of glorification has always been a source of controversy amongst evangelicals. Debates include the absence or otherwise of 'soul sleep' as well as the absence or otherwise of the millennium. If accepted, the actual sequence of the millennium (pre or post, with a range of qualifications and understandings) has been contested.

[15] R.T. Webber, *Ancient Future Faith: Rethinking Evangelicalism for a Postmodern World* (Grand Rapids, MI: Baker, 1999), p. 150.

[16] Richard Harries, *God Outside the Box: Why Spiritual People Object to Christianity* (London: SPCK, 2002), p. 105.

[17] Special Report, Background Information for Dr Paul Borden for Consultancy 2004 (Perth: Baptist Union of Western Australia, 2004), p. 45.

[18] It is interesting to note that when Vernall spoke of the rapid growth of his church it was attendance figures rather than membership figures that he referred to.

[19] Paul Tournier, *A Place for You* (trans. Edwin Hudson; Crowborough: Highland, 1968), p. 9.

[20] Psalm 27:4 expresses a comparable emotion.

[21] Matthew 12:46–50.

[22] See e.g. Matthew 18:1–6.

[23] Compare the titles of books on apologetics over a period of time. For example, Robinson and Winward entitle their 1949 work on apologetics *Here is the Answer* (London: Marshall, Morgan and Scott, 1949). In 1992 Alister McGrath entitles his book on apologetics *Bridge-Building* (Leicester: Inter-Varsity Press, 1992). In 2002 Richard Harries published *God Outside the Box: Why Spiritual People Object to Christianity* (London: SPCK, 2002). The difference in ethos implied by each title is striking.

[24] The work of Stanley Grenz and John Franke in this area is helpful. See e.g. Grenz and Franke, *Beyond Foundationalism*, and Stanley Grenz, 'Die Begrenzte Gemeinschaft' ("The Boundaried People") and the Character of Evangelical Theology', *Journal of the Evangelical Theological Society*, 45.2 (2002), pp. 301–316.

[25] See e.g. Richard J. Middleton and Brian J. Walsh, *Truth is Stranger Than It Used to Be: Biblical Faith in a Postmodern Age* (Downers Grove, IL: Inter-Varsity Press, 1995).

[26] Luke 19:1–10.

[27] Peter Brierley, 'Evangelicals in the World of the 21st Century', Occasional Paper for the 2004 Forum for World Evangelization, Pattaya (2004), p. 4.

[28] This section is a modified version of part of a paper I presented at the Mission to New Zealand Conference in 2003. Brian Harris, 'The Need for a Double Conversion', Mission to New Zealand Conference (Auckland, NZ: Carey Baptist College, 2003).

[29] MTV poll, 2002.

[30] Tony Jones, *Postmodern Youth Ministry*, pp. 30–37.

[31] Millard Erickson provides a helpful summary of some evangelical responses in Erickson, Millard, *Postmodernizing the Faith*. Particular concerns tend to centre around two of the shifts highlighted by Jones, viz. those towards pluralism and relativism.

[32] While it is impossible to give precise content to the notion of the 'average face' of the church over its 2,000 year history, it is an unsettling concept and one worth pondering. To counteract some of the negative images, an increasing number of apologetic works are drawing attention to the more positive aspects of the church's history. See e.g. Schmidt, Alvin J., *Under the Influence: How Christianity Transformed Civilization* (Grand Rapids, MI: Zondervan, 2001).

Chapter Eleven

[1] R. Paul Stevens, *The Other Six Days: Vocation, Work, and Ministry in Biblical Perspective* (Grand Rapids, MI: Eerdmans, 1999).

[2] Matthew 5:48. It is worth noting that Jesus' understanding of perfect is likely to have been shaped by his Jewish background, where perfection was not a competitive concept (the best there is), but a functional one. Something was perfect if it effectively achieved the purpose for which it was made. For humans, made in the image of God, the invitation is to reflect God's image in and to the world.

[3] Leland Ryken, ed, *The Christian Imagination: Essays on Literature and the Arts* (Grand Rapids, MI: Baker, 1981), p. 429.

[4] David W. Rushton, 'A Christian Perspective on Music', in *Christian Worldview and the Academic Disciplines: Crossing the Academy* (ed. Deane

E.D. Downey and Stanley E. Porter (Eugene, OR: Pickwick, 2009), p. 333.

5 Smith has written widely in this field, some examples being David I. Smith, *Learning from the Stranger: Christian Faith and Cultural Diversity* (Grand Rapids, MI: Eerdmans, 2009); David I. Smith and James K.A. Smith, eds, (Grand Rapids, MI: Eerdmans, 2011).

6 2 Corinthians 3:2,3.

7 1 Corinthians 13:13.

8 Cited in Placher, ed. Callings, p. 3.

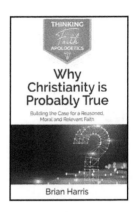

**Why Christianity is
Probably True**

*Building the case for a reasoned,
moral and relevant faith*

Brian Harris

Does the Christian faith lack intellectual, moral and experiential credibility?

These are the three most common accusations made against the Christian faith today. Brian Harris examines each of these arguments in turn by outlining the issue, looking at evidence against the claim before evaluating the argument as a whole.

This book explores these questions in a rigorous but accessible way. It doesn't offer easy, solve-everything answers, but it does build a cumulative case based on reason, history and experience to suggest that God probably exists, and that the Christian understanding of God could well be valid.

978-1-78893-106-9

Paternoster is the theological imprint of Authentic Media, and publishes books across a wide range of disciplines including biblical studies, theology, mission, church leadership and pastoral issues.

You can sign up to the Paternoster newsletter to hear about new releases by scanning below:

Online:
authenticmedia.co.uk/paternoster

Follow us:

.

Lightning Source UK Ltd.
Milton Keynes UK
UKHW021831310522
403794UK00009B/793